Conflict Resolution at Work FOR DUMMIES®

by Vivian Scott &
The Dispute Resolution Center of
Snohomish & Island Counties

WILEY

Wiley Publishing, Inc.

3 1257 01893 8729

Conflict Resolution at Work For Dummies®

Published by
Wiley Publishing, Inc.
111 River St.
Hoboken, NJ 07030-5774
www.wiley.com

WILEY

About the Author

Vivian Scott is a Professional Certified Mediator with a private practice in Snohomish, Washington. She has handled a variety of workplace cases, ranging from helping business partners end their relationship with dignity to creating a new working environment for a law firm. She has completed an extensive practicum and certification program with the Dispute Resolution Center of Snohomish & Island Counties, where she mediates on a regular basis helping parties resolve conflict in workplace, family, consumer, and landlord/tenant disputes. Scott is a member of the Washington Mediation Association and spends much of her time advocating for meaningful resolution.

Prior to retiring in 1999 from the competitive world of high-tech marketing, she realized that resolving conflict within the confines of office politics was paramount to success. She used her discerning negotiation, mediation, and problem-solving skills to forge and cultivate relationships with Washington, D.C.–based small business associations and departments on behalf of her employer, earning a rare personal honor from the Small Business Administration for her commitment to the business community.

Scott received the Silver Screen Award from the U.S. International Film and Video Festival for outstanding creativity for her role as developer and Executive Producer of the *America at Work* video series, which aired on the USA Network. She holds a BA in Interdisciplinary Arts & Sciences with an emphasis in American Studies from the University of Washington.

Scott lives with her partner of 11 years, Brent, and is the proud mom to a grown daughter, Vanessa, who will soon be a stellar attorney and mediator in her own right. Scott can be reached through her Web site at www.vivianscott mediation.com.

Dedication

To Vanessa and Brent, who always give me a soft place to land. Thank you for seeing my imperfections and loving me anyway.

Author's Acknowledgments

I'd like to thank all the people who played a part in bringing this book to life, including my Wiley friends Mike Lewis, Rhea Siegel, Sarah Faulkner, Elizabeth Rea, Elizabeth Kuball, Todd Lothery, and Gary Zimmerman. Big thanks also to the countless family and friends who candidly answered my questions about their personal struggles in the workplace.

The brilliant staff at the Dispute Resolution Center of Snohomish & Island Counties (in Everett, Washington) deserve much credit for their unselfish work and writing prowess. Thanks to the DRC employees for their level heads and warm hearts. Specifically:

Ryan Mattfeld, Certified Mediator and Senior Trainer at the DRC, who has a BA in Sociology from Western Washington University. Ryan is responsible for developing DRC trainings as well as designing new mediation products and materials. Ryan lives in Seattle with his wife, Christine, and their son, Reese.

Melissa Mertz, Certified Mediator and Mediation/Training Coordinator, who manages the Mediator Certification and Volunteer Mediator programs, as well as office operations. She has a BS degree in Criminal Justice from the University of North Dakota. She lives in Everett with her husband, Chris.

LaDessa Croucher, Certified Mediator and Ombudsman, who has mediated for the DRC of Missoula County in Montana and the Mediation Center of the Pacific in Hawaii. She has a BA in Communication Studies from the University of Montana and coordinates the Small Claims Mediation Program in Snohomish County.

Kathy Rice, Executive Mediator and Program Manager, who has mediated more than 1,000 cases in her career. She has worked in the field of conflict resolution for over 16 years, designing, customizing, and providing successful conflict resolution trainings, mediations, and services.

The Dispute Resolution Center is an alternative justice center that provides a wide range of ADR services, including mediation, training, and a full array of workplace conflict resolution services. Its program Director, Matt Phillips, JD, has worked in the field of ADR for 10 years. The DRC is a program of the Volunteers of America Western Washington. Special thanks to Gloria Elledge, Kathleen Rostkoski, and Anahi Machiavelli for holding down the fort while the rest of us wrote.

Publisher's Acknowledgments

We're proud of this book; please send us your comments at http://dummies.custhelp.com. For other comments, please contact our Customer Care Department within the U.S. at 877-762-2974, outside the U.S. at 317-572-3993, or fax 317-572-4002.

Some of the people who helped bring this book to market include the following:

Acquisitions, Editorial, and Media Development

Project Editors: Sarah Faulkner, Elizabeth Rea

Acquisitions Editor: Michael Lewis

Copy Editors: Todd Lothery, Elizabeth Kuball

Assistant Editor: Erin Calligan Mooney

Editorial Program Coordinator: Joe Niesen

Technical Editor: Gary Zimmerman

Editorial Manager: Christine Meloy Beck

Editorial Assistant: David Lutton

Cover Photos: iStock

Cartoons: Rich Tennant
(www.the5thwave.com)

Composition Services

Project Coordinator: Sheree Montgomery

Layout and Graphics: Ashley Chamberlain, Joyce Haughey, Melissa K. Smith, Christine Williams

Proofreader: Nancy L. Reinhardt

Indexer: Potomac Indexing, LLC

Special Help Publishing and Editorial for Consumer Dummies

Diane Graves Steele, Vice President and Publisher, Consumer Dummies

Kristin Ferguson-Wagstaffe, Product Development Director, Consumer Dummies

Ensley Eikenburg, Associate Publisher, Travel

Kelly Regan, Editorial Director, Travel

Publishing for Technology Dummies

Andy Cummings, Vice President and Publisher, Dummies Technology/General User

Composition Services

Debbie Stailey, Director of Composition Services

Contents at a Glance

Table of Contents

Introduction

· ·

Quarrels would not last long if the fault were only on one side.

—François de La Rochefoucauld

*E*very day in offices, retail stores, factories, and any number of other workplaces, people are having conflicts with co-workers. Whether you work for a nonprofit organization, a small family business, a Fortune 100 company, or a fledgling upstart, if you work with at least one other person, it's safe to say that you have disagreements and face difficulties at times. It's normal, natural, and nothing to fear.

You can drive yourself bonkers trying to create a workplace that's completely void of conflict all the time. And why would you want to create such a work environment? Contrary to what you may believe, conflict isn't inherently all bad. When handled properly, conflict can actually create positive changes and new opportunities in your organization. Successfully making the shift in your perspective from seeing only the negative in disagreements to seeing the prospect for positive change is the first step to resolving difficulties.

But how do you go about finding positive outcomes in what on the surface looks like a negative situation? You have to become skilled at calming the infernos by helping employees through discussions that prove to them that they can solve their own issues without always having to have someone (you!) in the middle, acting as referee. Become a coach for your team — someone they can trust to bring the real and right issues to the table for effective problem solving.

When it comes to your own workplace conflicts, if you broaden your perspective to include the other person's point of view, you're sure to come out of the dispute with a better working relationship. Being at the center of controversy is never a good idea for anyone, so decide to use the uneasy situation as an opportunity to improve systems, relationships, and your credibility.

In this book, I tell you what the most common causes of workplace conflict are and how to address them by using a proven mediation method and philosophy. And remember: Every story always has more than one side.

About This Book

This book is a tool intended to help managers (or anyone who has a job) work through conflict with peers, subordinates, and even bosses. It's primarily aimed at those employees in organizations who find themselves negotiating difficulties without the benefit of having professional conflict resolution or mediation experience. The chapters are chock-full of facilitation techniques and tools that come from successful conflict resolution experts, delivered in a way that's easy to understand and ready for you to apply right away.

Many employees who've felt helpless as previously functioning working relationships went south will appreciate that the information in this book shows them they're not doomed to repeat the past but instead can create a new way of dealing with problems when they arise — and they *will* arise. I lay out, and describe the function of, internal and external resources for you to turn to as the situation warrants. The information I serve up helps you build a customized plan for your unique situation.

In today's increasingly competitive job market, the insight I share with you about settling unsettling situations is invaluable. I share my personal experiences and the knowledge I've gained from mediating a variety of workplace, family, and consumer disputes, and I let you in on a few trade secrets.

I also enlist the expertise of some of the best mediators I know to show you exactly what to do to resolve conflict. Their collective proficiency in settling differences between 2 or 200 makes for an excellent chance of creating long-lasting and satisfying agreements.

Conventions Used in This Book

To help make this book easier to navigate, I include the following conventions:

- ✔ I introduce new terms in *italics* and then define them.
- ✔ I use **bold** text to highlight key words in bulleted lists.

What You're Not to Read

As an author, I'd be thrilled if you read every word I wrote. But from a practical standpoint, I know you're busy — with your day-to-day tasks at work and the conflict you're undoubtedly trying to resolve. To make this book even easier to use, I'm going to let you in on a secret. When you see *sidebars* — text in gray-shaded boxes — feel free to skip them. These asides are often real-life examples or other tidbits I've picked up during my years as a mediator. The stories can drive home a point I make in the accompanying chapter or offer a new perspective on a situation, but you'll get the main point of any section or chapter even if you don't read them.

Foolish Assumptions

I'm assuming you have a job, paid or volunteer, and that you interact with people. I'm also assuming you have some sort of management responsibility — be it keeping the line moving at the manufacturing plant or trying to keep your reputation intact as the star manager in the strongest department of an international corporation. And I'm thinking you're currently experiencing some trouble. You may be sick and tired of a conflict between two of your employees, or you may be bickering with a colleague, or perhaps you're at a loss as to what to do about the problems between you and your boss. My final assumption? I'm guessing you want to do something about it.

How This Book Is Organized

This book is organized into five parts.

Part 1: Understanding Conflict in the Workplace

Every book about workplace conflict should start with a broad understanding of how problems arise in the first place. This part describes how individuals and groups play a part in troubles at work. Understanding where people are coming from is key to solving the real issues, so in this part, I tell you how you as a manager can sometimes cause problems without even knowing it and what you can do not to make matters worse. I also give you a few signs to look for so you know when it's time to step in. The cost of doing nothing can be staggering, so I provide some points to think about that may spur you to take action.

Part II: Resolving a Conflict between Two or More of Your Employees

This part is a crash course in mediating a problem between two co-workers or an entire group. It starts by walking you through how to develop a plan, when and how to approach the people involved, and how to get a meeting started. I share my knowledge on the art of asking effective questions to get at what's really bothering folks, and then I tell you what I know about brainstorming and negotiating possible solutions. I show you how to help everyone write agreements that leave little room for confusion and how to take a mediation process and adapt it for a large group. Real resolution only comes when you can quantify it over a specified period, so I provide tips on monitoring agreements and noting progress.

Part III: Using Additional Resources to Resolve the Conflict

Handling problems yourself is all well and good, but what happens when everything you try just isn't working? This part outlines where to turn inside the organization and who may be able to help you from the outside. I describe what to look for in (and what to expect from) conflict resolution experts. I also give you ideas to keep your team functioning while you figure out the next step.

Part IV: Smoothly Handling Conflict When You're One of the People Involved

Oh my! Even if you're the best manager on the face of the planet, you can still have problems with people at work. Being at the center of a conflict puts you in a bit of a predicament, so I show you how to identify what the other person really wants, how to work through his resistance to meeting with you, and how to discuss the issues in a way that has the potential to result in a satisfying agreement.

If you're the boss, I give you tips on how to temper your power while still asking for what you want. If you're a peer, you'll discover how to honor your colleague's position without feeling as if you're giving in. And if you're a subordinate, I walk you through how to have a productive meeting with your manager. I also give you a few hints about how sometimes leaving your current job with grace and dignity can benefit you in the long run.

Part V: The Part of Tens

Here, I walk you through more tips and strategies to improve your odds of managing and resolving conflict effectively. Focusing on what you can't control in a conflict is far too common, so I give you a list of ten things that *are* in your control. Wicked-smart experts I know shared insight from their years of experience so I could provide you with some of the best advice around. I also give you a list of behaviors and attitudes to avoid. Pay special attention to the common reasons managers don't handle problems to avoid falling into the negative patterns yourself.

Icons Used in This Book

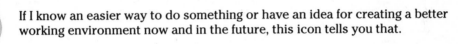

Throughout the book you'll notice icons to draw your attention to something I want you to pay particular attention to.

If I know an easier way to do something or have an idea for creating a better working environment now and in the future, this icon tells you that.

I use this icon to flag some important information that you don't want to forget.

This icon alerts you to common blunders that you want to avoid.

This icon is just what it sounds like — nothing beats a real life example to illustrate a point!

Where to Go from Here

Conflict Resolution at Work For Dummies is a book I hope you refer to again and again. You don't have to read it cover to cover to gain the insight you need to deal with conflict at work. You can flip to the chapter that best meets your needs today and come back to other sections as needed.

You may have a bookshelf full of management how-to tomes, but it's still a good idea to start with understanding what makes an employee tick and why she sees the world the way she does, so start with Chapter 2 to get right to the heart of the matter.

If you feel you have a pretty good handle on how emotions, values, and group dynamics contribute to conflict, and you're ready to mediate a problem between two or more people, head straight to Chapter 6 and follow through to Chapter 10. To gain an understanding of nuances to consider when you're one of the parties smack dab in the middle of the problem, go to Chapter 15.

Finally, if you feel you may be in over your head and you'd like to find out more about how to enlist the help of an expert, check out Chapter 13 to see what your company may be able to do, and turn to Chapter 14 to research external professionals. In the meantime, be sure to consider the tips for keeping your team focused in Chapter 12.

Although this book is designed so that you can start anywhere, don't feel obligated to jump around. If you're a traditionalist who likes to read every book from cover to cover, just turn the page!

Part I
Understanding Conflict in the Workplace

The 5th Wave   By Rich Tennant

"A large part of our success is based on our ability to resolve conflicts before we get to work."

In this part . . .

This part covers what you need to know to understand workplace conflict. I help you create a comprehensive framework to use in any conflict situation and fill you in on the various contributors to conflict. I discuss how difficult situations can either escalate or de-escalate depending on your reaction, and I identify common mistakes to avoid. I also provide information on self-reflection and point out behaviors that indicate it's time to take action.

Chapter 1

An Overview of Conflict Resolution at Work

*Y*ou may love your family and friends, but truth be told, you spend much of your time with the people at work. Not getting along with co-workers, or having members of your team at odds with one another can be stressful and distracting. In addition, problems in the workplace rarely stay at work; they can permeate every aspect of your life. So it behooves you to take the time to understand what's behind a conflict, to get beyond the surface issues, and to work to find satisfying resolutions for everyone involved.

Being curious about how to resolve conflict means you're probably ready to try something different. And being open to trying something different means you have a good shot at getting closure. Settling differences effectively requires you to step back and look at the broader picture, be mindful of another person's point of view, and take into account peripheral factors that may be creating or provoking problems, like group dynamics or workplace norms.

In this chapter, I give you an overview of conflict resolution so you can successfully mediate problems in your workplace, whether those problems are between two individuals or within a larger group. I also tell you about additional conflict resolution resources you may have at your disposal. Finally, I tell you how to adapt your newfound conflict resolution knowledge to situations that hit a little closer to home — when you're directly involved in the conflict.

Considering Common Contributors to Conflict

As much as you may think of yourself as a unique individual and see your problems as complex and one-of-a-kind, you actually have a lot in common with your colleagues when it comes to how conflicts get started and why problems escalate into unbearable situations. For the most part, workplace difficulties fall into common categories, such as

- Communication (and miscommunication)
- Employee attitudes
- Honesty
- Insubordination
- Treatment of others
- Work habits

Although most conflicts fall into these common categories, the company or organization you work for has unique DNA. The combination of its employees, policies, and culture has the potential to either create the most productive working environment you can imagine or ignite some of the most traumatic problems you've encountered in your career. Whether it's the former, the latter, or somewhere in between depends on how employees — and especially you, if you're a manager — handle conflict.

Effectively addressing conflict takes into account the obvious surface issue, the emotional climate surrounding the topic, and your knowledge of the viewpoints of the people involved in the dispute. In this section, I provide insight into how differing perspectives can cause employees to feel like ships passing in the night. I also discuss emotions, touch on the importance of communication in your organization, and look at group dynamics, including your role in the group.

Acknowledging differing perspectives

You and each of the employees on your team have a lens through which you see the world and one another. Everything you see, hear, and say goes through your filter on the way in *and* on the way out. These filters determine how you present and receive information. They color, distort, or amplify information in both positive and negative ways and act much like personal interpreters in every situation.

Your individual kaleidoscope is shaped by things like your personal history, education, values, culture, and the roles you play in your life, both at work and at home. Everything you consider important works together to create your worldview. The same is true for your co-workers. An employee who comes from the school of hard knocks may very well have a different perspective about educational opportunities in the workplace than a colleague who graduated top in his class from an Ivy League school.

When I discuss values, I'm not talking about tangible assets like your car, your house, or your diamond jewelry. Rather, *values* in this context are things like safety, respect, autonomy, and recognition.

Being familiar with your employees' values helps you resolve conflicts. For example, say that two employees are having an argument over where to stack some vendor binders. If you can appreciate that one employee sees respect as paramount in his environment, and his workspace is encroached by his colleague with a lackadaisical attitude toward boundaries, you have a better chance of helping the two resolve the issue. Rather than swooping in to tell the pair that the vendor notebooks they're arguing about should go on a shelf, you can facilitate a conversation about the real issue — respect. After you address the issue of respect, where the binders should go will be relatively easy to decide.

In Chapter 2, I go into more detail about filters, values, and the emotions individuals bring to conflict.

Recognizing emotions in others

Most organizations embrace positive emotions. The excitement over landing the big account, the revelry celebrating the product launch, or the congratulatory slaps on the back as the ribbon is cut for the newly completed project are all ways employees acknowledge optimistic emotions. Where managers often falter is in failing to recognize that every emotion — from upbeat to angry — is a clue to discovering people's personal values. Positive emotions are a sign that values are being met, while negative ones suggest that some work still needs to be done!

It's obvious that a situation has turned emotional when tears flow or an employee ratchets up the volume when he speaks, to the point that the entire office slips into an uncomfortable silence. What's a little more difficult is knowing what to do with such passionate responses. Emotional reactions are often seen as negative behavior in just about any workplace, but if you spend some time investigating and interpreting them, you can get a leg up on how to resolve the trouble. Check out Chapter 2 for a complete discussion of emotions at work.

Handling communication mishaps

Communication makes the world go 'round, and the same is true for you and your employees. Word choice, tone of voice, and body language all contribute to whether or not you understand each other.

Using vague or confusing language causes communication misfires. Phrases such as "when you get a chance," "several," or "sometimes" don't accurately state what you really mean. Similarly, words like "always" and "never" can get you in trouble. Choosing your words wisely, and in a way that invites dialogue, makes for a less stressful work environment and models good communication. See Chapter 2 for more tips on communicating effectively.

Deciphering group dynamics

Two employees can completely understand each other and work like a well-oiled machine. Then a third co-worker joins the team, and now you have group dynamics in play. Wow, that changes everything! A team that's cohesive and meeting its goals can be exhilarating from management's perspective. But if cliques form and co-workers start looking for allies to enlist in power plays behind closed doors, communication breaks down.

Teams have a propensity to label members — the caretaker, the go-to guy, the historian, and so on. It's good to know who's who in a group, but the responsibilities that come with those labels may be impossible (or undesirable) to live up to. Employees start to make assumptions based on the labeled roles, such as assuming that the go-to guy will happily accept any assignment you give him. Conjecture based on limited or selective information causes miscommunication, misunderstandings, and ultimately, conflict.

To address what happens when members of a group are undergoing difficulties, investigate how and when the problem started and determine if the problem stems from just a few staff members or if the impact is so great that you need to tackle the problem with the entire team. And flip to Chapter 3 for more information on the way group dynamics can contribute to conflict.

Assessing your own role

Something you're either doing or *not* doing may be causing friction on your team, and you may not even know what it is. Most people in conflict tend to spend more time thinking about what the other person is doing than looking at their own behavior and attitudes toward the difficulty.

Chapter 4 outlines some of the common missteps that managers make in their attempts to handle problems at work. I discuss ways you may be unwittingly pitting team members against each other, address the dreaded micromanaging accusation, and explain how underrepresenting your team to the higher-ups may unite them in a way that puts you at the center of a storm.

Mediating like a Pro

You can settle conflict in a variety of ways, including the following:

- **Judging (or arbitrating):** Hear what each party has to say and then decide who's right and who's wrong.
- **Counseling:** Listen with an empathetic ear with no expectation on your part for immediate action.
- **Negotiation:** Go back and forth between the employees while each suggests solutions until they land on something as a compromise that may not truly satisfy either person.
- **Mediation:** Monitor and guide a conversation between the two as they work toward understanding each other and creating solutions that work for both.

When I meet with clients in conflict, I prefer to use a tried-and-true mediation process that looks at both the surface issues and the underlying causes for the difficulty. In this section, I show you why mediation is your best bet for a long-term solution and improved working relationship.

Following eight steps to a resolution

Using a solid process to mediate a meeting between co-workers in conflict gives you a foundation on which to manage and monitor the difficulty. Follow these steps from a professional mediation process:

1. **Do preliminary planning and setup:** Carefully investigate who's involved and what you believe the issues are, and invite the parties to discuss the matter with you. Provide a private, comfortable, and confidential environment for the meeting.

2. **Greet and discuss the process:** Explain your role as a neutral facilitator, and go over the ground rules, including your expectation for open minds and common courtesy.

3. **Share perspectives:** Give each person an opportunity to share his point of view and discuss the impact the conflict has had on him. Reflect, reframe, and neutralize emotional content while honoring the spirit of what he's sharing.

4. **Build an agenda:** Allow both parties to create a list of topics (not solutions) they want to discuss. The list acts as a road map that keeps the discussion on track.

5. **Negotiate in good faith:** As co-workers discuss initial ideas for solutions, set the tone by listening to any and all ideas. Brainstorm and play out how suggestions might work and whether they satisfy what's most important to the employees.

6. **Hold private meetings as necessary:** If parties are at an impasse, meet separately with each to confidentially explore what's keeping each from moving forward. Discuss what each is willing to do (or ask for) in the spirit of progress and real resolution.

7. **Craft agreements:** Bring employees back together and let them share, if they so choose, any discoveries they made during the private meeting sessions. Begin to narrow down solutions and come to an agreement (with details!) on who will do what and when.

8. **Monitor follow-through:** Keep track of progress, address hiccups, and refine as appropriate.

Facilitating a conversation between two people

Before you begin the mediation process, you need to consider the following:

- ✔ **A suitable meeting space:** You want the employees to feel comfortable enough in the meeting location to open up about the real issues. Meet in a place that has lots of privacy — like an out-of-the-way conference room — and avoid any chance of turf wars by making sure the location is viewed as neutral territory.

- ✔ **Confidentiality:** You need to build trust for a mediation conversation (see Chapter 6 for details on setting up a meeting), so agreeing to keep the conversation between the colleagues is a must, whether you act as mediator or bring in an outside expert.

- ✔ **Time and interruptions:** You probably want to set aside at least four hours to work through the issues, and you want to clear your schedule of other responsibilities so that the meeting isn't interrupted.

When you make the decision to mediate a conversation between feuding parties, a few things change for you. It's imperative that you walk a fine line between manager and mediator. As a manager, you have the power to make decisions; as a mediator, you have the power to put the onus on the employees and act as a neutral third party (who just happens to be coming to the table with a skill set that the co-workers have yet to develop).

Practicing the arts of reflecting and reframing an employee's point of view may be an initial challenge for you, but it's worth it in the end. The employee will appreciate your efforts to respond to his emotions, your accurate descriptions of what's most important to him, and your empathetic recognition of what impact the conflict has had on him. And both parties will benefit from you listening to understand their perspective because they'll hear each other's story in a new way. Chapter 7 walks you through these steps and helps you keep your footing along the path of conflict resolution.

Negotiating a resolution to conflict starts with getting all the relevant information about the past on the table and ends with a clear definition of what the future could be. Get there by listening for what's really important to the parties involved and then asking directed, open-ended questions. In Chapter 8, I provide questions and cover the process of moving people through the negotiation stage of a mediated conversation.

The best solutions satisfy all parties involved and, perhaps more important, are lasting. Putting a bandage on a gaping wound stops the bleeding for a few seconds, but stitches will help it heal permanently. So it is with finding a solution to a conflict; it's much more rewarding in the long run not to have to address the same problems over and over. Be open to letting your employees try solutions for a while as you monitor the situation from a measured distance, and have them come back to the table, if necessary, until they reach a lasting agreement. Chapter 9 helps you work with your employees to develop good solutions and agreements. Chapter 11 gives you the tools you need to successfully monitor those agreements.

Managing conflict with a team

If the conflict making its way through your organization seems to affect each and every employee in your organization, planning for and facilitating a team meeting may be the answer.

The more upfront preparation you do, the better your odds are for a fruitful outcome, so set yourself up for success by following a few simple tips:

✔ Decide whether you're neutral enough to facilitate the conversation. If not, look to a professional mediator or conflict resolution specialist to help.

✔ Consider broad details like your goals and how you'll develop milestones that quantify progress.

✔ Plan for smaller details, like exactly how you'll organize small group work and handle hecklers.

In Chapter 10, I discuss how to resolve conflict when larger groups are involved.

Following up and monitoring the situation takes some attention on your part. Look for signs of decreased tension and increases in work quality and quantity so that you can get out of the hall monitor role and back into the position of managing the business you were hired to direct. Check out Chapter 11 for tips on following up and monitoring the progress your team is making.

Tapping into Conflict Resolution Expertise

You don't have to go it alone when difficulties evolve to the point that some sort of action is clearly necessary. And you don't need to panic or jump in and attack the situation without first looking at the tools available to you. Create a customized approach to fit your unique circumstances by looking at what's already in place and then determining how to augment that with a little help from your friends. If you find yourself working to mentor an employee through conflict, offer him training and educational opportunities, and always leave the door open for customizing what's right for him.

While you're doing that, keep your team focused on the work at hand by following the advice I give in Chapter 12.

Internal resources

Human Resources is an obvious place to start when you begin your search for advice and insight about a conflict. These personnel professionals can help you investigate an employee's work history and interpret company policy or employment law. They often lend a hand with customized trainings and can identify employee assistance programs such as counseling and addiction specialists.

They can also point you to other entities that may be able to help, including

✔ **Shared neutrals:** Common in large organizations and government agencies, shared neutrals are individuals selected from different departments with various levels of authority. They're trained in mediation and are brought together to purposely create a diverse group perspective.

✔ **The ombudsman:** An ombudsman is an employee in a company who provides a safe place to talk, vent, explore ideas, troubleshoot, or brainstorm any workplace topic.

✔ **Unions:** If your company has a relationship with a union, you can always tap into its strength and problem-solving expertise.

Flip to Chapter 13 for more about these and other internal resources you can utilize in a conflict.

External resources

The cost of doing nothing can far outweigh the budgetary impact of hiring an expert, but looking for the right entity to help can be overwhelming. Check credentials as you consider trainers, conflict coaches, and mediators to help with ongoing problems. Local dispute resolution centers, mediation associations, and professional training organizations can help you find experts in your area (see Chapter 14 for details about each).

Consider turning to an external specialist when

✔ The conflict is beyond your current abilities or the scope of internal resources.

✔ You're unable to stay neutral or unable to be seen as neutral.

✔ You can't guarantee confidentiality or would like to offer an added layer of privacy.

✔ It's important to you to create a personal or professional boundary.

✔ You want to communicate the seriousness of the matter.

✔ You want to participate in the process so you'd like someone else to take the lead.

Dealing with a Direct Conflict

Having difficulty with someone you work with can weigh heavily on you. Conflict isn't fun, even if you've somewhat enjoyed plotting the next move that will surely crush your opponent. Conflict takes a lot of energy, and when it gets to the point that uninvolved co-workers start directing attention toward you and your problems, or the work around you is affected, it's time to keep your reputation intact and figure things out.

Chances are that you're ready to resolve your differences and create a little peace and quiet. Take into account the unique characteristics that each of your working relationships has, but take care to treat everyone (subordinate, peer, and superior) with the utmost respect to avoid meeting that person again in what could be a horribly uncomfortable situation (like in the interview for a big promotion a year from now!). Knowing how to adapt your approach based on your co-worker's position on the org chart can make the difference between making matters worse and keeping your dignity in what may otherwise be an unbecoming situation. Staying true to yourself while you make room for a colleague's perspective is not only possible — it's necessary. (See Chapter 18 for details on how to tailor your approach to the org chart.)

Finding solutions that work for both of you

When you think about addressing a conflict, ask yourself, "What's motivating me to have this conversation?" If your answer is that you want to shame or threaten the other person, then the skills I share with you in this book won't do you any good. Being tricky to get your way and leave the other person in the dust doesn't really resolve conflict; it may hold it off for a while, but it's safe to say that the person you see as your opponent will find another opportunity to fight back.

How do you figure out what both people in a conflict want? You start by identifying core values. What do you *think* the other person wants when he says, "Don't touch anything on my desk ever again!"? Does he want you to leave his workspace alone, or do you think his emotional reaction indicates that he values respect? Perhaps from his perspective, co-workers show one another respect by asking permission before taking the stack of reports he's working on. And therein lies the real issue for him.

Figure out what you value (what's most important to you). Practice ways to communicate that information to your co-worker, and then create a productive meeting in which both of you share what's important. Be sure to reflect and restate what you hear him say is important to him, neutralize the emotions you see or hear, and get to work on coming up with solutions that fit the whole problem, not just your side.

If you're not sure what either or both of you really want, head to Chapter 15, where I help you look at both sides of the conflict. After you have an idea of what each side wants, ask your co-worker to meet with you (I tell you the best way to do this in Chapter 16). When you're ready to sit down to discuss the conflict, be sure to heed the advice I give in Chapter 17.

Look for ways to solve difficulties that give you both what you want. And if you really need to feel like you've won, consider the idea that including your co-worker in the solution expands the win rather than cancels it out.

Creating a different future

Use a different tactic when you start a conversation with a colleague or your boss to avoid some of the stale arguments you've been having. Taking a new approach is the first step in setting the stage for what happens next. Having the same old discussion over and over (and over!) may be a sign that one or both of you aren't really taking the level of responsibility needed in order to move on. If self-assessment isn't your strong suit, don't be afraid to ask for help.

Making an effective apology

In my experience, the right apology at the right time can significantly change a working relationship, even if it appears to be irrevocably broken. Your co-worker can get past the differences quicker and with more grace if you're able to acknowledge what you've done to contribute to the conflict. By giving a sincere apology, you eliminate the risk that he'll hold you hostage for a wrongdoing. Admit it and move on!

If you really feel that you've been a victim and can't see where you may have contributed to the tension, don't make something up just to have something to apologize for. Less obvious contributors to the conflict may be the tone you've taken, whether you've been avoiding him, or perhaps the fact that you didn't speak up sooner. Contemplate those and others that may come to mind before deciding an apology isn't necessary.

Genuine apologies, in my opinion, are more than saying, "I'm sorry." They include a description of what you're sorry for, an assurance that it won't happen again, and a request for an opportunity to make it up to the injured party. Your regret may model for your counterpart the apology you'd like to hear as well! Your statement should go something like this: "I'm sorry I waited to share the information with you. From here on out, I'll be sure to let you know about my findings as soon as I receive the data. What can I do to make up for my hesitation?"

Consider the strengths each of you bring to the workplace, and capitalize on those to move your relationship forward. The employee who nitpicks your daily reports may be the very person who saves you from embarrassing yourself with faulty data in front of the execs. Step back and consider that someone, somewhere thinks this person is an asset to the organization and that how you handle this situation makes a difference to that someone. Put effort into taking steps to building a new relationship and a more cohesive future. Be seen as a leader rather than someone who enjoys kicking up the dust.

Find the common ground you share (and you do have some!). At the very least, the two of you probably agree there's a problem, that you'd like it to end, and that you both most likely want the working conditions to get better. Outside of that, perhaps you and your colleague would like a process improved, want to find ways to foster teamwork, or want to make sure your reputations aren't tarnished by your not-so-private difficulties. How you've both gone about trying to achieve those goals, though, may be at the center of your conflict. Finding and examining common ground helps you both own the problem *and* the solution. Flip to Chapter 17 for tips on how to find common ground and negotiate resolutions with a colleague.

Chapter 2

Understanding What People Bring to Conflict

*E*ach person in your workplace is a complex system of past experiences, beliefs, values, opinions, and emotions. Each has different ways of communicating, processing the things around him or her, and handling conflict. Much like fingerprints, each individual is unique.

This chapter helps you gain a better insight into the people on your team — why they see things the way they do, why they react to different people in different ways, and how their emotions can complicate the whole situation. You'll understand how your colleagues' personal beliefs and attributes contribute to the team dynamic and sometimes contribute to conflict (which is normal, natural, and inevitable by the way) so that you can build better working relationships and a more productive working environment. You'll see the broader foundation of conflict and be more prepared to proactively reduce and perhaps prevent it.

Rediscovering Communication

Good communication is the hallmark of a productive working relationship. Easier said than done, right? Even when you believe you're being crystal clear, it's possible that the other person doesn't understand what you're really trying to say. This happens for a variety of reasons, including differences in goals, misunderstandings with language, ambiguous body language, and misinterpretations of tone of voice.

Changing the goal of communication

Not every conversation has the same goal. The workday is packed with a multitude of circumstances in which people communicate in various ways for a variety of reasons. You may approach a colleague to gather information you need for a project. A subordinate may start a conversation to explain her point of view on a memo you sent. Your boss may send you an e-mail reminding you of a deadline. Even people participating in the same conversation have different reasons for participating. Reaching agreement is commonly thought of as the goal, but this misconception is often one of the most unnecessary causes of conflicts.

In conflict, goals for communication often turn destructive. If someone in your group enters into a conversation for the sole purpose of proving that she's right, making the other person feel bad or establishing that the other person is an incompetent fool, the conflict is likely to get worse.

Instead of focusing on reaching agreement, use these opportunities to change the goal of the communication. The new goal is to create understanding — and understanding doesn't mean agreeing. It isn't necessary for the two people in conflict to see eye to eye and walk away holding hands, but it's helpful if they can talk to each other respectfully, feel heard by each other, and gain a greater understanding of the situation and the other person.

The old cliché "agree to disagree" may be coming to mind. In a way, this saying is both accurate and inaccurate. The two people in the conflict may end their discussion on this note, and that's fine as long as they both put forth a 100-percent effort to listen and understand each other. Unfortunately, most people use this saying as a quick way to end a conversation. They're tired of trying to talk with the other person so they agree to disagree as a polite way of brushing off the other person. That's not what striving for understanding is about.

Just listen to me!

Have you ever approached a colleague when you're having a bad day? You probably spent ten minutes venting to this person, only to have her tell you all the things you need to do to fix the problem. You knock down every one of her ideas, not understanding why she keeps interrupting you. The reason is that the two of you have different goals for the conversation. You simply want to vent and know someone is listening, and the other person thinks the goal is to fix the situation. Without this awareness, you'll both walk away from the conversation frustrated and irritated with each other. Instead, the next time you want to vent about something, be upfront with the person: "Hey, I'm having a bad day. Can I just vent to you for a few minutes? I don't need you to fix anything; I just want you to listen. Is that okay?"

Ultimately, if two people have a real and productive conversation where they both listen and feel heard, they'll probably find more in common with each other and find more points to agree on. For more information on how to have these difficult yet more productive conversations, see Chapter 16. Changing the goal of communication is a new way to think about it, and, as a supervisor, if you shift your thinking, you'll have a head start on working with employees to solve their issues.

Choosing words carefully: The importance of language

One of the most common contributors to miscommunication is language. The words you use can lead to misinterpretations and negative reactions, either because you choose words that don't accurately express what you're trying to say or you use words that the listener finds inappropriate or insulting. In some cases, the miscommunication is simply a matter of semantics.

Making sure you're on the same page

Semantics refers to the meaning and interpretation of words. The definition or understanding you attach to a specific word can be different from another person's understanding of the same word. Take "respect," for example. What does respect mean to you? How would you define the word? Now ask people on your team the same question, and it will quickly become clear that your group is made up of individuals who each describe the word differently. Don't be surprised if the group thoroughly dissects the word and a spirited conversation about respect's true meaning and connotation ensues.

The best ways to avoid misunderstandings are to be specific and to get creative. Take more time in a conversation, choose your words carefully, and ask clarifying questions. If you suspect semantics are getting in the way, take a moment to define the word in question. State what that word means to you, and ask the other person what it means to her. This clarification could shed light on the disagreement. When starting a conversation, try to avoid misunderstandings by giving thought to what information you're trying to relay or gather, and then formulate a statement or question that meets that goal. For example, asking a colleague to respect you isn't as clear as asking her to respect you by not playing practical jokes on you. Telling your boss that you want time off isn't as clear as requesting a vacation for the week of January 1st.

You can also get creative and find other ways to get your message across. If words are keeping people from a shared understanding, try a different method of communication. Visual aids like photos, maps, charts, and diagrams can be tremendously helpful. In some situations you may find that a demonstration or tutorial clarifies a point.

Being precise

Using words or phrases that are vague or too open to interpretation can cause problems. If you're using one of the following words or phrases, consider whether you can be more precise:

- ✔ Sometimes
- ✔ In a timely manner
- ✔ As needed
- ✔ To my satisfaction
- ✔ A few
- ✔ Several
- ✔ Often
- ✔ Frequently
- ✔ When you get a chance

To you, "sometimes" may mean twice a week, whereas to your employee it means twice a month. If your boss wants you to complete your project "in a timely manner," does that mean tomorrow or next Tuesday? Just because you know what you're trying to say doesn't mean the other person does!

Be proactive and use specifics whenever possible. If you have an expectation that the sales receipts need to be turned in "at the end of the day," say that what you really mean is by 5:30 p.m. each and every day. Being specific avoids confusion and uncertainty.

The president of a company decided to institute a new dress code. He relayed the information to the HR director and left it up to her to disseminate the details. Fearing that the information wouldn't be well received by the employees, the director decided to share the information by e-mail. He chose nice, fluffy language that he hoped would soften the blow. The e-mail instantly created confusion and stress among the employees, who couldn't understand what kind of dress was appropriate and what wasn't. The e-mail failed on two levels: It didn't accurately relay the new dress code to the employees, and it disrupted the day's work by causing conflicts among employees, who argued individual interpretations of the code with one another. The director could have prevented the stress and ensuing conflict by choosing words that accurately and specifically described the new rules.

Avoiding inflammatory language

Using the wrong language can also make a good situation bad or a bad situation worse. By choosing inflammatory words to get a message across, you can easily sound insulting, insensitive, hurtful, or just plain mean. Some inflammatory words, such as name-calling, are very obvious. Calling someone stupid, lazy, or incompetent can get you in trouble, not only with your team but also with Human Resources!

Beyond the obvious, some words are just easier for a listener to hear. For example, if an employee approaches you and says, "I hate my job," you'll probably have a negative reaction. If the same employee instead says, "I'm dissatisfied with my job," your reaction would be quite different. Some words have a negative impact, and the trick to getting a more positive reaction from listeners is to find more neutral words that they won't find offensive. I provide hints on neutralizing language in Chapter 7.

Body language: Reading others' and managing your own

Another important element in an individual's communication arsenal is body language. Body language goes beyond obvious gestures (like showing someone your appreciation when he cuts you off in traffic!) and encompasses everything people do physically while they're in a conversation.

Body language that's open and that encourages conversation includes

✔ Facing the person who's speaking

✔ Making good eye contact

✔ Nodding occasionally

✔ Having arms in an open position rather than crossed in front of the chest

Body language can also be closed and discourage communication. The following will shut down the conversation and probably earn you a reputation for being rude:

✔ Not looking at the person speaking

✔ Rolling your eyes

✔ Having an expressionless face, frowning, or squinting to indicate the speaker isn't making any sense

✔ Staring off into space

✔ Turning your back to the speaker

Pay attention to your group and make note of body language during tense or heated conversations. Do the same when things are going well and note the difference.

Be aware of the nonverbal cues you're giving off in the workplace, and be aware of the nonverbal cues you're getting from everyone else. Clenched fists, tightness in the shoulders, and increased breathing can all indicate stress, whereas a relaxed posture, leaning back in the chair, and a smile can mean happiness and contentment. What do these gestures say about the work environment, your team, and yourself? When you know what to look for, you can tell a lot about someone's day before she even says a word.

Use body language as a clue to discern what may be going on, but don't use it exclusively. If a co-worker walks into the office one day, doesn't say hello, and immediately sits down at her desk, maybe she's mad at you — or maybe she has a very busy day ahead and wants to stay focused. Making some assumptions about body language is fine, but check out those assumptions before acting or reacting badly. For more information on assumptions, see Chapter 3.

Discerning tone of voice

A largely under-recognized yet critical part of verbal communication is tone of voice. *How* something is said — either the tone used or the inflection given — can completely change the meaning of the words. Without knowing whether the speaker's intent is to be funny, sarcastic, serious, or sincere, a person may respond inappropriately. This often happens to people who communicate predominantly in writing. The written word leaves tone of voice open to interpretation, and you don't want to learn that lesson the hard way.

Dave needed to submit an article to his editor by 2 p.m. When 1:45 rolled around and he knew he'd need 30 more minutes, he sent a quick e-mail: "Janet, I'm putting the finishing touches on the article and will have it to you by 2:15." Minutes after he sent the e-mail, he received the following response: "Dave, I can't wait an extra 15 minutes for you. I'm on a serious deadline, and your lack of responsibility to adhere to your submission time will put us all in terrible trouble." Needless to say, this caused major panic in Dave. The words in the e-mail were very serious, and he wondered how this situation would affect his relationship with his boss. He immediately sent an apologetic e-mail and promised it would never, ever happen again. He waited anxiously to see how Janet would respond. After five long minutes, he received the following: "Dave, I was only kidding. I can't believe you thought I was serious!" This is just one example of how easy it is to misinterpret written communication, so err on the side of caution when using e-mails, letters, and notes. If you get a written communication that offends you, pause and consider that you may be misinterpreting the sender's meaning. Follow up with the individual for some clarification before you reply.

Depending on the kinds of interactions you have with employees, you may or may not be familiar with their style of communication. If you have a new team member, it may take some time before everyone can accurately identify when that person is being serious and when she's being sarcastic. Some guesswork comes into play, but the important thing is to be aware of the role tone of voice plays in communication and ultimately in conflict. Tone may be the whole reason for a dispute.

If you have an individual at work who's more sensitive to tone of voice than others, that person may be uncomfortable with raised voices. She may avoid working with someone who has a naturally loud voice, and the two could have a misunderstanding about each other's intentions, which could impact their ability to maintain a productive working relationship. Knowing some of the finer points of communication helps you consider conflict causes that go beyond the obvious reasons. Rather than letting the interpretation fester, address tone early on by asking a few questions to bring awareness to the speaker. For example, if I'm talking with someone who has an edge to her voice, I may ask if she's having a bad day or if she's upset with me. Sometimes the answer is "yes," and sometimes the speaker is simply unaware that she's coming across that way. This is a two-way street, so feel free to ask if the way you're speaking is getting in the way of the listener understanding your point.

Figuring Out Why People Think the Way They Do

People are unique in the ways they receive and process information. Experts have dedicated careers to exploring the scientific and psychological reasons for the differences in communication among people, and you could spend as many years trying to psychoanalyze your team. But to makes things a bit simpler, for now consider this section's practical overview of what makes individuals tick.

Values: Understanding what's important to people

Everyone has a set of core *values* — things that are fundamentally important to them. These values, which are sometimes called *interests,* are the underlying beliefs and principles that individuals carry around with them every single day. You'll notice with your co-workers that a particular value is very important to one but not as important to another. You'll also notice that a co-worker may value several things but not all to the same degree — some things are more important than others.

Being aware of the fact that values are common motivators for people gives you greater insight into why certain conflicts happen. Identifying the values in a conflict helps you as a manager find resolution to the conflict. When the conversation changes from individual positions to what's most important to everyone, you and your team can expand your options to include solutions that work for everyone.

People don't have just one core value; they have a whole set of values with varying degrees of importance. These values affect how they act, react, and interact with their environments. Following is a list of values you may see in your workplace. It's certainly not exhaustive, and you may even think of one or two values that matter to you that aren't here. That's okay — I just list the ones I run across the most so you can start to make the connection between a surface issue and a deeper motivation.

Acceptance	Equality	Order
Accomplishment	Family	Peace
Accountability	Freedom	Pride
Ambition	Friendship	Privacy
Autonomy	Harmony	Recognition
Comfort	Honesty	Reputation
Competence	Honor	Respect
Control	Inclusion	Responsibility
Cooperation	Independence	Safety
Courage	Innovation	Security
Creativity	Integrity	Stability
Dignity	Leadership	Teamwork
Efficiency	Loyalty	Trust

As you can see, even a short list of values is pretty long! In my experience, there are common values, and then there are a handful of values that are almost always at the heart of a workplace conflict. Take a closer look at these and see if you can identify any of them within your team:

✔ **Acceptance:** People who value acceptance want to be part of the team. They want to feel like an equal, be in on information as soon as it's out there, and generally feel a sense of belonging.

✔ **Accomplishment:** People who value accomplishment love it when the job is done and there's a finished product. Taking something from nothing, working it all the way through, and not giving up are important to them. They're often the person on a job site who enjoys the last turn of the wrench, or the individual who puts the finishing touches on the quarterly reports.

✔ **Autonomy:** Those who look for autonomy place a high value on being accountable to self over others. They like to work at their own pace, free from oversight and the influence of supervisors. They may enjoy working as part of a team but prefer to be fully responsible and accountable, demonstrating that they can be trusted to get the job done.

✔ **Competence:** Those who value competence may place a strong emphasis on knowledge, skills, and training. These folks like to do the job right the first time and look for others to do the same. They want to believe that management has matched the right person to the job at hand. They may be quick to complain if they feel someone is falling short on their responsibilities, but that's because at their core they care about the quality of the work.

✔ **Control:** These folks have a need to know all the details, and it's important to them to orchestrate every aspect of larger projects. Managing them, you may appreciate that they're able to see the big picture, but you may notice that they risk getting bogged down in the details.

✔ **Cooperation:** "We're all responsible for the work that gets done around here," says the person who values cooperation. These people look toward the sharing of information, tasks, and details to further the ends of the organization they work for. They believe that people are better and more successful working together than individually. Go team!

✔ **Recognition:** Those who value recognition may place a high value on giving and receiving credit for a job well done. They thrive on compliments, and they may have awards and certificates plastered on their walls. A pat on the back goes a long way with these team members. For them it's not always enough to know they did a good job; they want something to validate the results and will work hard to get it.

✔ **Respect:** Respect is one of the most common values and yet one of the most elusive to explain. Respect in the workplace can be acknowledging someone's expertise, validating a person's contribution to the group, or simply not stealing someone's lunch out of the refrigerator. On a basic level, those who value respect treat others in a way that doesn't diminish their self worth.

These values and others show up at work everyday. How someone reacts to a situation can give you a clue about her values. For example, if an employee becomes upset when a customer is rude to her, that employee probably values respect, or common courtesy. If your boss gives you a raise because you always get your work done by the deadlines, your boss may value responsibility. If you feel frustrated and angry because a colleague lied to you, you may value honesty.

Values are unique to the individual, so don't assume you've automatically identified the right value for a co-worker, or that you can label someone with just one value. If three staff members get upset because their meeting started 15 minutes late, that doesn't mean they all value the same thing. One may be upset because starting a meeting late is disrespectful of his time, or because he values order. Another may be upset because family is the most important thing to her, and she's missing time she could be spending with her family. And the third person may want everyone to show up for the meeting on time because that's how adults show they're responsible and accountable. All may additionally value honesty, which they feel has been violated, because previous agreements stressed that meetings should start on time.

When you're dealing with a conflict at work, a person's values show up in two ways:

- A particular issue becomes a problem for an individual based on her values.

- The people involved in the problem take certain positions because of their values.

As an example, look at a conflict between business partners where the issue is how to spend a $3,000 budget surplus. Jan's position is that the company should spend the money on new, ergonomic chairs for its eight employees. Marge's position is that the company should replace the old and outdated sign on the front of its building. What do these two people value? Possible values for Jan include employee health, happiness, and morale. Possible values for Marge include professionalism, innovation, and visibility in the community.

Filters: Sifting through information

Each person has her own filters or lens through which she sees the world. Imagine a metaphysical barrier around every person that filters all the information that she receives. Everything she sees, hears, and says has to go through not only her own filter but through the filters of everyone she interacts with. These filters can color, distort, or amplify the information in both positive and negative ways. Figure 2-1 shows that communication is a two-way street; each person in a conversation is sending out and receiving information. When speaking, you send out information that has been encoded or translated through your own filters. The listener receives the information and decodes or translates it with her filters. When filters are similar, the message gets through relatively intact. When the filters are very different (and they almost always are), the message can be distorted or lost.

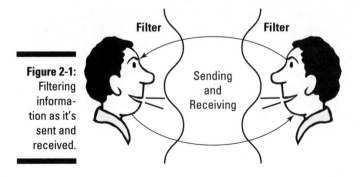

Figure 2-1:
Filtering
informa-
tion as it's
sent and
received.

Filters are a manifestation of self-identity, which is how people see themselves in the world. It's your belief of who you are as a person and the characteristics you place on yourself, whether you identify as being smart, funny, conservative, law-abiding, forgetful, or loving. Contributors to self-identity include:

- ✔ **Personal history:** Everything a person experiences in life affects who she is and how she sees the world. History helps people make decisions, put information into context, and create comfortable patterns or routines.

- ✔ **Culture:** Whole books are dedicated to this subject, so to keep it brief, culture on a basic level includes all the characteristics associated with a group of people that share something in common. What they have in common could be a physical location (a country), a particular kind of work (corporate culture), or a shared interest (pop music).

- ✔ **Values:** Values are what a person holds near and dear. They're concepts like respect, safety, comfort, health, family, honesty, and the like. They're not tangible items like expensive cars or diamond jewelry. They dictate how you react to the people and events in your life, and they add to the expectations you have for yourself, your co-workers, and society in general. See the section "Values: Understanding what's important to people" earlier in the chapter for more on values.

- ✔ **Roles:** Roles relate to the relationships a person has with those around him. Parent, child, sibling, friend, neighbor, co-worker, boss, confidant, and caregiver are all examples of roles people play. Roles affect interactions with others and create expectations for those interactions.

- ✔ **Education:** Everything someone has learned throughout her life, in both school and life settings, affects her ability to receive and send information. This can include information she learned firsthand through trial and error or something she picked up from a textbook or a colleague.

All these things create self-identity, and collectively, they help answer the question of why people say and do the things they say and do. (Because people are individuals, that's why.) In the workplace, you have a collection of people with different histories, values, cultures, and roles working together. Differences in opinions, work approaches, communication styles, and expectations are inevitable. Strive to understand everyone's diversity, and use it to create a strong, effective, and respectful work environment. Differences are the one thing everyone has in common!

History: Operating from the past

People use past experiences to predict the future. If Joe the delivery guy is always 30 minutes late, you're going to assume the next time you place an order that he'll be 30 minutes late. If he's been late the last seven times, why would you think he'd be on time now?

This phenomenon for using the past to indicate the future is both useful and limiting. You can draw from your experiences and knowledge to be productive. For example, a receptionist usually knows when staff members are in their offices and can refer calls and clients appropriately, or a supervisor may know that the majority of her team prefers to take a vacation day on the Friday before a three-day weekend and plans accordingly.

However, viewing the future as a continuation of the past can be dangerous because doing so doesn't allow for change. As a manager, how often do you hear, "Susan never gets her reports in on time," or, "Steve always comes in late"? When you hear these comments, don't accept them as the unwavering truth for future behavior. If these behaviors are undesirable and you want them to stop, consider what it will take to change the situation and make the future look different than the past. This may mean having individual conversations with employees, or bringing two or more employees together for a discussion. Chapter 5 gives you additional tools to assess the situation.

People have very different past experiences. What you know to be true because of a previous experience may not be true for someone else. Just because you've had a bad interaction with a co-worker doesn't mean that everyone else in the office has.

When differences of opinion escalate to major conflict, co-workers may lose faith in one another and form patterns of negative associations. These feelings can be compounded by unsuccessful attempts to correct the behavior. Hopelessness sets in, trust is lost, and individuals become unhappy, disillusioned, and dissatisfied. If you've inherited (or created) a team like this, all is not lost. The good news is that you can change it! State that current behavior or patterns of behavior are opportunities to change. Be clear with directives, investigate barriers to change, and address issues early as ways to demonstrate your belief that what has happened in the past doesn't have to be the recipe for the future.

Considering the Importance of Emotions

It's common to believe that work is work and that emotions have no place in a professional setting. You hear people refer to emotions as a sign of weakness, and employees who can bottle up their emotional reactions and behave like robots on the job are often praised. So if that's the goal, try a mental experiment. Strip all emotion out of your workplace. No anger, fear, frustration, or jealousy — this sounds great, right? Of course, you also have to take away pride in a job well-done, enthusiasm for the mission, inspiration to provide a better service, and satisfaction in an accomplishment. The workplace void of emotion is a collection of automatons going to work every day out of need or habit; such an atmosphere lacks joy, admiration, curiosity, or wonder. That sounds rather depressing and boring. Oh sorry — those are emotions, too.

Get past this notion of never needing or wanting emotions in the workplace. Focus on how to productively and professionally manage the emotional climate in the workplace, which allows you, the manager, to get the best out of your team. To discover how to do that, read on.

Listening to what emotions tell you

People have emotional reactions to many things in life. People like and freely accept emotions such as happiness, fondness, hope, satisfaction, and amusement. Emotions people dislike and prefer to avoid include sadness, suffering, hurt, torment, shame, and loneliness. You can usually link any emotion, positive or negative, to a satisfied or unsatisfied value. Contentment and satisfaction indicate that someone's values are being met. Sadness, anger, frustration, or disappointment indicates that someone's values are unmet or are being violated. This natural connection between emotions and values shows up throughout the day without you even noticing it. (See the earlier section "Values: Understanding what's important to people" for more information about these values.)

In the workplace, you'll see strong emotions around values like security, survival, and anything that impacts people's ability to maintain their basic needs. You'll also see strong reactions around issues of professionalism, accomplishment, or reputation from individuals whose sense of self is closely tied to their occupation. Keep in mind that what's happening *at* work may not stem *from* work. An employee may be feeling that core values in her personal life are at risk, which in turn can trigger negative emotions on the job.

Anger is a more complex emotion than most people realize. Anger has a natural tendency to mask or overshadow other emotions a person may be feeling. For example, a co-worker may be angry about a prank that made her look bad. If you dig deeper, her core emotion is embarrassment, and the anger is the outward expression of it. This is true for a lot of emotions: fear, worry, disappointment, confusion, and so on. Peel back the layers of the conflict and the emotions to get at what's really happening for that person. Ask open-ended questions like those in Chapter 8 to identify what's important so you can find a more accurate solution.

Dealing with emotional intensity and impact

Not all emotions are equal in intensity. Some are mild and unassuming, while others are strong and imposing. The intensity of an emotion may be a clear indication of how important that topic or subject is to someone. Figure 2-2 shows examples of levels of intensity.

The intensity of emotions can play a large role in the escalation of conflict. Visualize a conflict escalator — the higher you go on the escalator, the more intense and serious the conflict and emotions are. Also realize that the higher up on the escalator you go, the harder it is to come down.

Anger is a natural response to many negative conflicts; it prepares the mind and body to protect and defend itself. Therefore, anger is sometimes necessary for survival. However, far too often in conflict situations, anger takes a person up the conflict escalator and ends up making the situation worse instead of better.

As a manager, be aware of the emotional climate in your workplace, and address medium-intensity emotions and conflicts early on. It's easier to address a situation when someone is agitated than when she's irate. Low-intensity emotions or conflicts probably don't need your intervention. Let people have a bad day or be frustrated with a client's demands without investigating further. Keep an eye on things, and if you see a situation turn a corner or become worse, you always have the option to act.

Finally, be aware of the cycle of strong emotion. When people reach the very top of the conflict escalator, they're in crisis mode, and their emotions make it nearly impossible for them to think clearly. Reasoning and logic are easier for someone to access either before she gets to the point of crisis or after the crisis is over and she's had an opportunity to relax. After a blowup at work, don't try to reason and negotiate with the person right then and there. Be aware of the cycle and give the individual some time to cool down.

	Happy	Sad	Angry	Confused
High Intensity	Elated	Depressed	Furious	Bewildered
	Excited	Dejected	Enraged	Troubled
	Overjoyed	Heartbroken	Outraged	Desperate
	Thrilled	Crushed	Irate	
	Exuberant	Hopeless	Seething	
	Ecstatic	Woeful	Fired-up	
	Joyous	Sorrowful	Disgusted	
		Melancholy		
Medium Intensity	Delighted	Distressed	Aggravated	Baffled
	Cheerful	Hurt	Mad	Puzzled
	Jovial	Upset	Frustrated	Disorganized
	Satisfied	Disappointed	Agitated	Disoriented
	Fulfilled	Regretful	Perturbed	Lost
	Merry	Unhappy	Upset	Disheveled
		Dissatisfied		
		Dismayed		
Mild Intensity	Content	Down	Annoyed	Foggy
	Pleasant	Moody	Put out	Misplaced
	Fine	Blue	Irritated	Undecided
	Mellow	Sorry	Touchy	Mixed-up
	Pleased		Perplexed	Unsure

Figure 2-2:
Intensity of emotions.

Acknowledging and processing difficult emotions on your team

Positive emotions are accepted and encouraged in the workplace, but negative emotions cause dread, discomfort, or panic in everyone around them. People don't want to see anger, frustration, sadness, fear, or loss in their place of work. Ever been in a meeting when someone gets emotional about something, and everyone's eyes hit the table while they take imaginary notes? Uncomfortable!

Simply wanting these emotions to go away won't bring peace and happiness into your workplace. On the contrary, the emotions will continue to cause you and your organization conflict until you deal with them.

But most people — managers and co-workers alike — are unequipped to handle emotions. They can tell when someone is getting emotional, but the ability to accurately identify or handle the emotion is another story. As a manager, you've probably experienced the disruptive impact of negative emotions in the workplace, so focusing now on how to handle situations when they arise will give you a leg up on creating a more productive team.

First, be a good listener. Hear what the person has to say, and don't be compelled to fix the problem or offer solutions. Often, if a person can simply talk about what she's feeling, she can identify the emotion and gain the ability to move forward all on her own. Sometimes just allowing someone to get her concerns off her chest can resolve the conflict. Who hasn't benefited from a good talk, laugh, or cry about a situation? Getting it out means she can sift through all the emotions and you can help her discover what's really bothering her so she can create a fix that matches the problem. For tips on how to demonstrate that you're listening, see Chapter 7.

You're not the in-house counselor, and it's important for you to have boundaries. If someone is having serious emotional difficulties, know what resources are available through the organization and leverage them accordingly. Start with Human Resources for guidance, and check out other options I give in Chapter 13.

While you're showing that you're listening, help your employee identify the source of her emotion by asking open-ended questions like those found in Chapter 8. Helping someone understand why she's feeling frustrated or upset can bring her some relief. In particular, if you sense a strong degree of fear, uncertainty, or anxiety, you may want to look for something that has threatened her sense of security or caused a significant sense of loss. Things like budget cuts, downsizing, or fear of losing an important business account often cause these emotions.

Responding to Conflict

People react to and manage conflict very differently. Three people in the same situation may have three distinctly different reactions. And to make matters more complex, not only do people act differently in conflict, but the same person may respond one way in one situation and react another way in a different situation. How someone reacts can depend on the kind of conflict she's in, who the conflict is with, where the person is, and whether the issue is personal or professional. For instance, how you handle conflict with your spouse can be completely different than how you handle conflict with a co-worker.

Methods for managing conflict vary from person to person and situation to situation. Each method has its own distinct benefits when used in the right situations. Following are some common conflict management styles that people in your department may use and hints on how you can address them.

Giving in

This technique simply lets people have what they want. When someone who tends to give in finds herself in conflict, she's prone to sacrifice her own opinions or requests just to keep the peace.

You may manage an employee who's considered the ultimate team player. Everyone knows if they need help with something, they can go to this person because she never says no. Even when she has work up to her ears, she finds a way to accommodate requests. Above all, this person wants peace in the office. She doesn't want to hurt anyone's feelings, and she'll do anything to preserve working relationships, even at the expense of her health, happiness, or sanity!

The person who gives in rarely makes waves at work and is often considered by higher-ups (sometimes incorrectly) to be the easiest employee to manage. But managing an employee who doesn't put up a fight is more complicated than it sounds. Be extra sensitive to whether this employee is being overworked or taken advantage of. She may not verbalize her dissatisfaction with how she's being treated, and she may repress her emotions to the point of explosion. She's the type of employee who will up and quit one day, and you'll have no idea why. Check in frequently and let her know that it's okay to say no when she's overwhelmed. You may also need to help her set new boundaries and create more balanced relationships with her co-workers.

Avoiding the fight

This is the "flight" portion of the old adage "fight or flight." Rather than deal with the conflict, this person would rather avoid it altogether. She has a fairly low tolerance for conflict and places a high importance on safety and comfort.

You may have someone on your team who calls in sick frequently, prefers to work alone or at home, or would rather pass off problems or difficult conversations onto you, the boss. Her sensitivity to conflict is high, and she may have trouble working with more aggressive or demanding individuals. It's not uncommon for these employees to be passive-aggressive at times, asserting their power in ways that don't involve face-to-face confrontation, like communicating disagreements by e-mail, not passing along information to make co-workers look bad, or just not showing up to an important meeting.

An employee who avoids conflict needs encouragement to engage in difficult conversations, whether with you or with a co-worker. If you want her to open up to you, make sure she knows that you're receptive and ready to listen. If she has concerns, such as confidentiality, find ways to reassure her that it's safe to talk with you.

You may also want to increase her exposure to productive conflict. Holding staff meetings that allow for a free flow of ideas, some of which may be contradictory, is a way to place her in the midst of conflict without experiencing the force of it directly. Make sure the conversation is open and respectful; it helps if the team members trust one another well enough to be honest without taking any disagreements personally.

Fighting it out

These employees have no problem standing up for themselves. They're aggressive when confronted with conflict, and they may be the ones who start it in the first place. They may even view conflict as a game, and they enjoy competition because it's an opportunity to win. They're comfortable arguing and are persistent in fighting for what they think is right.

Often viewed as go-getters, these employees are focused and driven. It's not uncommon for them to be the most productive members on the team. When they find themselves disagreeing with someone, they can be insulting or dismissive without even meaning to be. If their aggression remains unchecked, they can become the bullies in the office.

As the manager, you may have to expand a fighter's focus to include the people around her. Help her concentrate on solutions that meet everyone's needs, not just her own. Let her know that working together allows her to reach her professional goals faster than her working alone. Do this in a private conversation in which you set an expectation for her new way of thinking. It's my experience that trying to swim upstream all the time only results in water up your nose, so point out that working against someone takes up valuable energy that could be used for everyone's benefit — especially hers!

Compromising

If you have a compromiser working for you, you'll notice that she isn't afraid of conflict but that she doesn't like to spend a lot of time on it, either. Conflict is a bother to her, a distraction from the real work that needs to get done. She tends to look for a quick and fair resolution. She's the first to suggest splitting a disputed dollar amount right down the middle, or she may support a proposal that gives everyone a little of what they want.

You should encourage an employee who jumps to a compromise quickly to look at the larger picture. Splitting something down the middle is fine in some situations, but sometimes that's not possible or advantageous. Help people with this style expand their thinking to include what it is that each person really wants. (Read the earlier section "Values: Understanding what's important to people" for ideas to get past the surface issues.)

I knew of a case where two employees worked in a small office where they shared the responsibility of answering the phone. One day the manager heard them arguing about who should be taking the calls that day, and both were saying that the other person should be doing it. The manager decided to intercede. He could have quickly made a decision for them and said, "Bonnie, you'll answer the phone in the morning, and Mary, you'll answer the phone in the afternoon." That sounds like a perfectly fair solution to a compromiser, right? Instead, he asked each of them, "What about answering the phones isn't working for you?" Bonnie said her severe head cold was making it next to impossible for her to hear anything over the phone, and both she and the callers were getting frustrated. Mary said she had a sudden influx in paperwork that day and would never be able to get through all of it if she was distracted by the phone. At that point, Bonnie suggested that she could process Mary's paperwork if Mary would agree to answer the phone. They agreed, both were satisfied, and the manager taught his team a valuable lesson in conflict resolution.

Working together

Some people really enjoy working with others. In all aspects of their lives, they'd rather work or interact with people than be alone. As employees, they're very social and enjoy a good, thorough conversation. You may notice that they seek out the opinions of others when making decisions and often get into long discussions with colleagues because they enjoy collaborating and sharing ideas. They approach conflict in a similar way — they want to work through the conflict by discussing all the possible solutions, looking for the perfect answer.

Working together, although great at creating and supporting relationships among employees, doesn't work well when quick decisions need to be made. It's often difficult for people with this style to know when the discussion is over and when it's time to make a decision. When working in groups, these employees may alienate or exhaust peers who prefer action over words.

One way to help is to provide focus. Given the information they have available to them, what decisions can they make now? It can also be useful to provide boundaries and deadlines well in advance. Give them structure with clear expectations and a little additional time so they can gather information, but let them know that there's a point when the talking stops and they must make a decision.

Chapter 3

Determining How Groups Contribute to Conflict

In This Chapter

▶ Identifying how your employees fit within your organization

▶ Highlighting common areas of conflict within groups

▶ Avoiding negative group behaviors

*P*ut two or more people in a work setting and you're bound to have conflict. The conflicts can range from minor squabbles about who drank the last cup of coffee to major disputes involving discrimination or sexual harassment. Anytime people interact, disagreements and disputes can result.

Whether you wear a white tie, a blue shirt, or a uniform, your workplace has naturally and artificially formed groups that add characteristics to the work environment and, ultimately, to conflict. You've probably heard phrases like *group think* and *mob mentality* used to describe what can happen when people get together. And with terms like these floating around, it's natural to assume that groups are bad. But, as a manager, you know that groups are essential!

Created based on similar job assignments (like the accounting department) or pulled together based on skill sets (like a selected task force), groups are required to get the work done. Teams can work like well-oiled machines that win awards, exceed sales projections, solve what seem like insurmountable problems, and build elaborate buildings in record time. So if groups have the capacity to do such great things, what is it about them that causes conflict?

In this chapter, I share how the company, its culture, and the phenomenon of group dynamics all have the potential to turn an otherwise functioning group into a fragmented team of distracted individuals.

Observing Your Organization's Culture

Conflict between two employees is one thing, but when conflict is between employees and the organization it's a whole other issue. When employees are up in arms, consider how the organization itself may be contributing to conflict. Start by looking at your enterprise and consider its culture.

Your organization's culture is made up of its philosophies, customs, and ethos, as well as the written and unwritten rules regarding policies, procedures, protocol, and conduct. These components are the basis for your establishment's culture and are evident in the organization's focus, how it hires and promotes employees, and how it adapts to change. Some examples of different kinds of workplace cultures include:

- Top-down, military-style organizations, which often have a very clear hierarchy. They stress the importance of structure and protocol, and decisions are made by those with power and rank. A structured company is a difficult work environment for people who prefer a more relaxed and flexible workplace or find value in the discussions that take place before decisions are made.

- Production or assembly-line companies, which focus on the individual and her role in the company. Like cogs in a wheel, employees are responsible for completing their part of a task so that everything continues to function properly. Employees who value creativity and like to do new and different things every day often don't appreciate this way of doing business and may feel stifled and unappreciated.

- Organizations with a looser configuration of employees, which put less emphasis on teamwork and more on individual achievement. Companies that have independent salespeople, for example, provide a lot of autonomy to their employees and focus more on the end goal than how the goal is achieved. This kind of environment doesn't work well for people who are motivated by collaboration and structure.

- Establishments that prioritize people and ideas over products. In these companies, titles and rank aren't important, and everyone has a vote in what happens. These environments don't work well for people who want to work independently or who don't appreciate a 20-minute discussion every time a decision needs to be made.

In addition to your company's culture, it has a distinct personality that's a combination of the culture and the unique personalities of its employees at any given time. Look at your establishment and consider what traits or characteristics you'd assign to the work environment. Have the majority of the employees created a fun, flexible, open-minded, creative, boisterous, ambitious, principled, driven, strict, friendly, spirited, serious, or conservative place to work? Conflict comes into play when the culture and organizational personality don't fit with the values or needs of one or more staff members.

Some employees expend a lot of energy trying to either fit into a workplace or make the workplace fit them. When neither possibility works, they have two options: create a change to meet their needs, or live within the structure that exists. If the conflict over culture is extreme and unworkable, then the company may not be the right one for that employee — and that's okay.

Identifying the organizational focus

Your organization has a goal, which is also called its purpose or mission statement — essentially, its reason for existing. This focus could be related to the kind of work environment you're in — corporate, business, government, nonprofit, public service, and so on — or it could depend on the philosophies and strategies of the leadership within your company, the management team, the board of directors, or the advisory council.

Each employee in your organization also has goals or reasons for going to work every day. How the goal of the whole organization fits with the goals of individual employees can explain why some employees stay with a company for 40 years and others high-tail it out in the first week. The difference in focus can be one source of conflict between employees and the organization.

For example, I mediated a case in which a handful of teachers had relocated to take positions with a small school district because it was the ideal place for them to create and grow a specialized learning curriculum. As the district grew, its focus changed and the teachers found themselves at odds with many of the employees who had been hired under the new regime. The old guard and the new guard both wanted what was best for the students, but the two groups couldn't see eye to eye on how best to achieve their goals. The powers that be, who were focused on new goals, sided with the newer employees, which caused conflict for everyone involved.

The scope of your company can also cause conflict. If the focus is too broad, some employees may become confused and uncertain about what direction the company is going. A nonprofit that wants to help everyone in the community with every need will end up with tired and overwhelmed employees. Equally, if the focus is too narrow, it can limit employee potential and miss out on ideas that contribute to its prosperity. A business that wants to sell only picture frames may miss out on opportunities if it dismisses an employee's suggestions to expand into the mirror market, leaving the employee feeling unsatisfied and looking for a company that'll appreciate her forward thinking.

Considering hiring or promoting practices

In a perfect world, every one of your staff would be a 100-percent perfect match to her job. All your employees would have the education, experience, and personality traits required to do their jobs better than anyone else. But this isn't a perfect world, and not everyone hired or promoted is a good fit. Because the organization, via HR or management, does the hiring and promoting, a misstep in personnel is considered the organization's fault.

Although there's no way to be absolutely certain you're hiring or promoting the right person, you need to consider a few intangible qualifications for a potential employee in order to keep possible conflicts at bay. Set aside the obvious criteria — like education, experience, and general ability to do the job — and then take some time to focus on how a new hire can affect a group.

Any change in personnel has a direct impact on a team. In a small business with only a handful of employees, everyone will be impacted by a change. In larger corporations, those who work most directly with the new employee are most affected. Whatever the situation, consider who's going to have the most contact or interaction with the new hire, and think about what traits in a potential employee are the most compatible with your current team.

Consider having your team's work styles assessed. You can easily find tools and assessments (online, in bookstores, or by hiring a specialist) to determine the strengths of each of your team members — and the exercise doesn't have to feel like a dreaded trip to the dentist. Not only will the assessment help you consider the traits and personalities you need from a new team member, but it also benefits employees, who need to work together on future projects.

Promoting an employee can be a little trickier than hiring someone new. You still want to consider the individual personality of the employee you're considering promoting, but you also need to be aware of how others will feel about the co-worker being promoted. Anger, jealousy, and disappointment are common reactions in employees who have *not* been chosen for promotions, and no matter how fair the decision may have been, those reactions may still be present no matter whom you choose to promote from within.

Be available to help others process the change. You can listen to those who are disappointed without necessarily having to do anything about it. You aren't required to justify your decision or act on their concern, but giving them a chance to say they disagree may help them put the issue behind them. (If you're not sure how to listen without acting, practice some of the tips I give you in Chapter 7.)

Serving up a reorg

A small university initiated a complete reorganization of its dietary program. What once was a university-run department was being outsourced and contracted to an out-of-state company.

Upon hearing the news of the reorganization, the dietary staff was instantly concerned. All the decisions regarding the changes had been made without their knowledge, and little information about the impact of the decisions was shared with the staff. What would happen to their jobs? What would happen to their benefits? Rumors and gossip started among the staff, and the uncertainty and stress became

unmanageable. The university organized an official information session on the subject, but by then, the damage had been done. The university did very little to help its employees adapt to the upcoming changes, and the results were disastrous.

Management missed an opportunity to explain how the changes would better meet the needs of the students, faculty, and staff. Providing accurate and up-to-date information throughout the reorganization, as well as an outlet for employee concerns (like those I give in Chapter 12) could have made the transition easier and smoother for everyone involved.

When you're hiring or promoting, think about the strengths of the people on your team and think about what's missing. What could a new addition to the team bring that would complement and benefit everyone? Create a list and consider these qualities in your applicants. Enlist staff members to add to the list as a way to get a broader view of the team's needs and to gain buy-in on your hiring strategy early on.

Considering how your company adapts to change

Structure and leadership determine how your organization views change. Organizations range from those that resist change and prefer the comfort and security of tried-and-true methods to those that thrive on new and innovative ways to enhance and grow the business. Most companies experience some level of change over the years, whether it's a large merger of multiple organizations or smaller changes, like hiring a new employee.

The important thing for any manager to remember is how dramatic *any* change can be for a workplace. Recognize the impact and address it quickly and effectively. Change can bring up fear, uncertainty, and stress for employees who are concerned about how the decisions will directly impact them, and they're relying on the organization to provide them with accurate and up-to-date information when it's available. Do just that.

When a substantial change in the workplace is going to occur, consider the following:

- ✔ Who will be affected by the change?
- ✔ Who needs to be involved in the decision making?
- ✔ How will those who are most affected have a voice in the decisions?
- ✔ What can you do to minimize rumors and inaccurate information?
- ✔ How much of what you know can you share with your team?
- ✔ What is the best method for sharing information?

After you determine what you can share and the best method for sharing, be consistent. You can create calm in the storm by keeping people informed on a regular basis. Even if nothing has changed since the last time you spoke with employees, you can keep them focused by letting them know that you'll tell them *what* you can, *when* you can, and that you're keeping them in mind during the transition.

From the opposite perspective, what happens when a group or team within an organization is more open and excited about change than the organization itself? Consider how an organization's resistance to change affects its employees. As staff create new and innovative ideas within an old, conservative structure, clashes can occur, valuable employees may leave, and others will be less willing to take on new projects or even give their best to existing assignments. If you're faced with such a position in a management role, acknowledge that you're in the middle. Do what you can to work within the structure that exists, listen to your team's concerns, and brainstorm with them to determine what you're willing to do on their behalf.

When you experience a conflict caused by change, prepare to do some damage control. Keep in mind that you're not 100 percent responsible for your employees' happiness, and pleasing everyone may not be possible, but consider a few of these ideas to help ease the tension:

- ✔ **Assess the fallout.** Find out which employees have been negatively affected by the change and how they're taking it.

- ✔ **Give people a voice.** Whether it's one unhappy employee or the whole bunch, give people a chance to voice their concerns. You can accomplish this in a variety of ways, including person-to-person meetings, anonymous surveys, suggestion boxes, and so on. (Chapter 12 gives you more details on creating a feedback loop for your employees.)

Be careful, though, not to set expectations you can't fulfill. Tell your staff straight up that there's a difference between having a voice and making the decisions.

✔ **Address concerns whenever possible.** Ignoring the impact or insincerely defending the company's actions just adds fuel to the fire. Listening to perspectives and acknowledging the reality of the situation is often enough to get people back on track.

✔ **Allow whatever control is possible.** Employees who are upset by change likely want some control over what's happening. If they're asking for small, manageable changes that can be implemented, consider doing so. It'll help them feel heard and respected. It also demonstrates how your team can pull together in the midst of chaos.

✔ **Bring in a professional.** If the change has caused more conflict than you or your organization can handle on its own, consider bringing in help. (See Chapter 14 for more information on how to choose outside experts and what to expect from them.)

Recognizing Team Dynamics

When the members of a group or team work closely together, certain dynamics start to surface. Those dynamics can be positive and productive (for example, when everyone is on the same page and they blow deadlines out of the water) or negative and counterproductive (when a team doesn't see eye to eye and the work stops). A number of factors can affect the energy of your team. In the following sections, I tell you about some common ones.

Dealing with mismatched expectations

Everyone in the workplace has expectations. Those expectations can be concrete, like not parking in the stalls reserved for the retail customers, or less tangible, like receiving respect from your colleagues. Conflict in groups comes into play when all the team members think they have the same expectations, but they really don't.

You may expect that your employees will arrive on time, take their breaks as scheduled, and leave on time. If one of your employees doesn't have that same expectation and decides to work more flexible hours, the two of you have mismatched expectations and a potential problem.

As soon as you get an inkling that your staff's expectations are different from yours or from other members of the team:

✔ **Ask each person to state *her* expectation and to expand on how she came to that point of view.** You'll find out more than if you only ask what they expect. Imagine your surprise if you find out the answer is "Because the person before you did it that way." Coming to resolution on mismatched expectations is easier if you all understand the background.

✔ **Be clear about *your* expectations and the impact of not meeting them.** And being clear doesn't mean barking orders — it means explaining your perspective in plain, concise language.

Acknowledging assigned and assumed roles

Groups tend to create official and unofficial roles for members. Much like a family or a sports team, individual employees take on certain responsibilities based on the needs of both the group and the person. After a role has been established, the group then relies on that member to fill that role.

Some roles — like a formal job description or a role specifically related to an assigned task — are officially handed down from the company. If your job description includes going to and from the post office to send and receive mail, you're now "the office mailperson." Other roles are self-selected — for example, maybe you enjoy planning parties, and you've taken it upon yourself to arrange all the upcoming birthday celebrations for the office. Event planning isn't an official part of your job, but you've decided to take it on, and now you're "the party planner."

Some roles are unofficially assigned to an individual by the rest of the group. You may have a colleague who's a particularly empathetic and compassionate listener. Other employees with a problem go to her because they know that they can share their problems and she'll listen. She's now "the counselor."

These roles, whether assigned or assumed, have an impact on both the individual and the group. When things are going well and everyone is happy with their roles, operations run smoothly and everything's fine. When employees become unhappy with their roles, you see conflict. Negative emotions — like resentment, irritation, and anger — often build in the person who no longer wants a particular role, and her dissatisfaction becomes more noticeable. She may start complaining, become snippy with co-workers who continue to enforce the role, or simply stop filling the part altogether.

REAL LIFE

That's not my job . . . or is it?

Kelly worked in a small office with six other real estate agents. They were all equals, sharing an office space to help reduce overhead costs. For the past few years, Kelly was the one who kept the front lobby tidy, stocked the break room, and managed the supply closet. She assumed this caretaker role on her own, but became unhappy and felt taken advantage of by her peers. Her attitude toward the other agents turned sour, and she stopped referring clients for listings.

The more Kelly tried to let the housekeeping tasks slide, the bigger the problem got. She finally decided to bring the issue to the attention of her colleagues, explaining that the work that she'd been doing the last three years had been voluntary, that she no longer wanted to continue in the role, and that she wanted solutions. After a simple discussion, the group thanked her for her past contributions and easily decided to split the cost of a part-time assistant. Everyone in the office was glad the issue was addressed and that a workable solution was found.

TIP

Times of transition can cause conflict because of the uncertainty involved. When an employee leaves, *all* her existing roles need to be filled. This includes roles that aren't attached to her job description but still impact the group. For example, if you lose an employee who was exceptionally proficient at trouble-shooting computer problems, even though it wasn't part of her job, the rest of the team will be greatly affected when you replace that employee with someone who isn't tech-savvy. Co-workers may automatically assume the new person can fill this role because she's the replacement, but the new person may not be happy with this imposed assignment because she doesn't think it's her responsibility. Consider adding assumed roles to the new hire's job description, or divvying up the responsibilities among your team as a way to ensure that all tasks and responsibilities are covered.

Redefining power

The most easily understood indication of power in the workplace is title or hierarchy. The CEO, the owner, the HR director, the boss, or the manager are common representations of the traditional view of power. Beyond title or position within the organization, power comes from other sources:

- **Physical attributes,** such as gender, appearance, and age
- **Mental attributes,** such as aptitudes, language, and problem solving

✔ **Skills,** such as industry-specific skills, verbal or written communication skills, and interpersonal skills

✔ **Experience,** such as knowledge of the field and years with the company

✔ **Status,** such as money, education, and social or professional networks

Don't kid yourself and think that power only rests at the top. In one way or another, every single person in your organization has some power because power is crucial to accomplishing work.

Clout associated with job skills and performance has a significant impact on the quality and quantity of work that gets done. Sources of power that relate to job performance, like the ability to persuade or the ability to track complicated details, are critical. Employees who constructively use their power are invaluable members of teams.

Power becomes problematic, however, when it isn't balanced. When a person or group has too much or too little power, team dynamics suffer and conflict is likely to arise.

Too much power

Be aware when power starts to become destructive — especially if you have a power-seeking group. Unchecked power coupled with a complete disregard for others is never a good combination. (See the "Groups Behaving Badly" section later in this chapter for examples of negative group dynamics.)

So before someone on your team successfully builds her army of doom, take a few minutes to consider these power-balancing techniques:

✔ **Be a good role model.** As the manager, you always have an opportunity to model positive behavior. Treat everyone respectfully and equally. Listen to the ideas of others and let them know that their opinions matter.

One of my favorite stories is that of two adults trying to figure out how to untangle the bumpers of two cars that were in an accident. They pushed, pulled, hammered, and tried for hours to separate the vehicles. A child who was watching the scene kept asking if she could help. She was repeatedly told that she didn't know anything about the situation and to keep quiet. Finally, the youngster said, "Why don't you let the air out of the tires of the first car?" The adults immediately saw the wisdom in the suggestion, let the air out, and quickly separated the vehicles.

Never assume that someone on your team doesn't have a great solution to a problem that's outside her area of expertise.

✔ **Be aware of emerging power imbalances in the office.** Address negative, counterproductive, or manipulative behavior early. A private conversation with the offending employee is always a good first step.

✔ **Help your employees use their power for good, not evil.** Power derived from job skills and performance can be channeled to help everyone, not just an individual at the expense of others. Point out the personal benefit in achieving group accomplishments in *addition* to individual accomplishments. For example, if you're a manager who values group success, let an employee know she has a better chance of receiving a bonus, recognition awards, or a promotion if she can identify specific actions on her part that have benefited the team.

✔ **If you can pinpoint a leader, focus your energy on getting her to work with you.** She already has influence over a group of employees who could be valuable contributors if only everyone would get on the same page. Address the issue upfront, listen to her perspective, and see if you can refocus her power instead of simply squashing her (as tempting as that may be). She could become an invaluable asset to you.

✔ **Encourage participation from everyone, and make sure those seeking power don't take over.** Create an equal playing field for all employees by bringing everyone together at the same time, not just the employees in the power-seeking group. This method allows you to give everyone a voice, not just the group. (For more tips on facilitating a meeting of this nature, see Chapter 10.)

Too little power

Just as excessive power can be problematic, so can a lack of power. Employees who feel as though they have no control over their situation can easily become disengaged and unhappy. A lack of power to change or affect a situation significantly diminishes motivation, causes poor job performance, increases sick leave, and potentially increases employee turnover.

When employees lose power or control over a situation, try the following:

✔ **Give your employees a forum to vent their frustration.** A private meeting with you will help them voice concerns and dissatisfaction.

✔ **Help them find things they can control.** These things could include other aspects of their job or how they want to respond to the situation, in either actions or words. As their manager, if there's something you can give them control over, consider doing it. For creative ideas on how to tap back into personal power, see the tips in Chapter 19.

✔ **Provide support and look for resources if needed.** Be there for your employees, as a stable presence who knows and understands what they're going through. When necessary, help them through difficult times by finding resources like an ombudsman, a conflict coach, or counseling service. These resources can help an employee talk through her situation and make decisions that are in her own best interest. You can find these resources either through HR or by accessing outside professionals.

Groups Behaving Badly

Groups that work well are an important component of the workplace. Often, nothing is more satisfying from a managerial perspective than the positive energy of a group accomplishing goals. On the other hand, groups that start behaving badly can become an absolute nightmare.

When employees join forces against each other, spread rumors, make false assumptions, and gossip, these actions can deplete morale and breed conflict. The following sections detail how staff associations can cause problems.

Joining cliques

I often hear executives say that the greatest asset an organization has is its people. I agree! Employees make significant contributions to the company's reputation, team morale, and the bottom line. But they don't go it alone. I'm no sociologist, but I know enough about the workplace to know that people are social creatures by nature, and that when they take on new jobs they seek out other people who will show them the ropes and help them assimilate.

Whenever I start a new job, I mark the calendar for 90 days out and look forward to that day, because it's ordinarily about the time when I've figured out who the major players are in each department, what most of the industry jargon means, and what time I need to arrive to get a good parking spot. You've probably noticed that for yourself, too. What usually happens around that time is you begin to recognize that you're part of a group — a clique, if you will.

Cliques form at work for a number of reasons, including shared interests, similar personalities, or proximity in working environments. Whatever the motivation employees have for attaching themselves to co-workers, the attachment has both positive and negative repercussions. I tell you about both the positives and the negatives in the upcoming sections, and I also give you some guidance on dealing with any clique that has become a problem.

Be aware of your own actions regarding cliques. As a manager, you walk a fine line when it comes to the strategic and social aspects of your job. If you're one of the players on the firm's basketball team, make sure discussions about last night's game include those around you, not just the other players. Asking what someone's experience is with the sport or limiting the conversation to a few highlights and moving on to another topic models appropriate attitudes and behavior toward social groups and cliques.

Focusing on the positive

If you're experiencing some negative fallout from a particular group, keep in mind that cliques aren't all bad. Groups can offer a lot to each other and the organization. Consider the following:

- **Cliques have power to get the job done.** There's safety in numbers, and cliques can have a lot of power, even if each member has little to no power in the company as an individual. Think of the jobs in your organization that, on the surface, may have the least authority to make decisions about strategy or company direction. Now think about the people in those jobs and their ability to get together and affect change.

- **Cliques play an integral part in team morale and create a sense of camaraderie that's difficult for even the most adept manager to replicate.**

- **Cliques can create a sense of safety and inclusion for their members, cultivating a multitude of positive experiences and workplace memories for employees.**

- **Cliques can work across departments and accomplish just about any task.** If you're part of a group or clique and your buddy calls for a favor, you make it happen. When personal relationships transcend company org charts, the give and take works for the benefit of the organization.

- **Cliques offer social benefits.** Who wouldn't want to be part of a group that offers them pats on the back and social invitations and reminds them that they're a part of something bigger than themselves?

Understanding the negative

Cliques start to go wrong when their power goes unchecked. Managers often overlook or dismiss grumblings about cliques because, to them, the grumbling feels like high school antics. Entertaining a discussion about how one of your team members feels slighted by a co-worker because she wasn't included in the group's lunch invitation may feel like baby-sitting to you. It's not your job to be the summer camp director, nor is it your place to act as an employee's personal therapist.

But if you're interested in ensuring that everyone on your team gives her best and is motivated to work hard to achieve the objectives you've set out for the year, then it *is* in your best interest to address the social aspects of cliques and how they impact the organization.

You know what's right for your situation, but consider intervening when

- Cliques are purposefully alienating others.
- Groups are closed to any perspectives other than their own.

✔ People are missing out on opportunities to expand their careers or view of the company.

✔ Alienation is causing employees to shut down and not perform to the best of their abilities.

✔ Bullying or inappropriate language and behaviors emerge.

Handling cliques

Sometimes intervening in cliques can be as simple as chatting with the group about how their behavior may appear to others. Not every clique-related issue needs to be addressed with the group, though. And there's often no need to take the approach that "If you don't have enough gum for everyone in the class, Johnny, then no one can have gum."

Begrudging the relationships of others doesn't do anyone any good, and it's unrealistic to expect that every person in every department should be included in every activity. If your company employs 36 people and only 9 spots are available on the baseball team, someone's not going to play. If one of your employees comes to you to discuss how she feels left out because some of her co-workers have formed a bowling league on their own time and they talk about it constantly during work hours, counsel her to participate in the conversation on a level that feels comfortable and sincere to her.

I facilitated a weeklong mediation training with a room full of students who were strangers to each other and a small number of staff mediators. The first few days, the group went to a nearby restaurant for lunch, where the staff mediators, who had worked together for some time, sat at the end of the table laughing and immersed in their own discussion. The rest of the group ate their lunch in silence, or made awkward attempts at conversation with the people next to them while the frivolity continued with the smaller group. At the end of the day, I talked to the staff mediators about the lunchtime experience. Of course, they meant no harm — they were merely enjoying one another's company. But when they became aware of the impact their actions had on the larger group, they adjusted their plans for lunch the next day and interacted with the larger group, creating a better experience for the students. I didn't have to go to HR or address their clique in front of the entire class — I had a quick conversation with the staff mediators, and the problem was solved.

Finding allies

One unhappy employee can quickly become a dozen unhappy employees. When people are in conflict or disappointed with a policy or a decision, they tend to look for allies; others who see the situation the same way they do and are willing to provide support. Finding allies bolsters people's beliefs that they're 100 percent right and adds fuel to the fire.

An unhealthy allegiance, one that has a negative impact on the workplace, can divide a workplace into factions and create a multitude of problems. Communication becomes difficult among members of different groups and an employee may feel that she needs to walk on eggshells to avoid saying or doing the wrong thing. This increased tension and mistrust creates more unhappy employees, and the cycle continues.

Even people who don't consider themselves part of any one group can become workplace casualties, growing dissatisfied with the tension in their environment and quitting or transferring to get away from it all. They become the innocent employees you lose by not addressing the problems.

Preventing the formation of negative groups in the first place is the preferred course of action. Encourage open communication and conflict resolution among all your staff. Be upfront about how you want everyone to resolve even minor disagreements among one another early on, instead of prolonging the dispute or going to others for coalition-building. Consider providing training on communication or conflict resolution as a way to demonstrate your support for early intervention. Look to your organization for additional conflict systems resources, like those I mention in Chapter 13, or look to outside resources, like those in Chapter 14.

So, what happens if an army of allies has successfully formed and you don't like the direction it's heading? One of the best ways to combat destructive groups or factions is to encourage more interaction among all your staff. Either create opportunities for everyone to interact together, or look for projects that include different combinations of employees. Encourage the formation of working relationships among different groups, teams, or departments as a way for people to build relationships and different associations. Refocus the power of the group by using the tips I list in the "Redefining power" section earlier in this chapter.

Creating inaccurate assumptions

Assumptions are a necessary part of life. When accurate, they keep you safe, save you time, and, generally speaking, make your life easier. For example, seeing storm clouds in the sky may prompt you to grab your umbrella, as you assume you may need it even though it's not raining at the moment. Noticing an expired date on your morning yogurt and assuming it's no longer edible may save you from having to use one of your sick days. Imagine how tedious it would be if you had to research and check out every minute detail of your day to make sure you had every piece of information available. No one has that much time!

But as useful as assumptions are, they can also get you into trouble. Not accurately processing the information in your environment or only seeing what you want to see can lead to incorrect assumptions. Acting on or perpetuating the assumptions by sharing them with others can start and escalate conflict. The following sections cover how people make assumptions and what you can do to prevent them from causing conflict.

Making assumptions in the first place

You and your employees view information and make predictions and assumptions to fit your previous experiences. Your assumptions are based on things you've learned from the physical environment and your previous experiences in similar situations. Factor in your emotional state at the time you make the assumption, and you have a general overview of how you and others come to certain conclusions.

History or experience also give you clues about a situation. Employees make assumptions based on the probability that something that has happened once will happen again, or that something that hasn't ever happened before won't ever occur. For instance, Emily always takes her morning break at 10:15 (experience). If you're having a good day (emotional state), when you walk by her office at 10:20 a.m. and notice that she's not there (environment), you'll probably assume that she's on her break. If, however, you're having a difficult day, your assumption about Emily may be affected by what you're feeling. When you see her empty office, you may come to more negative conclusions — for example, that she's slacking off or not paying attention to the assignment you just gave her. The exact same situation, viewed from two different emotional states, can lead to two different assessments.

Strong emotions can cloud your judgment and cause you to make quick and inaccurate assumptions. In important settings, like a private meeting with your boss, resist instant negative reactions to emotional assumptions you're making in the moment. Instead, suppress your urge to snap at your boss, and ask questions to clarify what she means by a particular statement.

Coming to selective conclusions

Be aware of how you and your team come to certain conclusions throughout your day, and encourage everyone to hold off making judgments until they can gather more information. Basing assumptions on cherry-picked information is dangerous and is a common contributor to miscommunication, misunderstandings, misinformation, and, further down the line, destructive conflict.

REAL LIFE

I assume you had a nice lunch

After starting her new job, Cheri was excited about getting to know everyone around the day care. In her first week, her co-worker Staci asked what she was doing for lunch. Times were tight until the first paycheck arrived, but Cheri made light of the inquiry and said, "I'll grab something quick when I have time." Staci offered to share her lunch and told her to eat all that she liked from the leftover pasta in the fridge. Cheri gladly accepted the offer and warmed up the tasty entree.

While Cheri was eating in the break room, Alice came in and began looking in the refrigerator for her lunch. Alice soon realized that the new hire was eating her food, so she sat down beside her and said, "That smells good. What is it?" Between bites, Cheri recounted how Staci had graciously shared the lunch with her. Alice replied with a grin, "Yeah, you have to watch Staci — she'll give away anybody's lunch." The two laughed as they realized that Cheri had innocently grabbed the wrong pasta.

Had Alice assumed that Cheri was rude or inconsiderate, they wouldn't have been laughing, and they would have missed out on a great friendship that extended beyond the day care. Assume the best in others and the results will be more rewarding.

When based on bad information or influenced by negative thoughts and emotions, assumptions can lead you down a false path. It's very common for employees to assume the worst or select only the information they want to hear and leave out the rest. If you want to believe that the CEO favors the marketing department, you'll scrutinize, file, and catalog every example that proves your point. For example, if one day you hear that the CEO cut the marketing department budget, you may not question your assumption of favoritism. Instead, you explain it away as a reality of the economy, and you may even assume that every other department in the company must've gotten it much worse than marketing. Your assumption isn't based on hard facts; instead, it's based on your overall opinion of how the company operates.

Asking rather than assuming

Be especially cautious when making decisions based on information that may actually be an assumption posing as fact. Combat the negative impact of inaccurate assumptions by gathering more information and asking questions. If you notice the till is $10 short at the end of the night, don't assume that the cashier pocketed the money. Instead, ask the question, "I noticed the till is a little short tonight — can you help me with this?" Try asking questions in an inquisitive, curious tone of voice rather than using an accusatory tone. You may discover that there's a perfectly legitimate reason for the discrepancy, saving you from scolding your employee and looking a little silly. (More details on how to gather information and ask different kinds of questions is available in Chapter 8.)

After you check out a situation, decide how you'll react. Does the new information change anything for you? Maybe it doesn't and you can proceed as planned. Maybe it does and you can adjust accordingly. Being wrong isn't the end of the world, and checking out assumptions doesn't have to be difficult or tedious. Assume the best, use humor when appropriate, and give people the benefit of the doubt.

Perpetuating gossip

A work environment can be a breeding ground for gossip. Both accurate and inaccurate information gets spread around the workplace from person to person and group to group. You may have employees on your team who really enjoy gossip because it makes the workday more exciting. But gossip can also have devastating effects.

Gossip is usually about a person or a group of people, and it's usually not very flattering. I could start a rumor about myself, claiming that I have an IQ of 170, but it probably wouldn't go very far! Instead, rumors and gossip that spread the quickest are embarrassing, salacious, and scandalous.

The effects of hearsay can be damaging on a variety of levels — an individual's self-esteem, a person's reputation with co-workers, and her comfort and confidence in doing her job can all be affected. Gossip on a larger scale can impact the cohesion of the workplace. No one trusts a gossip, so team members may have difficulty having honest and unguarded conversations. Co-workers never know when information they share is going to be used against them. Mistrust significantly hinders how a group gets its work done.

Shut down gossip when you hear it. Don't let your employees spread negative and hurtful information, and encourage all employees to be respectful of their peers. No one likes to discover that people are talking behind her back, so enforce a no-gossip rule. If you feel a co-worker just needs to vent or get something off her chest, listen respectfully, and then keep it to yourself. And absolutely, positively, never engage yourself in this unprofessional behavior. Be better than that.

Chapter 4

Practicing Self-Awareness: Understanding How Managers Foster Conflict

*I*f there's a problem on your team and you're wondering where to start, one of the first places to look for change may be with you. Without knowing it, you may be playing a part in creating or perpetuating a conflict.

Imagine if you were known for your great people skills, for your ability to grow even the most entry-level performer, and for your talent to get the job done successfully. You'd have people clamoring at the door to work for you! Imagine, also, if you were someone who had unintentionally made a few missteps as a manager but were given the opportunity to add new techniques to your usual approach. What would that mean for your reputation as a professional and as someone with an aptitude for problem solving?

This chapter outlines some of the common pitfalls you may make in your attempts to handle problems, whether the bickering is contained between two people or you think that a mutiny is about to happen. You also find proactive ways to manage a group, resolve issues firmly but creatively, and get on with the business at hand.

Micromanaging

Ask just about any employee what the number-one attribute of a "bad boss" is, and he'll probably answer with one word: *micromanaging*. Taking an inappropriate role in employee projects adds unnecessary friction to already stressful situations. Why? Because when an employee feels that his time has been wasted or that his work was for naught, he blames you.

"Hey, wait a minute," you say. "I'm not being a micromanager! I'm leading a team that's having trouble sticking to a routine and lacks the discipline necessary to complete their jobs!" That may be true — every organization has its share of wonky employees who aren't enthusiastic about hard work or creative thinking. The Wendy Whiners who want you (and everyone around them) to hold their hands, make decisions for them, and generally turn even the simplest of tasks into an excruciating exercise in patience probably *do* need additional attention from you, so manage them accordingly. But decide who's who before you take handholding to new heights.

Let employees take the lead on a project and it'll become clear pretty quickly which ones just need some independence to shine and which ones still need your assistance. This approach helps you direct your attention where it's needed most while allowing the employees who need less TLC to flourish.

Consider these ideas as a way to micromanage less and empower more:

- ✔ **Instead of relentlessly asking questions, set mutually agreeable check-in points for an employee to update you on his project.** He can prepare a thorough briefing that you can reference later if you feel the need to examine a particular area of concern.

- ✔ **Instead of stressing about every detail, add value where your strengths shine.** If you're not that into fashion, don't worry about the color of the golf shirts that the reps are wearing in the sales booth at the conference. Instead, offer to be a keynote speaker or simply a great cheerleader for everyone else's efforts.

- ✔ **Instead of swooping in at the last minute to criticize a detail, set a vision in the beginning of a project and trust your team to update you as necessary.**

A marketing coordinator I mediated for told me that he had worked for months putting together a large conference with a few co-workers. He put his heart and soul into the project working long hours and weekends to pull everything together. The employee had given his manager regular updates and, on the day of the event, was crushed when his boss arrived and, before he even said good morning, said, "I don't like the signage — who did it?" The signage may have very well been inadequate, but had the manager saved his comment for a later time, he could've avoided the finger-pointing and frustration that took place throughout the day.

✔ **Instead of allowing a temporary fix to become a long-term management method, do what you have to do to put out a fire, but then consider coaching an employee into more independent roles.** Pair him up with a co-worker so he can learn by example, or mentor him yourself while you observe his progress.

✔ **Take a hint!** Some employees will try subtle and diplomatic ways to get you to back off. Some may even tell you straight up that you're meddling or smothering them. Listen and find other ways to add value instead of steamrolling over them. If you want to feel like you're part of the group, the event, or the project, *ask* how your staff would like you to add value.

Hovering over employees makes for an untrustworthy workplace. You take away an employee's opportunity to show that he's proficient when you micromanage. Ease the burden on yourself by spending less time perched over shoulders and more time focused on building strategies, relieving stress, coaching him for the next big job, and showcasing your collective successes.

Stirring the Pot

Every person on a team isn't going to get along 100 percent of the time with every one of his co-workers — that's a given. Doctors take an oath to "first, do no harm," and you, as the leader of a group, will benefit from doing the same when it comes to setting the tone for workgroup relationships. Without even knowing it, you may be causing existing problems to inflate rather than settle down. At a minimum, assess to see whether you are

✔ Bringing up topics in public forums that you know are uncomfortable for one or more people in your group

✔ Pitting people against each other in what you think is friendly competition

✔ Asking members of your team to critique their co-workers

✔ Using sarcasm to make a point

✔ Publicly asking for updates on an already strained situation

✔ Using belittling or shaming language

✔ Allowing bad behaviors to become the norm

✔ Ignoring tension

✔ Playing favorites

Dividing rather than uniting

Every once in a while, you may feel like the scolding parent who wants to put the kids in timeout by separating them and telling the whole lot to go to the naughty corner. That approach may give you a bit of a breather, but it doesn't solve the problems. Even if the corner you're sending someone to is a different department or simply another task, one of the employees involved is going to feel as if he's being punished — and now you've possibly made a situation worse than it was before you intervened. Temporarily separating a team that's in conflict gives you time to think, but putting yourself at the center of their communication doesn't do much to meet a goal of solidarity.

Here are some not-so-obvious ways you could be dividing your team:

✔ **Using divisive language:** Using subtle language like "they" and "them" is a way of dividing a team. An employee is more apt to feel ownership in a solution if you use words like "us" and "we" and work to unite the sides instead of playing into any perceived or real separations.

✔ **Holding exhaustive general brainstorming sessions and staff meetings:** In your endeavor to include everyone in the decision-making process, you take it a little too far and spend too long in the idea-generating phase. Then people start taking sides and the dynamics of the meeting change. One person gives up the debate and shuts down, another pulls out the soapbox and demands that the others see it his way, and before you know it you've created an underlying animosity in the group that didn't exist before your attempt to "pull everyone together." (For tips on how to manage the brainstorming process, check out Chapter 10.)

✔ **Making concessions for an employee:** When a manager was given a new instruction about mandatory off-hours staff meetings, he immediately recognized that one of his employees wouldn't be able to attend at the appointed time due to a temporary commitment. The manager went to his team and asked their permission to make an exception to the rule for the sake of the employee, moving the staff meeting to a time when the employee would be able to attend. His heart was in the right place, but what happened next was, in his words, "the worst decision" of his career. The favored employee was shunned, other employees asked for their own exceptions, and he had unintentionally set a precedent that every decision would be up for a group vote. He later approached similar situations in which he needed to apply some flexibility differently — by letting his team know about temporary variations, without naming names or seeking permission.

✔ **Creating a false sense of security:** Even the most skilled listener can unwittingly create a feeling of betrayal in a staff member. Keep up the active listening skills, but be sure you're not just telling everyone what they want to hear. Set accurate expectations, coach employees through behaviors that may be contributing to conflicts, and be specific about how, why, and with whom you'll follow up.

I mediated with a team who initially gave their manager high marks for his ability to actively listen and truly understand their issues. An employee would leave a closed-door meeting almost walking on air because he knew that the manager had his back and trusted that he would make things right again. Then, time went by and two things happened: Some employees discovered that the manager made *everyone* feel that they were right, and he never did anything to move employees past the initial conversations. A day would pass, a week, and then months with no follow-up whatsoever. Because of their false sense of security, employees reacted to any new conflicts with a righteous attitude (based on the positive feedback each had received from the fatherly manager) and even small problems became World War III.

Appearing to take sides

You may wonder how you're not supposed to take sides when the higher-ups are looking to you to manage situations on your team. You should be able to make decisions, but how you go about making them matters to employees. There's a *big* difference between assuming Margaret is always right and Leonard whines too much, so you'll just go with whatever Margaret wants, and listening to all sides, asking pertinent questions, fully understanding the situation, and *then* making a decision.

Assuming that the sales team is always right or that the apprentice has no place having a different perspective than the journeyman may get you into trouble. If you manage a team, you're everyone's manager — not the manager of just a select few. You may take a lot of pride in your mentoring skills, but choosing just one or two of your staff members to groom could backfire by causing the other team members to turn against your protégé.

Instead of showing favoritism, demonstrate that you're equally interested in everyone's career and growth path by looking for opportunities to further individual education or experience levels.

Not Taking the Time to Gain Understanding

Busy, busy, busy. When you have your head down in the books or when you're barreling along to meet an important deadline, you may cause ripples in the pond without even knowing you threw the pebble! Not slowing down long enough to understand the broader picture or focus your attention in the other direction shortchanges your staff and weakens your reputation.

Overreacting

How you present situations to your team impacts their reactions. If you're always fired up, your crew will likely follow suit. A hyper-emotional approach to problems cultivates the feeling that no one has an eye on finding solutions. Keep day-to-day reactions below a simmer, so when things do get tough, your employees don't boil over. You set the example, and your team is looking to you for direction.

Misunderstanding the real issues

Looking at the surface issues of disagreements and ignoring the underlying values and emotions at play means you're missing an opportunity to find better, more durable solutions to problems. You can accomplish a lot more if you know how to read between the lines and capture what's most important for your employees. It may take some time and a little research to really get to the root of the problem, but it'll be worth it when you're able to help employees resolve the real issues. Assessing a problem can be tricky, so refer to Chapter 5 for some assistance. Chapter 2 can help you figure out what makes employees tick and Chapters 6 through 9 cover the steps for holding a successful mediation.

Looking the other way

You may be tempted to ignore a problem when you don't know what you can do to stop behaviors that adversely affect your team. But overlooking signs of unrest erodes your authority and your reputation. Watch for the following:

✔ **Bullying:** Bullying is one of the most obvious yet commonly overlooked behaviors. It can be subtle or overt, and you may find yourself ignoring it because, well, you're a bit intimidated by the bully yourself. Badgering and baiting is never acceptable, so gather whatever resources you need to address the situation, but handle it nonetheless.

✔ **Power struggles:** Playing tug of war is a fun activity at the company picnic, but it has no place on a functional team. If a staff member is trying to one-up a colleague, is putting a team member down to build himself up, or is lobbying against his co-workers, check out what may really be happening with that person. If it makes sense for the personalities involved, consider strengthening the weakest link rather than taking away from the strongest. (For more tips on understanding power issues, check out Chapter 3.)

Less obvious but perhaps just as frustrating for your staff is when you ignore their requests for your time. Sure, you're busy, but being available only via e-mail or agreeing to meetings and then not showing up is disrespectful to your crew. Scheduling, and keeping, face-to-face time is essential. And when you do meet with an employee, move away from the computer and turn off your cellphone — he'll appreciate the attention.

Being dismissive

If someone has the courage to talk to you about an issue, pay attention. Disregarding emotions or anxiety an employee feels about a situation with his co-workers (including you) may cause him to skip coming to you next time. Instead, he may go behind your back, go over your head, stew, or adversely affect the company by carrying out negative actions.

Here are some ways in which you may be dismissing an employee:

✔ **Telling him it's his imagination, that he's being hypersensitive, or even that he's exaggerating.** Just because you're not seeing what your employee is seeing, doesn't mean it isn't happening for him. Ask good questions, do a little investigating, and coach him to handle it himself (see Chapter 5 for tips on empowering your employees). Be sure to check back in with him to see how it's going, and if he still needs your help, consider mediating a conversation between the two parties.

✔ **Defending or speaking for the other person.** When an employee comes to you with an issue that involves a colleague and you immediately defend the other person's actions, you may be causing a tense situation to become even more strained. It's okay to offer a bit of conjecture as you ask him why he thinks his co-worker may be doing what she's doing, but taking on the role of defender won't sit well with the confider.

✔ **Saying, "Let's get back to some real work, okay?"** Listening patiently for a few minutes, acknowledging that what an employee is telling you is very likely taking place, and then dismissing his distress with an edict to get on with his job not only keeps a conflict brewing, but it also adds you to the list of individuals he's upset with. Choosing between a task and a person isn't necessary. You can do both by hearing out an employee and by working with him to solve his problems so he *can* get back to work.

✔ **Making a commitment to look into concerns and then not following through in a meaningful way.** You may wholeheartedly believe that what an employee is telling you is true and, with the best of intentions, promise to take care of the problem. However, if you take too long to address the issue, try to cure the symptom rather than the disease, or simply muff up the whole situation, the employee may interpret your actions as a way to dismiss him and his concerns.

For example, a lead shift worker assured an employee that he would handle a co-worker's abrupt and abrasive method of keeping the line moving. The lead had witnessed the behavior and knew the employee had a valid complaint. He went to the other worker and said, "Listen, Raj complained about the way you talk to the line and he can be sensitive about stuff, so just don't talk to him when you're giving instructions, okay?" Imagine what that did for the relationship between the two!

✔ **Limiting what you think an employee can contribute.** I mediated a case in which a conflict between a manager and an employee had been going on for three years. When we got down to what had sparked the clash in the first place, the employee recounted the day he walked into the manager's office while the boss was trying to cut spending and balance the budget. The employee asked if he could help, and the stressed manager abruptly responded, "You don't really have experience with this and I need to get it done." The employee had ideas about saving the company money, but he was so annoyed at the dismissal that he never shared them and, instead, enjoyed watching the manager struggle to find answers. The manager could've easily taken a few minutes to hear the suggestions — and saved himself some time and trouble in the process.

Talking about the Work Ineffectively

How you discuss what you're doing, what your staff are up to, and what's happening on a daily basis really matters to your team. If employees feel you have their backs, they're more likely to watch out for one another and demonstrate their loyalty to you. The more informed your team is the less likely they are to fill in the blanks with erroneous or hurtful information.

Not sharing your contributions

Though most employees complain about micromanagers (see the earlier section "Micromanaging"), your staff most likely wants you to show them you're doing *something*. Simply saying, "Wow, I can't believe how busy I am!" probably isn't enough. You don't need to share every detail from your calendar or spend hours going over your business plans for the year, but letting an employee know what you're doing and why you're headed in a particular direction makes it easier for him to have your back with others in the company and may keep him from badmouthing you as a manager.

Instead of trying to fly under the radar, try

- ✔ **Creating easy ways to update the group.** Staff meetings, conference calls, or e-mails go a long way toward getting the team up-to-date on what everyone is doing. Include yourself in any update conversations.

- ✔ **Doing what you say you're going to do.** If you assign yourself a task, do it. Taking responsibility for a job and then having someone else do the work erodes your integrity. If you know you don't have the time, energy, or skill set to complete a task, set expectations from the start.

- ✔ **Explaining yourself.** If you leave your employees in the dark, they'll find ways to assume you're doing nothing.

A frustrated employee told me about a field superintendent who would check in daily with each of his foremen via cellphone. During the calls, a foreman would make requests for materials he needed for his job. Instead of taking the information right then and there, the superintendent would respond with, "After I hang up, call back and leave it on my voicemail." The foreman would do so and the materials wouldn't arrive the next day. Though the field superintendent may have had a valid reason for this protocol, it was far too easy for the foreman to compare notes with the other project managers and then collectively wonder what the supervisor did all day long while they were laboring away on the job sites. The employees were united in their frustration with his poor management skills, which ultimately caused friction and eroded the company's reputation. Truth be told, none of the foremen really knew whether the field superintendent was busy or lazy because he hadn't taken the time to clarify why he preferred voicemail to taking the information down immediately or why material deliveries were delayed.

Underrepresenting your team

Spending more time schmoozing with the top dog than working with your crew in the trenches makes it hard for employees to believe you're in tune with their career needs. Even when you have the best of intentions and all you're trying to do is make sure your team is recognized, the appearance of catering and pandering to the powers that be can damage your reputation back on the shop floor. The only thing your staff sees is you distancing yourself from them, which leads them to think you're only in it for yourself.

To combat a self-serving perception, present your hard work as team-focused. Your employees will probably appreciate your efforts to lobby for additional funds or your endeavors to get them new tools. What they won't appreciate are overt actions that appear only to benefit you. People know the difference between the two approaches, and their reactions to you will be 180 degrees different. Working on their behalf and being a trusted representative of their concerns wins you loyalty.

Conversely, you may have a strained or difficult relationship with upper management that frustrates your employees. You can easily think negatively about the higher-ups when they make decisions you don't agree with, especially if it involves an ongoing issue. When continually fighting with the execs is the rule not the exception, you run the risk of alienating yourself and your team from the main decision makers.

Regardless of your approach with upper management, when an employee feels that you don't have his back, he takes steps to protect himself. His dissatisfaction most likely won't begin and end with you. He'll do what he feels he needs to do to step over others, deftly move around you, and capture whatever spotlight he can whenever he can. Elevators, lunch lines, and parking lots are great places for him to talk to upper management himself!

Just say no: Communication styles to avoid

Your workplace is probably chock-full of differing personalities and communication approaches. Some people have little time for chitchat and want to get right to the point. Others see themselves as great orators, or can't resist the opportunity to throw in a pithy zinger every once in a while to liven things up. Whether your business style is serious and straightforward or casual and jocular, be careful not to alienate your colleagues by

✔ Ordering, directing, or commanding

✔ Threatening

✔ Preaching, moralizing, or delivering monologues

✔ Advising without understanding the real issues

✔ Judging, criticizing, blaming, or accusing

✔ Name-calling, ridiculing, or shaming

✔ Withholding information

✔ Talking up or down, too fast, or too slow

✔ One-upping with bigger, better, more horrific stories

✔ Using sarcasm or snide remarks

✔ Reacting with over-the-top emotions

✔ Shutting down

If you place employees in the predicament of having to fight for attention, they fight among themselves. Avoid an employees-versus-management mentality by being the bridge between the two. Make sure your staff knows that you're working the company hierarchy for everyone's benefit, not just your own, and work to improve any strained relationships with executives.

Creating Ill-Defined Expectations and Responsibilities

You're probably already aware that not having detailed job descriptions is an obvious cause for concern among employees. But what may be less obvious are the directives you give on a daily basis that also have the potential to cause problems between your employees, such as:

- **Using hazy terms to give what you consider to be clear instructions.** Telling an employee "This is a priority" sounds pretty clear, but what's missing in that directive is a description of what *this* is a priority over. One person may construe your order to mean that he should drop everything and concentrate on the task. Another team member may take it to mean that she should make time for the priority task but continue with her other responsibilities, too. If he stops what he's doing, and she doesn't, she may be upset that he's stopped working on what she needs, and he may be upset that she's not giving the task enough attention.

- **Assigning a task or responsibility to more than one person.** When you assign a task to more than one person, it almost always causes tension between those people.

  A manager confided in me that he was often so passionate about his new ideas that he would share them privately with particular staff members, who would then jump on the bandwagon and look into how they could bring his concept to fruition. The problem is, he didn't tell them who should do what, so they would all go off and make the same phone calls, investigate with the same vendors, and write business plans based on the manager's initial thoughts. The co-workers would eventually realize that each of them was thinking he was the "go-to guy" on the project, when, in reality, their efforts were being duplicated and their time was being wasted. The otherwise friendly team members would get angry with each other for stepping on toes, and a conflict would follow.

- **Couching language because you're worried an employee may not react well to an instruction.** The people who work for you are pretty smart cookies, and if you're less than honest about your expectations, they'll soon figure it out. If you sugarcoat the fact that you need an employee to work overtime when you say, "Run those numbers when you can," he won't be too happy when he learns from someone else that you need the report for an 8 a.m. meeting tomorrow.

✔ **Making promises or setting expectations with vendors, customers, or people from other areas of the company and then expecting your staff to deliver disappointing news.** Putting employees' professional reputations at stake is always a bad move. If you've mistakenly set an unrealistic expectation, cowboy up and admit the error to the outsider instead of ordering your employees to do it for you. If you had time to make the promise in the first place, you have time to adjust expectations.

✔ **Setting expectations that are beyond what an employee can accomplish.** Setting unrealistic expectations can cause your employee to have low self-esteem and feel overwhelmed and stressed, which, in turn, may lead him to give up, quit, or talk trash about his situation. Brainstorm with him about what you can do to ease the burden — and set more realistic expectations going forward.

✔ **Employing a military-type approach that includes barking orders at subordinates.** On the surface, this approach may seem to be the most efficient way to get a clear and concise message out to the troops. But if you're leaving out important parts of the instructions (like the strategy behind them!), you run the risk of creating infighting while team members stumble into each other in their panic to react. It only takes a few more seconds to share with employees your strategy or thought process when you're handing out assignments. If your employees get where you're coming from, they have the opportunity to add to or refine tasks to help you meet your goals better, faster, and under budget.

Hiring the Right Person for the Wrong Job

Exemplary individual contributors commonly get attention and gain respect from management. You may have a staff member who does a bang-up job with every assignment you've ever given him. Perhaps the two of you have even developed a mentor-student relationship and you're ready to move him to the next step in his career. The only problem: You may be setting him, and the rest of the team, up for a conflict if you move him into a new role without first giving him the tools he needs to succeed.

It happens often — someone with no leadership experience gets promoted, and one of his peers, who didn't get promoted, reacts by quietly seething, publicly railing, or covertly looking for another job. Jealousy, disbelief, and hopelessness can infiltrate even the strongest of teams when a reward for one person feels like a punishment to the others. This is especially likely when the news comes as a surprise.

Hiring someone from the outside or allowing an internal lateral move can be just as tricky as promotions. Even though a person has received high marks for his work in one area, you can't assume that his skills will easily translate into another role. The best sales rep in the industry could be the worst operations coordinator your team has ever worked with. Any time a change occurs, it affects everyone — and not planning ahead can lead to an uproar.

Take steps to prepare a new employee and his co-workers for changes in team dynamics. Merely announcing a change and saying, "We're going to see how Ajani does" could make the rest of the staff wonder, "At whose expense?!" Here's how to prepare everyone for personnel changes:

- **Thoroughly discuss with an employee his strengths and areas for improvement.** Build a plan to baby-step him into the new role before he takes the job. Consider training for certain job functions or additional people skills. Take the time to groom and prepare him for the next steps.

- **Ask other employees to share confidentially how *they* see a potential employee's skill set.** What's his reputation in the industry? Where could he improve? Some of the answers you get may be the result of the employee wanting to be politically correct; others may be the result of jealousy and resistance to change. Use your best judgment to sift through the information and listen to the team. You may learn something!

- **Test the waters.** If you're planning to promote a team member from an individual contributor to a supervisory position, consider creating situations that allow everyone on the team to try out bits of the change a little at a time. Can you form a committee or task force, putting the employee at the helm, to see how he does in the new role? Maybe putting him in charge for an interim period of time — say, while you're on vacation — will give all parties an opportunity to get used to the idea and bring any potential pitfalls to the surface. Think in terms of milestones rather than sweeping changes all at once.

- **Lessen the impact of the change.** Be open with the team about the change and discuss how it will benefit them. Will the change ease the communication process, lighten workloads, or make for shorter days? What's in it for the team if an employee is promoted or newly hired?

Living in Fix-It Mode

There are only so many hours in the day and you have work to do, right? Moving projects forward, meeting deadlines, and getting some tangible results under your belt are all seemingly reasonable justifications for fixing a mess yourself instead of putting the onus for solutions on employees. After all, you're the boss and solving problems is your job. When a fire is burning, people appreciate the guy who grabs the extinguisher and puts it out pronto!

But being a good listener, mentoring employees, and fully investigating the source of problems takes time. When there's a ton of work to be done, time is of the essence and you may have developed a few survival tactics that are causing strife among your employees. Avoid the following approaches to solving issues because they could be giving you more — not less — to do.

Talking instead of listening

Who likes to listen to long-winded lectures and dry-as-dirt sermons? You probably don't, so why assume any of your subordinates like it. If you're guilty of pulling out a soapbox and spouting your view before fully investigating a conflict, consider a change.

Even though you're expected to handle flare-ups as they arise, be sure you really listen to what your employees are saying before you make decisions that don't consider their needs. If your only focus is on telling your team what you want to see rather than listening to what's happening, you miss out on key information and opportunities to improve the overall work environment. Your team is in the trenches every day, and they know what's getting in the way of good business or causing conflicts to recycle. Asking questions to understand gives you a better view of what's happening, so you can implement a strategy that reduces future conflict and increases productivity.

And, while you're at it, fake listening isn't a good idea either. Don't spend time asking your employees what they'd like to see happen or what ideas they have for viable solutions (making them feel as if they're part of a remedy) if you've already decided what's going to happen. You'll add another layer to the conflict — even if you have the best of intentions.

Being judge and jury

Jump into a sticky situation, make a few quick decisions, and everything's fixed, right? The problem with that is that not only are you most likely missing some of the key elements of the dispute, but you're also placing yourself at the center of every difference of opinion.

Being the judge and jury inadvertently creates a dependence on you as the only decision maker in the group. Over time, employees either resent you for not letting them be involved in solving their own problems or become completely paralyzed when faced with a decision: "Should I have chicken or fish? I don't know. Who can make this decision for me?"

Work with individuals to come up with their own answers. People are capable of solving their own problems — sometimes they just need some assistance. Be a sounding board by listening to your employees' concerns and then ask questions to help them consider options. Questions like the ones in Chapter 7 help your staff get to the heart of a dispute and find satisfying solutions.

Rescuing instead of coaching

Occasionally, an employee in the center of a conflict may tug at your heartstrings. Taking on the role of caregiver every once in a while isn't unusual, but feeling sorry for or empathetic toward an employee's social awkwardness or lack of training keeps a conflict going. Telling his co-workers to overlook his need for development shortchanges everyone and doesn't solve anything; it can actually make the situation worse, by creating resentment in the employees who end up doing more and limiting the potential of the person you're trying to rescue.

An employee who wants and expects you to fix the situation for him may actually end up resenting you. He may even get angry when you tell him that you won't do for him what he can do for himself. Plus, you run the risk that you'll be put in a bad spot if things don't go well. The very person you're trying to help can easily turn on you if he doesn't get what he wants.

Coach and empower an employee to handle situations himself so that he gains the necessary skills to handle future situations better, improve his working relationships, and expand the skills that lead to less conflict overall. Help him identify the problem areas and brainstorm ways he can be more independent.

Always putting yourself in the role of the lifeguard makes for some pretty weak swimmers! If you've created a team of dependent employees, it's not too late to strengthen the aptitude for problem solving you already have. Use the skills in this book to mediate conflicts, arrange group meetings in which the team finds their own solutions, and reach out to others to find the resources your team needs.

Denying Shortfalls

Owning up to the possibility that you may not have every skill or quality it takes to be a perfect manager is tough. I won't ask you to reveal all your shortcomings to your team, but I will ask that, when you make a mistake, you're humble enough to admit that you were wrong. If you don't have all the information, be willing to ask for help. Admitting that you made a mistake or need assistance makes you human. It also allows your team to show its strength and feel closer by supporting you when you need it. Demonstrate your willingness to be vulnerable, and your staff will be more likely to admit their own shortfalls instead of going to great lengths to cover them up.

Letting egos get in the way

Taking credit for work you had little or no part in, dismissing the efforts of employees, or clamoring to get your name mentioned before those on your team is not only egotistical, but it also turns the very people who are there to support you against you. Be a cheerleader for your team, and they'll return the favor. Pushing a boulder uphill with all hands on deck is easier than going it alone.

The best manager I ever had was a man who figured out early on in his career that he could get farther up the corporate ladder by shining a spotlight on the people on his team while he stood just far enough in the shadows for others to see he was still part of the limelight. My success was his success. Because he set such a solid example, it was pretty easy for the rest of us to revel in one another's accomplishments and genuinely celebrate a co-worker's accolades.

Pulling rank is your prerogative, and yes, sometimes it's necessary. Play the boss card when you feel that doing so is absolutely essential. Your team knows you're the manager — you don't have to remind them daily. They'll appreciate you *showing* them you're the manager rather than telling them. Use motivating language such as "I know you have what it takes to do the job" instead of "Because I'm the boss — that's why!"

Lacking training or skills

Every once in a while, you'll come up against a situation that tests your knowledge and capabilities. Maybe it's that one employee who doesn't respond to your usual approaches or techniques. Or maybe your boss is pushing for more than you can deliver and you're simply out of your element.

Knowing that you should do *something* but not getting the help you need to pull it off can get you in trouble. Take, for example, the manager who sensed problems between himself and a subordinate — problems that were starting to affect his entire group. Instead of addressing the issues with the individual directly, he decided to throw that person a surprise birthday party. The problem was, the boss ordered the other team members to put the event together, didn't explain the sudden interest in birthdays three-quarters of the way through a year in which no one else's birthday had been celebrated, and ignored the fact that the man's birthday was two months ago! The manager was on the right track with his attempt to acknowledge the tension, but his method resulted in an awkward party and created bad feelings with the rest of the team. The featured employee was mystified and irritated. The manager would've gotten much better results had he just admitted that he didn't quite know what to do and listened to a mentor or HR for possible solutions.

Being uncomfortable with change

Reorganizations, budget cuts, new clients, or fresh strategies that are outside your comfort zone can be exhilarating for some people . . . and gut wrenching for others. I worked with a company whose employees had the saying "If you don't like the way things are, wait 20 minutes — they'll change." The only predictable thing in the organization was the constant unpredictability!

If you're a manager who doesn't do well with change and you're stuck in the middle of one, you may resort to

- ✔ **Hiding:** Dropping off the face of the Earth when uncertainty is in the air gives you a few minutes of calm, but it doesn't change the fact that you have a responsibility to your team to keep them informed and to keep the chaos in check. If you're not available, employees have to deal with the stress and confusion on their own. Leaving your employees to fend for themselves breeds discontent. It goes without saying, then, that you have to show up and have a calm, consistent presence in the face of change.

- ✔ **Fighting:** If you're uncomfortable or unhappy with changes that are occurring, you may decide to fight the new world order with everything you've got. You may be putting 110 percent of your effort into stopping what's happening and completely lose sight of the big picture.

Yes, fighting for what you believe in is important, but don't forget to take a break once in a while and reassess the situation. Remind yourself of your ultimate goal, and keep your employees' interests in mind at all times. As the situation evolves, you don't want to find yourself so caught up in "winning" that you miss a key opportunity for positive change.

✔ **Surrendering:** So you got some bad news. Maybe you tried to make things better, but now you're just phoning it in. Often, accepting the inevitable makes sense, and finding ways to communicate the benefits of a change (even one that on the surface doesn't appear to have any good points!) helps your employees work through disappointing decisions. But if your team is willing to come up with viable alternatives to a decision, and you just want to give up, their morale can be seriously affected and you could be setting the stage for irreparable harm.

A period of change is not the time to inadvertently bring your team together against you or sit on the sidelines as people get their résumés in order. Instead, put your energy to good use and help the group formulate a cohesive response that takes all sides into account. If the ideas are shot down and the group receives a clear "no," at least they can move on *with* you rather than against you.

Chapter 5

Knowing When to Address Conflict

*A*s a manager, it's inevitable that you spend a considerable amount of time involved with employee conflicts. But knowing there's a problem and knowing when to do something about it are two very different things. Trying to guess when you should let something ride, how much you can trust employees to work out a problem on their own, or where to turn for help if you're not terribly comfortable handling a conflict yourself isn't easy.

It may not always feel like it, but resolving conflict at the lowest level possible saves you time, money, and energy. Managers often overlook the cost of conflict, or the cost of doing nothing about a conflict, when considering the impact of disagreements. An executive once told me, "I provide conflict resolution training for my employees so I can implement their ideas rather than solve their problems." Smart cookie!

This chapter provides insight into whether you should step in to mediate a conflict on your team. It also gives you ways to monitor progress if you decide to put the resolution process in the hands of the employees involved.

Assessing the Cost and Severity of the Conflict

Even the smallest squabble takes away from important projects and deadlines. So when a conflict at work is increasingly taking more of your attention and you have less time to focus on the bigger picture, you may be tempted to look the other way and hope the problem disappears. You may find some benefit to giving a conflict time to work out on its own, but you won't know whether you're doing the right thing without investigating to see whether your strategy has an impact on your teams' productivity and the bottom line. Taking a broad view of the situation and considering both hard costs (like lost inventory) and soft costs (like team morale) helps you determine whether it's time to step in. Use the costs worksheet in Figure 5-1 to see how conflict affects the bottom line.

Hard costs associated with unresolved conflict

Hard costs are measurable costs that can be deducted from your financial statements. These are items like lost inventory, legal fees, and revenue decreases from lost sales. Though they're tangible and usually easy to find and add up, managers often overlook them in the midst of conflict. If you're curious what a problem is costing you, it's time to put pencil to paper. Here are some of the more common hard costs that could be attributed to unresolved conflict:

- ✔ **Wasted time:** Time is money, and if people are avoiding one another and delaying outcomes, there's a cost to that. People in conflict have to have an outlet for their emotions and can often waste time by commiserating with anyone who will listen as a way to vent what's happening. Talking about conflict is a good thing, but complaining without any progress toward resolution is just, well, talking. Employees start avoiding one another, taking longer lunches and breaks, and coming in late or leaving early as a way to cope.

  Pay attention to the number of hours being wasted in a day or week and consider whether you can afford to wait this out.

- ✔ **Lost workdays:** When people are uneasy in an environment, they seek comfort. Staying in bed with the remote in one hand, chocolate in the other, surrounded by a pillow fortress is inviting. If you're expecting people who are in conflict (or who are surrounded by conflict) to work without resolution, they may be taking sick days just to avoid the stress.

  If you've noticed that your group is without the information it needs to move forward on a project or you're short a staff member during the busiest day at the store, you're enduring an unnecessary cost that could be directly related to conflict.

- ✔ **Reduced productivity:** People often find their thoughts drifting to a conflict and replaying it over and over, thinking about what went wrong, why they're right, and then snapping back to reality when the phone rings. It's not a stretch to say *you're* probably spending precious work time thinking about the situation, too — and you may not even be one of the people directly involved! When you have to work on a project with someone you're not getting along with, the job takes longer and the final product is affected.

	Your Calculation	**Annual Cost**
Wasted time		
Sick days due to stress		
Reduced productivity		
Missed deadlines		
Parts, inventory		
Decision-making ability		
Healthcare premium		
Sabotage and theft		
Loss of employees		
Recruitment		
Training		
Termination		
Potential legal fees		
Morale		
Lost customers		
Lost potential customers		
Reputation		
Restructuring		
Additional supervision		
Market share		
Stock price		
Other		

Figure 5-1: This worksheet helps you measure the costs of conflict in the workplace.

✓ **Performance and quality:** Even if you don't notice a marked drop in productivity, you'll probably notice a diminished quality in the work that's being delivered. Maybe your employees are able to carry as many projects as they always have, but are they as responsive to the details? Someone has to pick up the slack and correct mistakes that are made due to other distractions, and that someone is often you, the manager.

Are you still getting the same quality you were before there were problems? Distractions get in the way of an individual's ability to be creative, and the company may be losing out on good ideas and clever solutions to problems.

✓ **Healthcare costs associated with stress:** Stress can contribute to a number of health problems, such as high blood pressure, headaches, and stomach ulcers. Some workplace stressors may not be avoidable, but allowing the stress of unresolved conflict to continue only adds to the pressures your employees may already face. More health issues mean more visits to the doctor and potential increased healthcare costs for your company. They may also mean more on-the-job injuries.

✓ **Sabotage and theft:** If employees reach a point where they feel no one cares about a situation, it's not all that unusual for sabotage and theft to ensue. This possibility may sound extreme, but in some cases employees have gotten so angry with one another that they hid equipment the other people needed to do their jobs, just to cause them additional frustration. Theft can be as simple as an employee removing inventory or as underhanded as taking ideas to another company where the employee will be rewarded and not looked at as the person with the problem.

✓ **Turnover:** Regardless of the size of your organization, there's a dollar amount associated with the cost of hiring, processing, and training every new employee. Even if you run a job site and call the union hall to hire someone off the bench, there's a cost involved in getting that person up to speed on the project.

✓ **Termination packages:** If your HR department determines that a conflict carries a potential legal risk to the company, it may negotiate a termination package that includes additional financial remuneration. Unresolved conflict can lead to a termination package that's more costly to the company than if someone stays or leaves on good terms.

✓ **Legal costs:** How far an employee is willing to take a conflict to prove a point, to get you once and for all, or simply to buy himself some time while he considers other career options is often unpredictable. After a lawsuit is filed, you'll spend money on legal fees and wages for all the employees who are addressing the court case, not to mention that the money you pay out isn't going toward productivity or more sales. You never really "win" when a conflict reaches the courts, and your bottom line suffers along with the confidence of your employees.

Soft costs associated with unresolved conflict

Soft costs, on the surface, are those things that may not seem measurable or easily assigned a specific dollar amount, but they still affect your bottom line. Soft costs often distinguish you from your competitors — they're the intangibles that contribute to or detract from your success. Here are just a few examples of soft costs:

- ✔ **Morale:** People are likely aware of an ongoing conflict, and this awareness can affect morale on all levels. Over time, when employees are unhappy and they share their disgruntled attitude with others, the situation wears on those who have to listen to them and shades their view of the company as a whole. Even staff who aren't directly involved in the conflict may start to believe that the company doesn't care, so why should they give it their all?

- ✔ **Decreased customer service:** Taking care of employees who interact with customers keeps clients satisfied. If someone who deals with clients is unhappy, you run the risk of her taking it out, knowingly or not, on customers. The cost on the bottom line could be devastating.

- ✔ **Reputation:** Word gets around fast when people find a great enterprise that really values its employees. When conflict goes unresolved, it also affects a company's reputation. When employees and customers begin speaking negatively about their experiences, reputations erode. Disgruntled employees' comments can scare off a future valued employee and potential customers.

- ✔ **Loss of skilled employees:** In addition to the hard cost associated with employee turnover, consider the soft cost when a skilled employee leaves out of frustration and you have to retrain a new hire. In addition, when a highly skilled employee leaves, he takes with him everything you taught him and he gives his expertise to your competitors. Retaining skilled employees keeps production high and training time to a minimum.

Determining severity

Thoughts of screaming in the hallway, threats of physical harm, or slashed tires may come to mind when you hear the words "severe conflict." The truth is, though, that a problem between employees is severe when it costs you more to ignore than it does to address it. If an employee has placed a letter of resignation on your desk, or if important documents have come up missing, for example, the problem has moved from a minor disagreement to a severe conflict. Use the lists in the previous sections to help you determine whether the few people involved can work things out on their own or can manage to get beyond the problem with a little coaching from you. If minimal intervention doesn't resolve the problem, it's severe enough to require a mediation meeting like the one I outline in Chapters 6 through 9, or you may need to call in resources like those I give you in Chapters 13 and 14.

Approaching Employees and Gathering Information

If you've determined that the cost of doing nothing about a conflict is too high, then it's time to take action and address the issue. You may already know most of the details about how the situation escalated, or you may be the new kid on the block who has inherited a big problem. Either way, tactfully approach those impacted and see if you can get at what's really going on.

Knowing your intent

Before you begin any conversations with your employees, know what your intention for meeting is. Will you call them in for a disciplinary action, or will you have a discussion that encourages them to be a part of the solution? Determine whether you're on a fact-finding mission and going to HR for documentation, or you're going to allow room for a confidential conversation. There's nothing wrong with either course, but be sure to communicate your intention so the employees don't feel blindsided after they open up.

Try to resolve the conflict at the lowest possible level. Plan a resolution strategy that uses the least amount of escalation. Start with the employees before you bring in anyone else. Your intention should be for those involved to save face, for them to see that they can work out disagreements on their own, and for you to keep the cost (and exposure) of the conflict down. Let your employees feel empowered by their ability to work things out rather than afraid of what may show up in their personnel files.

Although your intention may be to act as an objective facilitator, tell the employees upfront what your organization requires you to report so they can determine for themselves what they're comfortable sharing with you.

Sorting out the players

You may think that determining who should be involved in a discussion about a conflict is relatively easy, and that the only people you need to speak with are the two culprits. But unless you ask around, you could be missing crucial players.

Create a list for yourself that includes those directly involved, and then add any other staff members who may be impacted by the problem. If you learn from your initial conversations that another person needs to be involved, you can easily add her to a mediated conversation.

As you meet with each person, ask whom he or she sees as key players in resolving the conflict. You may be surprised by how many names you get. If it becomes apparent that a number of people are involved and their presence in a meeting is necessary to reach a resolution, look to Chapter 10 for processes to facilitate larger meetings.

When employees are in conflict, they often build armies as a means to strengthen their point of view. Make sure to check in with secondary players to determine their level of involvement and whether you think they'll be valuable in resolving the issue. They may be satisfied just knowing that the conflict is being addressed and learning about the outcomes at a later date. You don't need to involve the whole gang if you can resolve the conflict with just a few people.

Considering the meeting place

Where you meet communicates a lot to other employees. If everyone sees one closed-door meeting after another, fear and stress can escalate. Your employees will be more focused on what's happening behind the door than on their work. Similarly, publicly walking up to someone's cubicle and starting a conversation where others can overhear can cause your staff to shut down and share very little, causing you to miss important information.

Consider what's commonplace for you and the least disruptive for those involved. If it's not out of the norm for you to ask someone to stick around after a meeting, do that. If it's going to raise concerns and curiosity, think twice. Whatever you decide, your goal should be to choose a place that is private and inconspicuous, where people can speak freely.

Being consistent in your inquiries

When you begin approaching employees to gather information, be consistent with all parties. Communicate the same message to each employee and demonstrate that you're not in this to take sides. Prepare a simple statement that explains the approach you're taking to resolve the matter. I like to use language as simple as the following:

> I'd like to talk with you about your working relationship with Ted. I'm going to be talking to him as well to get his perspective. My intention is to understand each of your perspectives, and I hope we can resolve this ourselves. I won't be sharing anything you tell me with Ted or anyone else. Can you share with me what's been happening for you?

End the discussion by letting both parties know what type of follow-up you've planned, even if it's just to give the situation more thought. Give them time to consider how they want to proceed and let them know when you'll be checking back in with them. Provide a way for them to correspond privately with you if they think of any other information they'd like to share or just want to touch base.

The simple act of having a chat that starts with "I'd like to get your perspective" helps employees see their role as a problem solver, so being consistent in your approach with all sides multiplies your odds of success.

Asking questions

Keeping the questions open ended rather than asking questions that only require a yes or a no draws out more information. Open-ended inquiries allow your employees to tell their stories while you get beyond the surface details you may already know.

Here are some of my favorite questions to get you started:

- ✔ What's been happening for you in this situation?
- ✔ What have you tried to do to resolve the conflict?
- ✔ What do you think the next steps are to resolve this situation?
- ✔ Who do you believe needs to be involved to resolve it?
- ✔ Is there any additional support I can offer you?

Evaluating the Details of the Conflict

If the conflict in your workplace involves a threat to safety or a glaring legal issue, deal with it immediately. Beyond an emergency situation, put the pieces of the story together to determine whether you need to intervene.

What you know

After your individual conversations with the main players and those employees affected by the conflict (refer to the earlier section "Approaching Employees and Gathering Information"), you should have a pretty good idea about what's been going on. You can probably even see that those involved may have had the best of intentions, but a miscommunication has kept them from seeing each other's perspective and moving past the problem.

You should also have a clear idea of the timeline of events. This conflict may have started at different times for different people. The individuals involved may not even be upset by the same incidents! When you know who the key players are, how long things have been brewing, and who needs to participate in creating solutions, consider what you've observed in the working environment. These are the kinds of things you've probably noticed but haven't thought to add to the list. They're important, so pay attention to

- ✔ Reactions from team members when those in conflict interact

- ✔ Contradictions in the stories being told by those involved

- ✔ Body language, such as rolling eyes, avoiding eye contact, not acknowledging one another, and just plain tension in the room

- ✔ Expressed (or overheard) frustration by other team members

- ✔ Resistance to working on group projects

Don't be surprised if, at this point, you feel you can solve the problem in record time. All you have to do is call everyone together and announce your decision. Problem solved, move on. But wait! If you take full responsibility for deciding the outcome this time,

- ✔ You're signing up to take full responsibility for resolving every future conflict.

- ✔ You'll have lost an opportunity to show employees how they can proactively resolve future issues.

- ✔ You'll have taken away the chance for them to understand (and not repeat) what got them to this point in the first place.

Instead, follow these recommendations based on your unique situation:

- ✔ **If you know that both employees see a problem and express an interest in finding an answer,** allow them to try to resolve the conflict on their own (see "Empowering Employees to Handle the Issue Themselves" later in this chapter). You can still step in to mediate later if necessary.

- ✔ **If you know that one employee acknowledges a problem but the other doesn't,** help the employee who's denying the difficulty see the benefits of having a conversation with the other person. They could have a productive conversation on their own, or you may need to mediate their meeting. (For guidance on facilitating a meeting, see Part II.)

- ✔ **If you know that neither party believes there's a problem,** you need to consider a course of action that takes into account the impact that the conflict is having on the rest of the team and what it's costing the company. If the impact and cost is minimal, you can give it some time. If you're not comfortable with the level of impact, act by either mediating a meeting between the two parties (see Chapters 6 through 9) or begin planning for a team meeting (see Chapter 10).

- ✔ **If you know that a conflict is affecting your entire team,** use techniques customized to resolve group conflict effectively. (Chapter 10 provides a detailed process you can use.)

Follow-up conversations

If the problem isn't affecting the whole team, give the parties a little time to figure things out on their own. Even if you learn that one or both employees seemed oblivious to the conflict, the fact that you had initial conversations will highlight the need for them to do *something*. Allow time for them to connect to resolve the issues, and then schedule individual follow-up conversations. Here are some questions to ask at the meetings:

- ✔ How have things been since we last met?
- ✔ Do you feel the situation is improving?
- ✔ What have you tried?
- ✔ What do you need to do to move forward from here?
- ✔ Would you be willing to meet with the other person if necessary?

Empowering Employees to Handle the Issue Themselves

It's common for people to want to save face and try to resolve a problem without their manager's involvement. So, if those involved all feel confident they can handle the situation on their own, let them work it out.

Even though you aren't guiding them through the conflict resolution process, you can help employees prepare for the conversations that they'll have with each other. Communicate your expectations for follow-through clearly, and include housekeeping details and decisions such as the following:

- ✔ Whether their communication will be part of their personnel files
- ✔ Confidentiality — who needs to know about the meeting and agreements
- ✔ The timeframe in which you expect them to meet
- ✔ Your availability for the meeting if needed and how they'll let you know
- ✔ What type of feedback you'll need from their meeting (written or verbal)
- ✔ How they plan to address future disagreements
- ✔ How often and in what format you'd like to be informed about progress
- ✔ The exact date you'll be checking back in with them
- ✔ When and where they'll meet (think safety, comfort, and time of day)
- ✔ Resources they may need from you, such as access to a private meeting room or someone to cover their shifts
- ✔ Whether agreements will be in writing or a handshake will do, as well as the level of detail needed in an agreement (such as a summary for you but a detailed document for them)
- ✔ What they'll do if they come to a standstill
- ✔ What homework or preparation is needed prior to the meeting so they have important information on hand

Providing each person with information from Chapter 15 (which details how to have a successful one-on-one conversation) is a good way to set everyone up for a productive discussion.

Providing tips for success

Let both parties know you're rooting for them, that you have confidence in their ability to look at the situation from each other's point of view, and that you're ready to help them as needed.

Coach the parties at various points in the process doing the following:

✔ **Ask them to treat each other with common courtesy and to walk away from the conversation without doing additional damage to each other.** In our everyday lives we're generally courteous people — we're kind to those we meet and liked by many. But being your best can be difficult when you disagree with someone. Frustration can set in, and you can find yourself responding defensively. Get a firm commitment from both employees that if either person becomes frustrated to the point that he wants to verbally attack the other person and the conversation goes south, one of them will ask for a break and the other will honor the request when asked. A walk around the block may give them enough time to cool off before continuing.

✔ **Ask them to listen, and assure them that listening doesn't mean agreeing with what the other person is saying.** Listening demonstrates that you respect the other person enough to hear what's important to her. Ask them not to interrupt one another, and encourage note taking when the urge to say something out of turn arises. Discuss the importance of restating what they heard the other say as a way to demonstrate a willingness to begin to see the other person's perspective.

✔ **Encourage sharing.** In one-on-one conversations, you may have heard some key information that, if it were shared, would help create understanding and move the parties forward. When one person doesn't see things the same as someone else does, he'll often hold back information. People do this out of fear of being ridiculed for their point of view or so they can use it against the other person later if needed. Let both employees know that sharing certain details would help. Simply say, "I don't think he's aware of that and if I was talking with you and you shared that with me, it would change my view of things." Help them see the value of getting all the information out on the table so they can make the best decision and move forward.

Motivating your employees to succeed

People are more motivated to put their energy into something when they can see the benefit in trying. Help both parties see that they're in the driver's seats here. Tell them that, as the manager, you could decide what they'll do to resolve their conflict but there's a good chance one or both of them wouldn't be happy with the result. They have the opportunity to tell each other what's important and to ask for what they need. They'll be more likely to follow the solutions if they reach them together than they would if they had to carry out a mandate handed down from "the boss."

If they need you or someone else to make a decision, they can always ask for that, but let them know now's the time to try it on their own first.

You may be tempted to encourage them to focus on resolution as the primary motivation to put this conflict behind them and be done with it. Unfortunately, that approach can put pressure on them to find an answer — any answer — even if it's not something that'll work. Let them know their time will be well spent if they come away understanding what's most important to the other person, that you're not interested in a quick fix. Assure them that you have other resources available to help them if needed.

Wrapping it up

No matter the outcome of their discussion, they'll want to know what to do next and how to end a meeting. They'll need to discuss and share the logistics of their next steps. Let them know that you'll expect some sort of feedback, even if the information they share is that they're giving it more thought.

If they come up with a number of steps that they need to carry out in order to resolve the conflict, make sure that they've taken the time to consider the order and timeline of the steps — the how and when. Have them put their agreement in writing — this strategy can prevent future conflicts if one person forgets an important step.

Finally, tell them that you'll expect them to consider the future. How do they want to approach one another if either person feels a need to meet? Have the parties consider how they'll follow up with you and how they intend to meet the expectations you gave them from the "Empowering Employees to Handle the Issue Themselves" section earlier in this chapter.

Watching their progress

Your employees have met and all seems well after their conversation. You're hopeful that the conflict is behind them and that they're both moving on. So how will you know if things are on track or if you need to step in with another course of action? You have to pay attention to determine what's next.

Complimenting their progress

Give your employees a little recognition for the risks they took in trying to resolve a conflict themselves; they'll appreciate it even if they were unsuccessful in resolving the situation. Say something like, "I appreciate your willingness to give it a shot. It's not always easy to see eye to eye on things. Your willingness to try indicates to me that we'll find an answer. We may just need to try a different approach."

Keep in mind each person's comfort level with receiving compliments — some people are a bit uncomfortable with praise. Even if one of your team members is the most humble person around, you can find a way to compliment him. A sincere e-mail, handwritten note, or after-hours voicemail can go a long way in helping him know he's on the right track.

Knowing what to watch for

Look for a number of different indicators to determine whether your employees have been successful in putting the past behind them. There's no need to run around playing Sherlock Holmes with an oversized magnifying glass, but look for subtle indicators of how things are going.

Your answers to the following questions can help you pinpoint trouble spots:

- ✔ How do they interact? Are they respectful of one another? Are the other team members comfortable with how the two are behaving?
- ✔ Are they able to share information freely?
- ✔ Can they work together when necessary?
- ✔ Are they finishing projects in a timely manner?
- ✔ Are they working through problems or pointing fingers?
- ✔ Do repeat issues keep popping up?

Responding to progress

Keep a watchful but subtle eye on the situation. If you overdo it, your questions will remind them of their troubles and may indicate that you don't trust them to follow through.

If you think that they're doing really well, you can casually say, "How's it been going since you talked?" and give them space to share their good news. If you see specific concerns, bring those to light and ask for any solutions. You may say, "I noticed whenever we have a new order come in that the two of you seem a bit tense. Is there anything we can do to prevent that?"

Your check-ins should be matched appropriately to specific, observable behavior. Not checking in at all could lead them to feel unsupported and uncomfortable asking for additional resources that they feel are necessary for continued success.

Part II

Resolving a Conflict between Two or More of Your Employees

The 5th Wave   By Rich Tennant

"In your complaint, you said you felt you were being manipulated by Mr. Prabhakar. Can you be more specific?"

In this part . . .

I walk you through a step-by-step mediation process designed to help feuding co-workers find solutions. As the mediator or facilitator, I show you how to identify the source of the conflict, help employees respectfully share what's important to them, and brainstorm mutually acceptable agreements. I also pass along tips and techniques for setting benchmarks and monitoring future progress.

Chapter 6

Developing a Plan and Preparing for a Meeting

In This Chapter

▶ Informing employees about the meeting

▶ Setting boundaries and expectations

▶ Creating an inviting meeting space

▶ Preparing to facilitate

Managers often have to address the conflicts of the people on their team. You've probably worked with managers who've tried to rush headlong into a conversation with the people in conflict, without giving much thought to the process or the techniques that could maximize their chances of success. You may have taken such an approach yourself because it was quick — and possibly even necessary for a temporary answer. But rushing into a conversation doesn't usually yield good long-term results.

People in your organization probably see you as a problem solver, because you're one of the people the company wants on the front lines. And that's a good thing. But solving your employees' conflicts for them actually does more harm than good. Think about your own life for a moment: You're more likely to support an idea when you have a stake in creating the solution than you are when someone else arbitrarily decides the answer for you. The same thing is true for your employees. They want a say in how a conflict is resolved because they're the ones who have to live with the consequences.

This line of thinking may represent a dramatic shift for you, but don't worry — I fill you in on a proven process that not only solves problems but also strengthens people's ability to tackle future issues.

This chapter is dedicated to all the front-loaded work you can do to prepare your employees for a productive conflict resolution meeting. In this type of mediation, you facilitate discussion — you don't make decisions or even offer suggestions, odd as that may sound. The responsibility for creative solutions and decisions ultimately will rest on the shoulders of the folks who are in conflict, so you can focus on other tasks.

Preparing the Parties for a Conversation

You may have had your eye on a conflict for a while and perhaps even chatted briefly about the problem with one or more of the people affected by it. Regardless, if your employees have reached the point where they need some help, it's time to intervene and facilitate a mediated conversation. (See Chapter 5 for information on knowing when to address conflict.) Follow this strategic process that takes your employees from preparing, to sharing, to understanding, to brainstorming, to agreement. I give you all the preparation details you need in this section; Chapters 7, 8, and 9 help you work through the remaining stages of the process.

In the upcoming sections, I cover the elements of a good preparatory approach. I break them out and discuss each in detail, but you should include them in one succinct communiqué or conversation.

Inviting your employees to the meeting

Every meeting starts with an invitation, and mediation is no different. You have some decisions to make regarding the way in which you'll notify your employees about the meeting — and the option you choose depends on your relationship to the parties involved.

This step of your strategic process can vary, depending on the kind of workplace you're in and the policies surrounding dispute resolution. I outline two good invitation options in the upcoming sections. Regardless of how you opt to let the parties know it's time to talk, the goal of the invitation is to

- Share information about the process
- Allow the parties to voice any initial concerns
- Prepare them to share their perspective at the meeting

The timing of this invitation may be as important as the invitation itself. Whether you choose to inform your employees that you're requesting their attendance in person or in writing, do so in a manner that allows them enough time to process their thoughts, but not *so* much time that they dwell on it. And unless you feel like doling out cruel and unusual punishments, don't set the meeting for a Monday and send the invitation on a Friday afternoon — your employees' entire weekend will likely be ruined worrying about the meeting.

Issuing personal invitations

Your employees may not yet see a mediated conversation as a helpful and constructive thing, and that usually means resistance. If you choose to approach them in person, do so in a private and confidential way. Dropping a bomb during your next staff meeting that Jarred and Kelly have been having some difficulties and are expected to talk things out with you may not generate a lot of goodwill. Plus, it drags others into the conflict. Instead, find a time when each employee is alone and has a few moments to chat with you. They'll both likely have a number of questions, so allow some time for them to process the request and come back to you if they feel the need.

The benefits to a face-to-face meeting request include the following:

✔ **Your employees have the opportunity to hear from you firsthand what your intentions are for the dialogue.** They'll likely initially see this conversation as a disciplinary action, rather than as an opportunity to solve problems. You can do a lot to reinforce a positive, creative approach to the conversation ahead of time, simply by talking about the meeting as just such an opportunity.

✔ **Your employees have a chance to process with you how they're thinking and feeling in real time.** Processing those thoughts and feelings now is better than brooding and worrying over the course of a few days while they prepare for the meeting.

Expect, however, that if you offer a verbal invite to your meeting, you may begin to hear more than you're ready for right away. Knowing that a mediated conversation is imminent, employees may try to deflect or defer the meeting. They may even try to convince you that the other one is clearly the problem.

If that happens, just reiterate your desire to talk about anything they'd like to share during the meeting and tell them that, for now, you're just letting them know the particulars and your expectations for the meeting. Use summarizing skills and clarifying questions to keep them on track and focused. (For more information about communication skills, refer to Chapter 7.)

A personal invitation is *not* the best bet if you're not comfortable relaying all the details about your role, their roles, the goal of the meeting, the process you'll be employing, what will be different about this meeting, and what will happen with any agreements. In that case, use the written option (see the next section).

Sending written invitations

You know your workplace, and you know what's appropriate and not appropriate when it comes to written meeting requests. If possible, make this invitation informal rather than formal. An e-mail or personal note is better than written instructions on company letterhead using very businesslike language. The best-written invitations are simple, personal, and confidential.

Provide both employees with an opportunity to talk to you if they have any questions or concerns. You don't want them going into your meeting with false impressions or preconceived ideas about your intentions and goals.

The benefit to putting the request in writing is that it provides your employees time to consider their reactions and thoughts before engaging anyone in discussion. Many employees find taking some time to gather their thoughts is a great boon to their ability to address the conflict with the right frame of mind.

A written invitation has some limitations as well. Specifically, the employees may be concerned about

- ✔ The formality of such a meeting
- ✔ Who else knows about the conflict or the meetings (for example, how involved other departments — particularly Human Resources — are in this conversation)
- ✔ Whether your letter will be part of their permanent files
- ✔ Whether their jobs are at stake

Anticipate concerns and include those items in the text of your invitation. Put their minds at ease with language that's clear, concise, and inviting.

Here's an example of a written invitation that includes concepts I go over throughout this chapter. Your memo should look something like this:

> Dear Barbara and Pat:
>
> Thank you for spending a few minutes to talk with me the other day about the conflict you're experiencing. I know this hasn't been an easy time for you, so I've arranged for the three of us to meet on Tuesday at 9:30 a.m. in the south conference room. My intention in calling this meeting is to mediate a conversation in which you'll both be able to share ideas on how we might resolve the issues. Your attendance is mandatory, but I'd like you both to voluntarily prepare a number of ideas for possible solutions.
>
> During the meeting, I'll act as a neutral facilitator. That means I won't be taking sides, nor will I be advocating for one idea over another. If at any point you feel it's necessary for me to act in a managerial capacity to determine how a particular idea might play out, I'll certainly be able to do that. Otherwise, consider this _your_ meeting with _your_ agenda.
>
> Our department head has asked that I report the result of the meeting to her, and I've agreed. I will not, however, be sharing anything other than whether an agreement is reached and any follow-up is needed. I would like you both to keep the meeting to yourselves, and we can decide who else needs to know about the outcome at the end of our discussion.
>
> I expect that you both will come prepared to discuss all the pertinent topics and that you'll be open and willing to hear what each other has to say. Between now and the meeting, consider your specific issues, possible solutions to the problems, and how you'll respectfully communicate these things to each other.

Clear your calendar for the better part of the day. I'll have lunch brought in so we won't have any distractions. This meeting is a priority for me, so I'll make sure I'm not interrupted. Please do the same.

I'm confident you each have what it takes to work this out. If you both give this a good-faith effort and you're not able to resolve the problem, I can offer additional resources. If I can clear up any questions you have about the meeting details, please let me know. Otherwise, anything you'd like to share about the situation should be saved for the meeting.

Explaining your role

In your (verbal or written) communication about your meeting, discuss and clarify a number of concepts regarding what your employees can expect from you during the meeting. You'll be fulfilling dual roles during the course of the meeting. You'll need to act both as a manager and a mediator, but for very different reasons and at very different times. There may be times when you'll need to clarify policies and procedures that are specific to your workplace.

The majority of the time, however, you'll want to be acting in a different role. Specifically, you want them to see you as something entirely separate from your job as "the boss." You want them to see you as both of the following:

- ✔ **Facilitator:** Essentially, you'll be facilitating the conversation. This means that you won't be taking anyone's side or speaking on behalf of either party. Reinforce that both employees are responsible for representing and speaking for themselves.

- ✔ **Guide:** Clarify that the responsibility for making all the decisions comes down to your employees. This means that, although you may help them in crafting and living up to any agreements they make, all decisions ultimately need to come from them.

If your employees can see you as a facilitator and a guide rather than as an enforcer of policies or a disciplinarian, they'll be more likely to speak openly and thoughtfully. Seeing you in such a way frees them up to think creatively about possible solutions and allows them to speak more freely about information that may be essential to getting to the root of the problem.

Helping employees get into the right frame of mind

For many employees, and indeed maybe even for you, the process in this book is a new way of looking at conflict, so they must have a clear understanding of your expectations of them during the mediation meeting process. They may think that this conversation will be an extension of what they've already done or, worse, that you're going to spend the time chewing them out.

When you invite the parties to the meeting, do a couple of things to prepare them and to help them create some opportunities that will make this conversation go well:

- ✓ **Ask them to come fully prepared to discuss all the topics that are pertinent to their conflict.** It's important that they're willing to participate fully and give the meeting an honest-to-goodness effort. Encourage them to be open and willing to discuss any possible items that may come up. Essentially, encourage them to think creatively and come to the meeting with a number of ideas for resolving the issues, rather than entering the room with only one fixed way of solving the problem.

- ✓ **Remind them to be aware of their language — which includes tone of voice and body language.** The best conversations are ones in which your employees, though they may disagree with each other, speak respectfully and without interruption. No one genuinely receives an apology that includes eyes rolling and ends with a *tsk!*

This part of your process really only serves as a means to get the parties in the right frame of mind prior to the meeting. You'll be repeating these instructions again in a much more formalized fashion when the meeting begins, so don't spend too much time discussing specific expectations right now. (For information about setting the tone and orienting your employees to your process, refer to Chapter 7.)

Assuring confidentiality

There's no getting around it — people are going to talk. When employees are in the midst of conflict, you can pretty much guarantee that they've brought others into the mix. In some cases, it's merely to blow off steam and vent some frustration. In other cases, it's to draw others to "the cause" and gather strength for their positions. Either way, other people are involved, so you need to attend to it.

Start by addressing the extent to which you'll be acting in a confidential manner. Specifically, clarify with your employees exactly what you *will* and *won't* share with others. If you'll be reporting to your manager the results of the discussion, be clear and upfront about it.

By including confidentiality details in your invitation, your parties will have a sense that, indeed, this meeting will be different. They'll also be more apt to share crucial information about the situation and the impact it's had on them.

Additionally, you must address the confidentiality expectations you have of the employees. Because others are likely interested in this conversation, you need to tell the parties involved how they should speak about the upcoming meeting with the rest of the staff (if they talk about it at all). Encourage them to limit any conversation with others regarding your meeting or the person they're in conflict with. Although expecting them to remain completely silent on the matter may be unreasonable, at the very least you're planting the seed that other voices may only complicate matters rather than help, and that this conflict, along with its resolution, is their responsibility.

When you're in the meeting (see Chapter 7 for more about the actual meeting), you can create some specific and mutually agreed-upon language surrounding the confidentiality of the conversation. For now, however, you're just trying to do some damage control and limit the problems that can arise when other employees throw in their two cents.

Defining meeting parameters

Your company may already have a very formalized dispute resolution procedure, and this conversation may fall somewhere within that process. Or your workplace may not outline *any* specific procedures or guidelines for handling meetings of this sort. Either way, having a clear understanding of the degree to which this process is voluntary or mandatory is important.

I encourage you to describe this meeting as mandatory with voluntary elements. Though you may require your employees to participate, let's face it, the conflict may not be something they can resolve in one meeting. So give them some insight into your intentions right upfront. Let them know that you're expecting them to attend, participate fully, and give it a good-faith effort, but that they are *not* required to reach a solution at any cost during the session. Also, though the meeting may be mandatory, any offers they make or solutions they arrive at are entirely voluntary. Discuss this point in the meeting request to demonstrate how this discussion will be different from past attempts and to alleviate any fears that they'll be stuck in a room for hours only to finally give in just so they can leave. Let them know that other options are available if they come to a standstill.

Giving pre-work/homework instructions

Your invitation to the meeting should include assignments. Give the parties some specific tasks to work on in the days leading up to the conversation. Depending on the nature of the conflict, you can vary your approach and instructions, but consider the following topics as possible pre-work:

✔ **Specific issues:** It may be difficult for employees to pinpoint exactly which concerns and issues they have with the other person. By encouraging them to spend some time identifying specific behaviors that upset them, you're helping them put language to their conflict.

✔ **Language:** Not only do you want your employees to examine their specific concerns, you also want them to be thoughtful of the *way* in which they discuss them. Encourage them to find language that expresses their concerns without making the other person defensive or resistant.

✔ **Possible solutions:** You want your employees to be open to ideas and proposals that are generated through brainstorming, but it never hurts to have them prepare some ideas in advance. Ask them to think about what would make them *most* satisfied *and* what they'd be willing to live with.

✔ **Their own responsibility:** It's all well and good to get them thinking about what they want from the other person, but it's another thing entirely to ask them to consider what they're willing to do. Help them see that their own responsibility is not so much a concession, but a strategy. Can they think of anything they may be able to do to bring the conflict to an agreeable close?

Setting Up the Meeting

Before your employees are ready to sit down with you and get the conversation started, you have some work to do. By preparing the space for your meeting, you maximize your potential for a successful conversation.

Choosing a neutral location

You must maintain the appearance and substance of neutrality at all times throughout your conversation. Any suggestion — whether real or imagined — that you've compromised neutrality will derail your process. (For more information about neutrality, refer to Chapter 7.)

Here are a few things you can do to create a sense of safety and neutrality:

✔ **Consider the location of the room itself.** Make sure the room you choose doesn't hold more or less power for either party. Specifically, try not to schedule your meeting in any location that could be described as either employee's "turf." Work to balance the power early to avoid having to address a power struggle during the meeting.

You may think that your office is the ideal spot, because, as a manager, you'll be calling the shots and your employees will be more likely to follow your lead. But the truth is, your office only reinforces the idea that this meeting is a disciplinary action — which is a message to avoid.

✔ **Choose a meeting room that's as private as possible.** Meeting someplace where other employees are wandering in and out or lurking (and listening) won't create the kind of environment you want. So find a place where the curious eyes of others won't affect your discussion.

Private should also mean minimal distractions. A room with a telephone constantly ringing or computer beeps announcing the arrival of new e-mail serves only to distract from the conversation. Listening well is hard when you have distractions competing for your attention.

Avoid creating a situation like that of a manager at a local mortgage office who held a mediated conversation between two employees in an area of the office that the team collectively referred to as the "fishbowl." The room was a raised platform surrounded on all sides by windows in the center of the office. Needless to say, every time another employee would wander past the area, there were stares and uncomfortable glances. Everyone in the office had some idea that *something* was happening between the two employees, and their curiosity got the better of them. In the midst of the meeting, one of the employees turned to the manager and said, "I feel like I'm in the middle of a three-ring circus. It's absolutely humiliating. I think I'd rather just quit."

Allowing enough time

Successful mediated conversations take some time. If you're following the process in this part and following each step to its fullest potential, your conversation may take upwards of three to four hours (including the occasional ten-to-fifteen-minute breaks you'll take for personal needs). Make sure that the parties allow for such a time commitment when you schedule the meeting. You want them to treat this meeting as a priority, not an afterthought. It's reasonable to assume that the demands of the workplace may intervene in the conversation, but setting clear expectations about the importance of the meeting should create the space for the parties to devote enough time to reach solid agreements.

Facilitating a comfortable environment

These kinds of conversations can be difficult and uncomfortable for employees. You can help create a more positive response to the conversation, however, by improving the comfort of your surroundings.

Holding the meeting on neutral ground is important, but location is only part of that equation. Both of your employees must have equal access to all the amenities that you provide. Yes, it sounds silly to discuss these finer details, but trust me, they matter. I had a mediation go south from the get-go because one party's pen didn't work and the other person couldn't stop laughing!

Consider the quantity and quality of everything in the meeting. For example, if you provide three pieces of paper to one employee, make sure the other employee also has three pieces of paper. If you provide a black pen with a cap to one, make sure that the other person has the same. Any indication of partiality can disrupt your process.

Make the process go more smoothly by setting up your room in a fairly bare-bones way. The fewer distractions the better. That said, consider including a few of the following items to help the parties make the most of their time:

- ✔ **Blank paper:** To jot down any notes or thoughts they have during the process, or for documenting important decisions that come from your discussion. This is also a great way to remind your employees not to interrupt each other when they're speaking. By drawing attention to the paper, you can subtly remind them to wait their turn.

- ✔ **Pens/pencils:** If you're going to have paper, make sure to provide something they can write with. Oh, and make sure that both pens work or that both pencils are equally sharp!

- ✔ **Comfortable chairs:** The meeting is going to last approximately three to four hours, so provide comfortable chairs. Lengthy and difficult conversations can be made even *more* lengthy and difficult if you're constantly readjusting, trying to find a comfortable position.

- ✔ **Water and snacks:** Your employees may appreciate some simple amenities like water when their voices get tired from talking, or something to munch on to help keep their blood sugar stable. Providing water and snacks also prevents the need for too many breaks.

Some snacks are better than others. Nervous employees who gobble down handful after handful of candy may have a quick burst of energy followed about an hour later by a pretty nasty sugar crash. I provide protein bars or granola bars and a small bowl of candy.

- ✔ **Facial tissue:** Don't be surprised if you see tears from either of your employees. It may not happen, but if it does, you need to be prepared. I knew an employee who would bring her own box of tissue to every discussion she thought might be difficult. She'd plop it on the table and say, "This is a topic I feel strongly about, and I just might start crying once we get into it. If I do, I've got my tissue ready, so just ignore my tears and listen to what I'm saying." Because she was able to acknowledge upfront that she might cry, she never once produced tears. Do the same for your employees and let them know you're prepared.

✔ **A way to keep time:** You may keep a clock in the room with you for the purposes of monitoring the length and timing of your meeting. Because you'll be the facilitator of the process, it's less important that your employees have access to a clock. If you do provide one, however, just make sure each employee has equal access to it.

Preparing yourself

With all the work you've done to prepare your employees, you also need to take a few minutes to focus on yourself. Getting caught up in the conflict is pretty easy to do. Don't allow yourself to get over-invested in the outcome, though. In fact, the less emotionally invested you are, the better.

This is your employees' conflict. They own the problems, so they own the solutions! If you allow yourself to become attached to the conflict, and you become invested enough to make suggestions or offer solutions, you've effectively become responsible for those outcomes and whether they succeed or fail. Your employees will be more likely to buy in and follow through on an agreement when they themselves propose and refine it.

Before your meeting begins, take about 30 minutes and prepare yourself for what's to come. Strong conflict creates strong emotions, not only on the part of the participants, but for any observer as well. Expect to hear language that's affected by emotions, and prepare yourself accordingly.

Prepare yourself in these three ways while waiting for your meeting to begin:

✔ **Mentally:** Be ready to listen for facts, figures, and timelines so you can keep it all straight in your own mind.

Be sure to clear whatever time is necessary for your meeting. If you can, take care of any issues that may be hanging over you. You won't be giving your best to your employees if you're thinking about your own project that's due at the end of the week!

✔ **Emotionally:** This is the self-preparation that comes with expecting to hear difficult language and raised voices. Remind yourself who the conflict really belongs to (them!) and who is responsible for solving the problem (them!). This approach will help center you before the meeting.

✔ **Personally:** Whatever helps you clear your mind and focus on the present will help you make the most of your time in the coming meeting. Anyone who does mediation for a living knows that high emotions and negative energy can exhaust even the most prepared facilitator, so some folks I know meditate, some read over a favorite passage, and others listen to music. I prefer complete silence before I bring parties in.

Chapter 7

Starting a Mediation Meeting and Creating a Working Agenda

*A*fter you meet privately with individuals in conflict, you have the option to facilitate a discussion (or mediation) between the two. The way you set up the meeting room is important, so look for tips on how to do that in Chapter 6. When you're ready to bring the participants in, take a deep breath and steady yourself so you can be the neutral facilitator they need.

In this chapter, I give you skills and techniques to direct the conversation in a meaningful way as well as step-by-step instructions on how to demonstrate your neutrality by reflecting emotions and issues back to the parties. I also share tips on ordering and structuring a productive agenda.

Unsure how all this fits together? Not to worry — the flowchart in Figure 7-1 will help you keep track of where you're at in the process and what the next steps should look like.

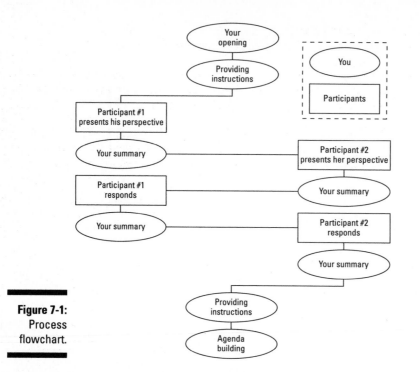

Figure 7-1:
Process
flowchart.

Facilitating Effectively

Mediating a discussion is a lot more than just positioning yourself between two people who aren't getting along and blocking verbal punches. There's an art to reading the situation in a way that puts you in the facilitator's seat but allows you enough involvement in the discussion to move the conversation forward. It's not refereeing; it's guiding. And it's guiding without the parties feeling manipulated. Stay on top of the conversation without getting too involved in it. For instance, don't talk too much or say things like, "Well, Vanessa made a good point there, Brent. It's hard to argue with that."

Establishing rapport and making the employees comfortable

The extent to which your employees feel comfortable with you mediating their conflict is a concept that's difficult to quantify. It's vital that they see you as a neutral and impartial facilitator of their dialogue, even if you're required to wear the Manager Hat when you leave the room.

The words you choose and the tone you take set the stage for either a productive conversation or a gripe session to ensue. Draw on the following tips to establish rapport and make everyone feel comfortable:

- ✔ **Use open language.** Use words that encourage positive interactions, like *share, create, explore, encourage, clarify,* and *guide.* Avoid words that detract or shut down interactions, like *must, require, expect, demand,* and *impose.*

- ✔ **Be brief.** Lengthy oration about expectations may do more harm than good. Your opening comments should be lengthy enough to describe the process and expectations but not so long that you lose their interest.

- ✔ **Project confidence.** The folks at the table are looking to you to keep the meeting on track and civil, and to help them focus. If you appear nervous or uncomfortable, you may send a signal to your employees that they, too, should be nervous or uncomfortable.

Showing your neutrality

Present yourself as neutrally as possible. If the time arises when you have to step back into the management role and make a decision, the decision will be better received if the employees feel you were impartial during the rest of the conversation. Be equally interested in what each has to say by providing the same opportunities to each throughout the process; allow equal opportunity for them to share their stories and to add content to the meeting agenda.

Here are some easy ways to show and keep an impartial role in the process:

- ✔ **Position yourself in the middle.** Your chair should be in a position that maintains an easy balance between the parties. For example, you may place yourself at the head of the table with the parties on either side. You don't want to have to turn your back to either of your participants.

- ✔ **Strive for balanced eye contact.** Manage the amount of time you make eye contact with each party. Spend most of your time connecting with the person who's speaking, but be sure to check in periodically with the other person. You minimize outbursts and create a sense of awareness of their needs if they both feel you're paying attention.

- ✔ **Watch your reactions.** You may hear some things that you'll find surprising, but keep your poker face! A raised eyebrow, a rolled eye, or a dropped jaw at the wrong moment can send a pretty clear message that you've made up your mind and have lost your objectivity.

✔ **Balance your feedback.** It may not be possible to provide identical feedback for your parties, nor is it reasonable to expect that your feedback will take exactly as long for one as it does for another. You do, however, want your feedback to be roughly in balance in terms of timing, tone, and content. For tips on giving feedback, see "Summarizing and Reflecting Back What You Hear," later in this chapter).

✔ **Facilitate dialogue.** Your goal for this meeting is not to assign blame or responsibility for the problem, nor is it to solve the problem for them. Instead, your job is to give them the space to create their own conversation, to acknowledge and validate their perspectives, and to facilitate them solving their own problem.

Actively listening

When it's time for your employees to share their perspectives (which happens later in the meeting) demonstrate active listening skills by taking good notes, and begin thinking about how to summarize each party's viewpoint in a way that speaks to what he *does* want instead of what he *doesn't* want. And on top of that, periodically check in with the other person. No small feat, right?

While each party tells you what's been going on for him or her, demonstrate that you hear and understand what the speaker is sharing by doing the following:

✔ Display open body language by assuming a comfortable posture with your arms at your sides or resting on the table.

✔ Try to lean forward just enough to demonstrate your interest but not so much that you're sitting in the speaker's lap.

✔ Be aware of environmental impacts on your body language. If you've folded your arms because the temperature of the room is chilly, a participant could read that as a judgmental posture.

✔ Take simple notes (not a word-for-word transcript) on what each speaker is saying, but also listen carefully for any values and emotions you hear. Make note of important dates, numbers, or other facts, and take special care to note any potential common ground that the two parties share, so you can provide that in feedback as a way to illuminate mutual interests.

It's difficult for a listening co-worker not to interrupt, so make sure you're doing enough to stay connected in some way with her. Simple movements like a glance in her direction or sliding your hand toward her side of the table can be enough to say that you haven't forgotten that she's there and that in a moment you'll be sure to provide her an opportunity to speak about her perspective. Both will be more likely to sit and listen quietly if they know that you're periodically checking in with them to see how they're doing.

Saving your questions for later

You may be tempted to ask a number of questions while your parties are sharing their thoughts. Resist that urge! This isn't the time or place for it, even if you hear things you feel you can clear up or address in the moment. This meeting isn't an inquisition, so wait until later to test assumptions or address misinformation. Chapter 8 explains more on how to do that.

This part of the meeting isn't about the facts; it's about the experience. You want your participants to feel open to share information. It's more important that they relay their thoughts and emotions and feel heard than it is for you to clarify or fix information that they provide. Your only job here is to make sure that you're hearing and understanding what's said.

Reviewing the Ground Rules for the Discussion

Set the right tone for the meeting from the get-go. It's important that your participants are clear in your expectations of them and are as comfortable as is reasonably possible given that they may not have spoken to each other in quite a while or have been at each other's throats. Bring them in together, and begin by inviting both of them to take a moment to relax as you outline some of the housekeeping items that will make the meeting run smoother. Set up the parameters by using clear language in an organized and professional manner. With that said, don't freak everybody out by being so scripted that it sounds like they're on trial. Set boundaries, but let the employees know you're willing to be flexible.

If this is the first time the two have been able to talk, be aware that a lot of new information will be exchanged, and it's up to you to make sure they're really hearing what the other has to say. On the other hand, if they've tried talking to one another before, they've probably shared most of the details but can't agree on a solution. If the latter is the case, let them know you'll focus on helping them brainstorm solutions that work for both sides.

Also let them know that you'll spend most of the time together understanding from each person what keeps them in conflict and then working to find what each needs in order to limit further problems. For now they've probably prepared some pretty tough language about the other person (or even regarding their thoughts about this meeting) that may threaten to derail your process. But don't panic! Go over rules of common courtesy, and point out that you won't tolerate name-calling or disrespectful language.

Emphasize collaboration by stressing to your employees that this conversation is their opportunity to come together and work on a solution that's satisfactory to both of them. Include language that emphasizes the responsibility that each shares in brainstorming and implementing solutions.

In this section, I walk you through a sound way to describe what's about to happen, what you will and won't be doing for each of your participants, and what you expect from everyone at the table.

Explaining roles and responsibilities

You're the manager, and your employees are used to you being in charge. This meeting is different, though, and it's vital that they understand your objective role as mediator. Explain that you aren't acting as a decision maker, an advocate, or even a counselor. You aren't influencing outcomes, offering advice, or determining liability. You're here to help them explore their issues and concerns, assist them in brainstorming options, and aid them in creating their own mutually agreeable outcomes and solutions.

This is *not* your conflict! Though you may have a stake in the outcome, it's important to remember that the conflict and its solution rest in the hands of your employees. If you become invested in the outcome, take sides, or offer solutions and ideas, you risk alienating one (or both!) employees.

Additionally, you may find that if your ideas or suggestions don't meet their needs, in their eyes you've effectively become responsible for the failure of the process. By reinforcing that the responsibility for solution rests on their shoulders, you effectively reinforce ownership and buy-in for the process.

After you state your role, clearly stress the importance of the participants' roles. Specifically, outline the kind of behavior you'd like to see from them during the course of the conversation. Discuss these key points:

✔ **Willingness to listen:** Asking employees to communicate respectfully means allowing time to finish sentences and thoughts and choosing not to interrupt when the other is speaking. It also means not monopolizing the floor when speaking.

✔ **Willingness to share:** Encourage them to speak from their own perspectives. Remind them that it's important to hear what each person has to say and that this meeting is a safe setting in which to do so.

✔ **Courteous treatment:** Most people are fairly courteous in their day-to-day interactions with others, but when in conflict it often becomes difficult to maintain the same manners. Acknowledge this fact, and then ask your employees to remember that courteous treatment of one another is a simple way to make your meeting go smoother.

✔ **Openness to new ideas:** Although each employee has likely come to this meeting with only one way of addressing the conflict, encourage them to remember that there are multiple ways to solve problems. There are no wrong answers while brainstorming; ideas they never imagined may come from the most innocuous comment.

Directing the flow of information

Encourage your participants to start out by speaking directly to you. They'll have an opportunity to speak to one another later, but for now, you want all their energy and attention focused on you. They likely have prepared scripts running in their heads, which include a laundry list of things that the other person has done, and they may use language that isn't terribly helpful. Rather than have them lob this language at one another, ask them to give it to *you*.

Stressing uninterrupted time

Uninterrupted time means that while one person is speaking, the other is listening. Seems pretty straightforward, right? They may have agreed not to interrupt, but face it: It's hard to sit and listen to someone say things you disagree with. Encourage your employees to honor the agreement, rather than calling them out. If you blurt out, "Don't interrupt!" you dismiss the fact that the topic is uncomfortable for the interrupter. You may have to be stern later if they continue to talk over one another, but the best first step is to ask them to jot down their thoughts for when it's their turn to speak.

Supply your participants with some notepaper and pens before you begin (see Chapter 6 for tips on setting up the meeting room). When the inevitable interruption comes, simply gesture to the paper as a reminder to make note of the interrupter's thoughts.

Giving the Participants a Chance to Present Their Perspectives

Up until now, you've been outlining ground rules and maybe sounding to your employees a little like Charlie Brown's teacher droning on and on. Trust me when I tell you that they may have been looking at you and nodding as if they were taking in every word you said, but in reality if asked to repeat your instructions, they'd probably reply with, "Well, you said something about being a facilitator and maybe something about not interrupting."

The reason your employees have only caught about every third word you said is that they're likely concentrating on what they're going to say, what they're going to keep to themselves, and how they're really going to let the other person have it when it's their turn to talk. From the moment the first person opens his mouth, your job is to move them from blaming to eventually creating solutions. Do this by listening to both parties, pulling out pertinent information, acknowledging emotions, and neutralizing statements.

Deciding who speaks first

Ask the parties which of them would like to speak first, and allow them to make that choice on their own. No matter how tempting it may be, don't make the decision for them. You can inadvertently set the expectation that when things become difficult you'll step in to solve the problem (both in this meeting and in the future!). Instead, be patient and allow them some time and space to work it out. If they still struggle, comment on the fact that there's no benefit to going first (or second, for that matter) and ask for a volunteer.

Although it's important for your parties to make the choice on their own, watch for power moves. An employee may bully his way into speaking first, or he could gallantly let his co-worker go first because he feels certain he'll be able to rip her perspective to shreds. A quick check with the other person ("Is that okay with you?") lets him know it really is a joint decision.

Sample script: Describing the process

When I'm mediating, I summarize the ground rules and instructions for sharing perspectives in one statement that sounds something like this:

> Thank you for giving me the opportunity to describe this process. Now I want to give both of you the chance to share with me what it is that brought you here and what it is you're hoping to accomplish. This will be uninterrupted time, so while one of you is speaking, the other is listening. I've provided some paper and pens for you, so if you hear something you want to respond to, go ahead and jot down your thoughts. For now, I'd like you to direct your comments to me, even though it may be difficult for you to hold off on speaking directly to one another. You'll have plenty of time for that in a few minutes. So, who would like to start? There's no benefit to going first, since both of you will have two opportunities to speak with me. Who would like to begin?

Listening to the second participant

After the first employee has had a chance to express his thoughts, take the time to summarize what you heard (see the upcoming section "Summarizing and Reflecting Back What You Hear" for details). Then turn your attention to the second party. Start by thanking the first party for his statement and the other party for waiting and being patient (even if she really hasn't shown a lot of patience!). Reaffirm that this is the second party's chance to share her thoughts, and then put some additional parameters around your expectations.

Tell the second party that although she may be tempted to respond to what the first speaker has just said, you want her to speak as if she's sharing first. This mindset gives her an opportunity to present her story in a fuller way.

After the second employee has shared her point of view and you've reflected back to her, turn your attention back to the first party and say, "Is there anything you'd like to add that hasn't already been discussed or a particular point you'd like to respond to?" It's my experience that any more than one response during opening statements just makes for a prolonged back-and-forth that looks more like a tennis match than a productive conversation.

You may find that your parties attempt to begin the negotiation process here by turning to one another and bypassing you as a facilitator. It's important to prevent this from happening because it can seriously derail the meeting, but bear in mind that this action is actually good news! It means that your parties are active and engaged and ready to get to work, so use their desire to talk to each other to your advantage. To guide the conversation back on track, say, "I can see that the two of you are anxious to get started. Let's complete this part of the process and then we'll move forward."

Summarizing and Reflecting Back What You Hear

After the first party shares his perspective, briefly summarize what you've heard before moving to the other person. Likewise, after you listen to the second person, summarize before giving the first person a chance to speak again. Summarizing not only allows the speaker to know that you've heard and understood what he had to say, but it also gives the other employee the opportunity to hear the concerns from a new source (you) and with new ears.

Think of it this way: There's probably not much chance your employees are going to hear anything new if the same old script keeps running. But when you skillfully craft your response to the speaker in the form of reflecting and reframing the information, you create the opportunity for the other person to hear something in a new way. Imagine that they each hear your perspective not as a list of all the things that were "wrong" with the way they handled things, but rather as a conversation about what's important to the speaker.

In the following sections, I show you how to reflect emotions, reframe statements, and neutralize perspectives. Each of these skills on its own makes up only a small portion of the kind of feedback to provide participants at the end of their statements. The truth is, you need to combine all the elements together into one succinct, summarized package. You can use each of these skills independently, but it's better when you bring them all together.

Reflecting, reframing, and neutralizing take some practice. You may not be accustomed to speaking in such a way, and to be sure, the parties may not be accustomed to hearing it. Give yourself some leeway while you practice these skills. In the meeting, take some time and be reflective about how you'd like to say what you're thinking. Try not to worry so much about getting it *exactly* right. If you're pretty close, you'll see subtle clues and hints that your summaries resonate. I always know I'm on the right track when I see someone's eyes light up, nodding, or body language that goes from crossed arms to an open posture. And if you notice quizzical looks, furrowed brows, or a shaking head, feel free to ask for an opportunity to try it again.

Before you jump into a mediation meeting, spend some time listening to other people having conversations. Try to pick out the specific emotions and values that you hear when others speak. Practice listening for the core of the message. When you've begun to identify some of the emotions and values, the language you use to frame them will come fairly quickly and easily.

Be careful not to use the same language over and over again. You may become very comfortable framing responses in a certain way, but it can be distracting for the listener. For instance, you've probably heard someone start a reflecting statement with, "It sounds like you're feeling. . . ." In and of itself that's good language. But you start to sound artificial if each time you reflect emotion you begin with, "It sounds like you're feeling. . . ." People don't like to feel like they're being handled or processed.

Find different ways to frame your response, such as:

"It sounds like. . . ."

"I hear [blank] is important to you."

"You feel strongly about [blank]."

"When you said [blank], I understood. . . ."

"So for you it's important to. . . ."

Reflecting emotions

Conflicts create strong feelings. It's important to recognize emotions and speak to them in others, so as the mediator of the conversation you need to spend some time understanding how to reflect another person's feelings.

Reflecting isn't just repeating what you hear. It goes way beyond that by putting a voice to the emotions that you see or hear, and it creates an openness and curiosity about the emotions you may not observe.

To reflect effectively, start by identifying what you think the speaker's emotion may be. For example, imagine that you're mediating a conflict between Carol and Peter. In the midst of her opening statement, Carol says, "Peter never finishes any of the projects he starts, but he's always there to get the accolades when we finish."

What are Carol's emotions? How is she feeling? She certainly sounds pretty frustrated, annoyed, and maybe even a little disappointed. When you relay your understanding of her emotions back in a way that allows her to know she's been heard, you're halfway to understanding why this conflict has had such an impact on her. Here are some examples:

Statement: "I can't believe she botched another presentation!"

Reflected: "You're concerned that the presentations haven't gone well."

Statement: "She places way too much demand on us. We can't do it all!"

Reflected: "It's been difficult to accomplish all the assigned tasks."

Statement: "Our project was an utter failure. He really screwed it up."

Reflected: "You're disappointed at the way the project turned out."

Notice that in the examples, nothing is intentionally said about what was supposedly wrong about the other person. The idea is simply to speak to what the speaker is feeling. It may be true that she's frustrated *because* of the other person, but the point of effective reflecting is to highlight the emotion itself.

You may have also noticed that in the reflection, the emotion is toned down just slightly from what the speaker describes. That's intentional, too. Your goal is to soften the language used to help reduce the emotion so the participants can create the kind of conversation that moves them forward. For example, if you hear "angry" and reflect instead "frustration," you're purposefully acknowledging emotion while calming the situation. Similarly, you may hear "crushed" and reflect instead "disappointment." Reflecting just below where you think the emotion may be goes a long way in softening the participant who's experiencing the emotion. You'll be pleased at how different (and positive) the reaction is from the parties when you reflect back emotions rather than regurgitating exactly what was said.

Conversely, if you hear an emotion and reflect it stronger, you run the risk of taking the speaker beyond that emotion. For instance, if you hear "anger" and reflect instead "rage," you may find the speaker using much stronger language and, in fact, becoming angrier than she was before!

Reframing statements

Parties involved in mediations have a tendency to talk about the things they don't like or disapprove of in each other rather than what's personally important to them. Reframing is a way to capture what's important to the speaker while leaving out what's supposedly wrong with the other person.

Reframing is also a way of highlighting and drawing out interests or values, which is a tremendous asset to you as a facilitator. (Check out Chapter 2 for a definition and explanation of values.) Highlighting the values shifts the conversation away from negative descriptions and toward describing what's important to each party; and that allows your participants to talk about the same thing without requiring them to see it the same way.

For example, Jacob says, "Katherine is the real problem here. She has to create a timeline for everything! I have to juggle multiple projects, and I don't need her trying to make my work process fit into her little plan."

What is it that Jacob really wants? Look past what he says to what's underneath it all — what are his values? Perhaps what he's really after is the ability to work to his own schedule and at his own pace. You may reframe that as "autonomy," "independence," or "freedom."

Here are more examples of statements and their reframed summaries:

> Statement: "He never shares any information. I don't understand why he can't just provide me with the numbers."
>
> Reframed: "It's important for you to work cooperatively."

> Statement: "She's so dismissive of everyone's proposals. She always says 'no' to everything and insults us when we come up with ideas."
>
> Reframed: "You'd like to have a respectful talk about proposals."

> Statement: "He has been late for every single meeting we've ever set up. Does the man not own a watch? How hard is it to show up on time?"
>
> Reframed: "Timeliness is important to you."

By reframing language to include the values you hear, you create the opportunity to discuss what each value means to the parties. Then they can begin to think about how they may be able to ask for the important things they've described rather than only asking for resolution to a surface issue. For example, asking someone to respect a need for autonomy is a much different request than asking her to quit checking the reports.

Neutralizing the perspectives

When summarizing statements and providing feedback, neutralize difficult language to take the sting out of words without taking away from the message. You can capture the spirit of a message without minimizing or downplaying the meaning.

Putting it all together

Imagine you're facilitating a conflict discussion between Charles and Mike, who have similar jobs and titles. They've worked together for only a short time and are having trouble working together on several of the same projects. They had a blow-up in the middle of the office that many of their co-workers witnessed. Charles starts by saying, "I've been working with Mike ever since I was hired around six months ago. I was told to follow him around for the first couple weeks so I could get the hang of things."

He then describes the structure and pacing of his job, how he came to be employed, and generally how things function for him day to day. Charles describes the trouble that he and Mike encountered: "Recently, facilities moved me into his pig sty of an office to create space for some new employees. He's sloppy and disorganized and his work always spills over onto my desk. And now I'm stuck having to deal with him on a daily basis."

Charles goes on to detail all the stylistic differences the two have and follows with a description of the incident that brought them to this point: "Well, a couple of days ago, I'd been having kind of a tough day, and I screwed up on one of my reports. Mike saw it and launched into a diatribe about me and how incompetent I was, and he did it loud enough that everyone could hear."

Charles describes the shouting match that ensued and the fact that their boss overheard the entire exchange. Not exactly Charles's best moment, as he describes it.

Combining reflecting, reframing, and neutralizing, how would you summarize Charles's experience for him? Reflect his emotions, reframe what he doesn't want into what he does want, highlight his interests, and neutralize any hot-button language he may have used.

✔ **Reflect:**

"You enjoy your job."

"You're frustrated at having to work with someone with a different style."

"You're embarrassed over the way the mistake on the report was handled."

✔ **Reframe:**

"You would like to work independently."

"You appreciate it when communication is respectful."

✔ **Neutralize:**

"The two of you encountered some difficulty."

"There was a conversation about an error."

"There was an exchange that was heard by others."

Your job in this example is to provide feedback that's clear, succinct, and acknowledges Charles's perspective *without* alienating Mike. Remember that both participants are looking to you to make sure you've understood what they've said and to make sure that there isn't any bias in your feedback to the other person.

Here are some examples of statements and their neutralized summaries:

Statement: "That meeting was a total catastrophe."

Neutralized: "The meeting didn't go as you had hoped."

Statement: "We got into a shouting match in front of the staff."

Neutralized: "There was a loud conversation that others observed."

Statement: "The project has hit a total dead end. It's done for."

Neutralized: "The project is facing some difficulties."

Creating an Agenda

You may be wondering why I'm asking you to create an agenda midway through your meeting process. What gives? Well, an *agenda* in mediation is *not* a pre-generated list of topics that you use to guide the discussion. Nor is it a schedule of events and activities for your dialogue. Instead, it's a list of topics the employees want to talk about that they collaboratively create after hearing each other's perspective. By generating the list together, they're much more likely to see each topic as belonging to both of them rather than feeling that you're forcing topics on them.

Up to this point in the meeting process, there's been a lot of talk about what brings the parties to the table and maybe a little bit about what they're hoping to see from one another. Now the agenda creation is about clarifying and naming issues and creating a road map for the discussion that's to come. This is your opportunity to help put some structure to the conversation.

Start by standing up and moving to a whiteboard or easel. Tell the parties it's time to build a meeting agenda that will cover the topics and issues that are important to them. They talk; you write. (Manage what gets written down so you can ensure that inflammatory or hurtful language stays off the list.)

In the following sections, I show you how to take what might seem like a random stream of consciousness from the parties and turn it into an organized list. The agenda is your silent co-mediator and helps you keep the parties on track and further define issues, and it acts as a visual reminder of their progress.

Transitioning from the past to the future

Use the agenda to make an important point: It's time to move from the past to the future. Set the stage for the conversation to come by saying, "Thank you for sharing your perspectives. As we begin to build an agenda, keep in mind that you'll discuss each of these items thoroughly, but you'll do so with a focus on the future rather than rehashing the past." Your statement should focus the employees to move them away from where the problems have been and head toward where the solutions are.

Sample script: Asking for agenda items

As with all stages of the mediation process, professional mediators often summarize the information about creating an agenda in one statement. I say something akin to:

> Thank you both for giving me the opportunity to hear your perspectives. I want to shift our conversation a little bit and invite the two of you to help me create a list of the

topics that you feel we need to discuss in order to reach a resolution today. I'd like to hear from you a couple of words or phrases that you think capture the essence of your conversation. It's not necessary that you agree on topics; if it's important to one of you, we'll go ahead and list it up here. So, what are some words or phrases you think capture what we need to discuss?

Demonstrating accessibility and ownership

As you begin to create the agenda, make sure the list is visible to both employees, meaning that one won't be able to look directly at it while the other has to crane his neck to see it. In effect, your employees should be facing almost the same direction, working side by side. Also, make sure both participants know that they can add to the list at any time and that it's flexible. It should be seen as a living document rather etched in stone.

Whatever you do, don't let go of the marker! Take responsibility for creating and editing the list so one of your employees doesn't hijack the process by erasing all your hard work or adding language that derails the conversation.

Let the parties know that it's not necessary for them to agree on the topics listed on the agenda. In other words, if one wants to have a conversation about a topic, it goes on the list as a potential topic for discussion. This point is important, because it creates ownership in the topics an employee suggests and in his co-worker's suggestions as well.

Separating their topics

It's likely that the parties will see all the difficulties they're having as one big mess and lump everything into the same category on the agenda list. It's a lot like a big ball of holiday lights: It's hard to know how many and what color lights you have until you've pulled them apart, strand by strand. Unraveling the lights may take a little time and care, but it's worth it in the end. And conflict topics are no different.

Unravel complicated agenda suggestions by asking questions. Don't rush to write something down. Instead, take a few minutes to gently challenge your employees to give you more. For example, ask what someone means when he says that he wants to talk about "the problem." How would he break that down into a small handful of specific topics?

Labeling and defining issues

Your employees need to see the agenda list as belonging to both of them rather than see each topic as either "mine" or "not mine." So when possible, point out commonalities and reiterate that this is a collaborative agenda.

Make sure all the topics you list are neutral and presented objectively. Creating neutral topics is an important part of generating buy-in to the process. But if you're relying on the parties to create the topics, how can you expect them to keep the list civil? The truth is, you may not be able to. What you can do, though, is reframe their language to make it more palatable.

For example, one of your participants says that she wants to talk about the fact that the staff meetings run way too long and end up in shouting matches. She wants to cut the meetings in half and has a pretty good plan to make it work. But the other participant quickly responds that, in fact, the meetings are a necessary way of exchanging ideas and information, and it would be good to extend the time to make sure everyone is on the same page about projects.

If you list the topic as "Cut staff meetings in half," you've essentially recorded a position (or solution), which is only one person's way of resolving the issue. And if you list "Extend staff meetings," you've done the same thing in reverse. So what's really the topic here? The staff meeting is what's important, so list that. How the participants feel and what they think about the meeting remains intact, and neither of them is alienated by the topic as it appears on the agenda.

Make sure the agenda includes all the issues. You don't want to finish the meeting only to realize a key issue has gone unnoticed and unaddressed. Ask both parties after the list is made if there's anything else they need to discuss in order to find a resolution.

If they feel the list is complete, let them know again that items can be added or erased if they change their minds. It's a flexible list that belongs to the participants. Tell them for now it's "a good place to start."

Considering common agenda topics

Although it's true that every facilitated conversation is different depending on the participants and their concerns, a few common themes tend to surface when dealing with work issues. Having some sample language at the ready helps you frame topics in an objective, constructive manner. I use the following agenda topics quite often:

- ✔ **Roles and responsibilities:** This topic can describe a number of situations in which employees see their job responsibilities differently. Put this on the board if you need to discuss disagreements about job descriptions and areas of influence.

- ✔ **Respect:** Another common theme in workplace scenarios is the hard-to-define yet all-important concept of what respect means to employees. Although each party is likely to describe it differently, they get an opportunity to speak about how they wish to be respected and what it means to show respect to others.

- ✔ **Communication:** This agenda topic is a simple way to discuss differences in how employees speak to one another. Many workplace conflicts boil down to either a lack of communication or different approaches to communication.

- ✔ **Confidentiality:** Confidentiality is huge in mediation, so even if your employees don't bring it up, you should. This is a great topic that covers other employees' interest or curiosity in what's happening in the meeting or when to share details about the conflict.

Using the agenda for negotiations

The agenda helps you structure brainstorming, aids in problem solving, and creates an organized way to kick off negotiations (check out Chapter 8 for a discussion of the negotiating process). Breaking the conflict into smaller pieces helps your employees feel the situation is little more manageable.

The agenda is a tool you'll use throughout the negotiation and agreement phases, and it will serve you best in these areas if you

- ✔ Have the parties choose one item at a time to discuss.

- ✔ Be thorough with each item and do your best to work through one topic completely before moving on to another.

- ✔ Move on to another point if the two participants get stuck on something. You can always come back to the topic later.

- ✔ Talk about each and every concern on the list.

Chapter 8

Negotiating Possible Solutions to a Conflict

. . . .

. . . .

*N*egotiating any sort of resolution to conflict is tricky. It reminds me of the plate-spinning guy I used to watch on TV as a kid. Just when he thought he could move away from the first set of plates he had going and move down the line, he'd have to rush back and catch one of the first plates as it started to topple and threatened to fall.

The same can be true when you're helping employees through a mediated conversation. You may think that because they shared their perspectives about the impact of the problem a few times, you won't have to address the impact again. But not so fast! Get ready to twist, turn, and adapt to whatever your employees need to assess their unique situation while they shift into the negotiation phase of the meeting.

In this chapter, I give you the information you need to move your employees beyond a list of discussion topics onto collaboratively addressing the conflict and brainstorming possible solutions. (See Chapter 7 for information on starting a mediation meeting, getting employees to share their views, and building an effective agenda.) You also find tools to work through resistance so you can reposition your employees from a state of blaming one another to a problem solving mind-set, creatively enabling them to tackle future difficulties using a new skill set.

Encouraging Communication

The part of a mediation meeting in which participants try to negotiate a solution is notoriously complex, largely because each and every conversation of this sort is different depending on the people involved, the issues tackled, and the conflict's intensity.

Up to this point, your meeting has been clear and sequential, with some identifiable benchmarks and goals. Now, however, you need to be flexible and adapt to wherever your employees take you while keeping in mind some overarching guidelines that focus and organize the conversation. Get the parties to talk, talk, and talk some more, but direct their conversation and guide them to stay positive, think creatively, and move beyond their immediate problems. Talking in circles never gets anyone anywhere. This section helps you steer the conversation in the right direction.

Transitioning from past to future

When asked earlier to share their point of view, your employees probably spent a lot of time talking about the past (see Chapter 7). That makes sense, after all, because the problems they've experienced have already happened. They likely focused their attention on each other's actions that caused harm. They may have even given you a litany of dates, times, and specific moments when the conflict escalated or became especially troublesome.

But now it's time for them to begin moving forward. Make a statement about moving out of the past and into the present so you can set the stage for dialogue about solutions rather than problems. If you encourage them to speak to what they'd like to see in the future, or how they believe the issues can be solved, they're much more likely to find solutions than dwell on past difficulties.

To get employees to talk about the future, use the agenda they created as a visual tool (see Chapter 7) by standing next to it or pointing to it. Then say something like, "Thank you for sharing your perspective on what's happened so far. What we're going to do now is take what we know about the past and apply it to the future. Looking at the list you've created, I'd like the two of you to choose a topic together and decide where you'd like to begin your conversation. Stay focused on what you'd like to see, and try not to rehash what's already taken place."

You can also give them a physical clue that it's time for something different. For example, I tell my clients, "So far, you've been talking to me about the past, and now I'd like the two of you to turn your chairs and face each other so you can speak directly to each other about the future. Where would you like to start?"

Motivating and encouraging your employees

Face it — conversations about conflicts are hard work. Creating a dialogue in the midst of problems takes courage and energy, so validate and praise your employees for their efforts and find ways to acknowledge the good work they accomplish. In other words, encourage the behavior you *want to see* more than discourage the behavior you *don't want to see.*

Look for areas of common ground between your employees. Even if the two seem miles apart on everything, they still have one or two things in common — both are likely frustrated with the situation, and both are anxious to get some solutions on the table. You could note that each has a stake and a responsibility in creating a stable and comfortable workplace. And anytime that you detect values they have in common — like respect or autonomy — point them out. Allow them to talk about how they define those values differently and what actions need to be taken for those values to be fulfilled.

Don't treat this conversation as some sort of disciplinary action. Instead, emphasize that this discussion is an *opportunity* to create what they want their ongoing relationship to look like. Encourage them to see the conversation as a turning point in their interaction with each other rather than as a trial for you to judge who makes the better case.

Listening and interjecting

The negotiation process is about your employees working together to create their own answer to the conflict. If you consistently jump in with your insights and observations, you're apt to get in the way, so do more listening than speaking. And when you do interject, use the strategies I outline in the following sections.

Ask questions

The majority of the speaking you do should come in the form of good questions (refer to the "Asking Great Questions" section later in this chapter for more information). Focus on encouraging your employees to negotiate together rather than on drawing their attention to you. Think of yourself as a conversation starter, not an investigator.

Clarify and summarize

Listen for any language that threatens to derail the process such as blaming, antagonizing, pushing hot buttons, or name-calling. Be aware, however, that because of the emotional state your employees are in, they may be more apt to misinterpret or misunderstand what the other person says. This is where your summarizing skills become so important (see Chapter 7). If you hear your employees struggling with language, summarize what you've heard with more neutral language and help them clarify their intent.

However, sometimes the words your employees use aren't simply misunderstood — they're clear and downright hostile! In this case, intervene by reflecting their emotions, reframing their language to focus on their interests, and neutralizing any hot-button language you hear (see Chapter 7 for more on reflecting, reframing, and neutralizing language). Remind the speaker that he made a commitment to follow the ground rules for this meeting, and warn him that he needs to manage the way he speaks about his emotions.

Capture proposals

When you hear proposed solutions from either party (see the "Fostering Brainstorming" section later in this chapter), summarize the important points and frame them in language that's easy for the other party to digest. Ask the other party what she likes or doesn't like about the proposal, whether she accepts it as is, or if she'd like to make a counter proposal.

Make note of any *possible* proposals you hear that the employees may not be quite ready to offer. Doing so gives you a reference point down the road, when they begin to make a little more progress. I sometimes ask if I can jot down a word or two next to the agenda item the two are discussing as something they might discuss later in the meeting.

Focusing on Values Rather Than Issues

During the course of the meeting, you're likely to hear a lot from both people that describes how the conflict should be resolved. The language will likely come in the form of a position they've taken, also known as their *issues*.

It's important for you to hear and understand the issues, because they give you a sense of the nature of the conflict. However, it's more crucial to understand *why* those issues are of importance to your employees. As such, you need to focus more on discovering their *values* — the things that drive them to act the way they do and make the decisions they choose. (See Chapter 2 for an extensive list and information about how values surface in the workplace.)

The following sections help you drill beneath the surface of your employees' issues and draw out the values that are at the heart of their conflict.

Discovering what's really important

Employees often come to a mediation meeting with a win-lose approach in mind, arguing about the merits of each other's position. By focusing the conversation on values, you can help them find common interests — or at least those that aren't in conflict — and develop a collaborative approach to negotiating.

Both your employees may feel, for instance, that they need to improve their communication, or that being a professional is important, even though they describe each of those values differently. At the very least, by encouraging them to concentrate on common values, you move them away from speaking about what they *don't like* and nudge them toward talking about what they *would like*.

Understanding and validating your employees' values helps you identify and articulate appropriate responses to emotional outbursts. Acknowledging these values is the best intervention strategy in many conflict resolutions.

Reading between the lines to find values

Uncovering values takes a little work. The key is to listen for what lies beneath the statements your employees make. Tune your ear to strip away the things you hear them saying, and listen instead for what drives their positions.

Take the following example. Imagine that you're meeting with two employees, Wendy and Allison. Wendy becomes emotional when the conversation turns to the difficulties the two experienced at the last staff meeting. She says, "Allison is late for every single meeting we schedule. Does she even own a clock? The rest of us are always forced to wait while she saunters in at her leisure!"

Clearly, Wendy is upset. Having to wait for others when you come to a meeting prepared can be frustrating. So you want to summarize that idea for Wendy: "It's important to you that schedules are respected, and timeliness is something you very much value."

Don't express what's *wrong* with Allison (she's always late; she doesn't respect others' time). Doing so doesn't add anything constructive to the conversation, and besides, Allison likely has a different point of view. In addition, you're liable to lose your neutrality and credibility!

Responding to a person about what she values rather than adding to the criticism of what the other person has done wrong allows the second party to explain her view of the situation without becoming defensive. So in this example, stating Wendy's values back to her instead of knocking Allison for her tardiness leaves Allison with enough room in the conversation to describe her position. When you reframe and reflect a person's statement, you also model good communication for both people. To get more familiar with effective reframing and reflecting, check out Chapter 7.

Fostering Brainstorming

After your employees have had a chance to vent some of their frustrations, and you've validated their emotions, summarized their concerns, and neutralized any tough language you heard, it's time to start turning your attention to problem solving. Do this by encouraging your employees to start brainstorming.

Good brainstorming draws on the best that each of the employees has to offer, but you need to do a significant amount of coaching during the brainstorming process. Motivate your employees to think creatively about problem solving, let them know that this is their process, and remind them that there's no *one right way* to solve difficulties. The following sections give you some brainstorming guidelines and help you evaluate the results of your efforts.

Defining brainstorming ground rules

Encourage your employees to view brainstorming as an opportunity to create any kind of solutions they can imagine. Give them the freedom to suggest anything and you'll find that their ideas and proposals are as creative as they are effective.

The best brainstorming occurs without limits to creativity but focuses on one area at a time. Suggest a few ground rules, such as:

- ✔ **Use the agenda:** The agenda (see Chapter 7) isn't just for show. Ask them to choose a topic from the list and focus their conversation on that point until they're ready to move on. This technique helps prevent them from jumping around from topic to topic.

- ✔ **Remember that any idea is a good idea:** Brainstorming is about articulating any and all possibilities before deciding on anything.

✔ **Follow time limits:** Some of the best ideas come when people are pressed for time. I worked with a large group facilitator who would give groups five minutes to come up with ideas. If he gave them more time than that, the ideas that came in 20 minutes were no more creative than the ones that surfaced in the first few minutes. Keep the brainstorming short, and then spend quality time *refining* the ideas.

✔ **Say then weigh:** Generate as many ideas as possible before weighing and evaluating a single one. Don't let the brainstorming process derail by getting bogged down in the details. I like to capture the first few ideas and then start saying "and" after every suggestion. Keep the ideas coming!

✔ **Create a parking lot:** If one of the parties has an idea for a different agenda item, quickly jot it down next to that topic (I call that "parking it") until you're ready to move to that point. Similarly, if the employees think of something they need to check out or want to add another topic for discussion, into the parking lot it goes.

Narrowing the possible solutions

After the employees generate a number of ideas, start making some decisions. Help them establish evaluation criteria for their proposals, and determine how best to choose agreements that meet both of their needs. Such criteria are typically related to common values, or expectations and guidelines set forth by your workplace.

Ask questions that address the benefits and limitations of each proposed solution. Specifically:

✔ What do each of you like about this proposal? What don't you like about it?

✔ How might the idea be improved?

✔ Does it meet the needs you both stated as being important? If not, what can be changed for it to do so?

Asking Great Questions

Good questions are the primary tools of a skilled mediator. Throughout the negotiation part of the meeting and in any private meetings you have, good questions are an important way of encouraging your employees to find their own answers. Asking questions allows you to gather information, expand your employees' perspectives, generate options, and orient your process to the future. Additionally, good questions help you reinforce that this conversation is a dialogue, not a monologue (no lengthy speeches!).

The following sections cover the different types of questions you can ask, the order in which you should ask them, and the kinds of questions you should avoid.

Knowing which questions to use when

Different types of questions accomplish different tasks. The trick is knowing which questions to ask and what kind of response each type generates.

Closed-ended questions

Closed-ended questions require a specific and direct answer to a specific and direct question. The answer is often implied by the question itself. You may think of closed-ended questions as those that only elicit a yes or no answer. This is true to some extent, but they can be very useful when trying to help your employees sort through and narrow down a number of options.

Here's an example of a closed-ended question you would frame after hearing a few proposals: "If your options are to continue working on this program with William or begin a new program from scratch, which option best meets your needs and the needs of the company?"

Use these questions to clarify a situation with employees in order to develop a common understanding, or to call attention to a situation that you believe needs some action or further steps. For example: "Is this the kind of communication the two of you typically use together? Is it working for you? Would you be willing to try something different?"

Open-ended questions

Where closed-ended questions can give you specific information and can help narrow down choices, *open-ended questions* give so much more. These questions are designed to widen your discussion and invite your employees to participate in a dialogue. For example: "What possibilities do you see? What solutions can you imagine that would work for both of you?"

These questions don't presume any answers. They do, however, require more nuanced and thoughtful responses than just yes or no. In fact, they encourage the listener to look toward the future and consider potential solutions for the problem. They also open doors and expand the conversation in ways that you never expect, because they invite listeners to provide more information and expand their thoughts. For instance, "How is this impacting you? How could you get that information? What else might work?"

These questions are short and sweet, but they leave open the possibility that your employees can take their thoughts almost anywhere, which is usually where you need them to go. Keep a couple of questions in your back pocket and come prepared to ask questions that give everyone a broader view of the situation.

Sequencing your questions

People in conflict can have a hard time getting out of a circular conversation mode. If you watch two people having an argument, it often appears that each party is talking to a wall. In addition to their emotional attachment to issues, their problems stem from the fact that they can't stay focused on one thing before moving onto another.

Use your power as the facilitator to change the circular conversation by sequencing your questions. Each question you ask should follow from the answer to the previous question. For instance, if you discover that the conflict revolves around a disagreement at the last staff meeting, your next question should be about that specific encounter. You might say, "Let's talk about that meeting. What happened that was difficult? What would the two of you liked to have seen happen differently?" Help the parties fully explore the topics of discussion and truly flesh out the important ideas. Keep them on track and make sure they see you as being interested and invested in their discussion.

If your questions don't flow with the direction of the conversation, they can come off as jarring or abrupt, and your employees may lose momentum, or become confused about what you're asking. For example: "What happened at the meeting that was difficult? Do the two of you use e-mail or face-to-face discussions when you communicate? Who else do you think was affected by the argument?" These are all good questions, but if you put them one after another, you make it difficult to explore any one area of concern.

Sequence questions follow thoughts in such a way that each one follows directly from the answer to the previous question. Here's an example:

> **You:** What is most important for you to accomplish today?
>
> **Your employee:** I just want to have a professional working relationship with Angela.
>
> **You:** Tell me about that. What does a professional working relationship look like to you?
>
> **Your employee:** I guess I just want the gossip to stop. I'm sick of listening to her talk about everyone else's business and creating drama.
>
> **You:** You'd like to limit your conversations to work-related activities. How do you think the two of you can create that?

In addition to being sequenced, questions like these follow a subtle path by moving people from identifying values to describing and defining them to designing a path to achieve them. In this way, you can move employees who are stuck arguing about what has happened and who's at fault to working together to create a plan for the future.

You can word great sequenced questions any number of ways, but you should often follow a very basic pattern:

- ✔ What is it that's most important to you? (Name values)

- ✔ What does it look like? (Describe values)

- ✔ How do you get there? (Brainstorm solutions)

Avoiding unproductive questions

Some questions can bring the meeting to a screeching halt, or at the very least, make it difficult for your employees to work constructively. Good questions expand, explore, and create, while unproductive questions tend to minimize, limit, and place blame. I recommend avoiding the following types of questions.

Leading questions

Simply put, *leading questions* are your answers with a question mark tacked on to the end for good measure. Often, people ask these questions with the best of intentions, trying to provide insight or options, but in actuality, leading questions limit the creativity and ability of your employees to come up with their own solutions. Some examples:

- ✔ Have you ever considered getting some training in the new software?

- ✔ Can you think of any reason why you wouldn't want to share resources with Bill?

- ✔ Couldn't you come in at another time and take care of the paperwork then?

Assumptive questions

Assumptive questions assume that the answer to the question is obvious. In addition to being limiting and closed-ended, they tend to create negative reactions in listeners and usually shut down the conversation, rather than expanding it.

- ✔ You realize your actions make you look really unprofessional, right?

- ✔ Don't you want to have a successful career here?

Why questions

Questions that begin with the word *why* rarely give you anything from the listener other than defensiveness. And with good reason! Essentially, you've asked the listener to defend the position he holds, or the actions he has taken, rather than discussing what's important to him *about* the positions and actions. *Why* questions don't allow for an answer that provides much of anything except for excuses and defensiveness, and they often elicit nothing more than an "I don't know" from the listener. Plus, they run the risk of making people feel like kindergarteners being scolded by the principal. For example:

- Why did you write that e-mail to accounting?
- Why didn't you call Christina to tell her about the change to the staff meeting?
- Why did you think Reece would be okay with that?

With the right inquisitive tone, some why questions may be okay (especially in private meetings, like those I describe later in this chapter). But instead of fretting whether you've mastered the correct tone, you can simply use an imperative statement if you think finding out why an employee did what she did will help you understand her perspective: "Tell me about the e-mail to accounting."

Working through Resistance

Employees may be resistant to your mediation skills and strategies, regardless of how hard you work to keep an open, safe, and respectful environment.

The truth is, this is pretty normal. You'll likely experience resistance in a number of forms, and that's okay. In fact, to some extent, you should expect it.

No magic formula exists for moving through resistance. Every one of your employees is unique and carries his own experiences, personalities, and core values. And because each person comes to this conversation with different needs, each one will likely respond differently to different techniques.

Your goal is *not* to bully your employees into working through resistance. As satisfying as it may initially be to headbutt your way through an impasse, that approach rarely gives you anything but a migraine. You have a lot of power in your role, and if you use it to force your employees to find a solution, they may not arrive at an appropriate or sustainable answer.

In the following sections, I reveal some of the causes of resistance and give you strategies you can use to overcome it.

Identifying common causes of resistance

Before you address how (or even if) you want to work through resistance, have a sense of where it's coming from. Take a look at some of the common causes of resistance to discussions:

- **Strong emotion:** The parties involved are either stuck in the past, reacting to each other's actions or language, or are unable to hear what each other is saying. Strong emotions tend to limit people's ability to think critically and can hamper progress.

- **Distrust:** Your employees may not trust each other to keep the conversation civil and on track, or they may not trust your process. This can be because of their work history, their relationship, bad experiences, or even threats, both real and perceived. They may not trust you, either, as a neutral facilitator. Don't take it personally — do your best to prove them wrong.

- **Failure to communicate/listen:** Lack of communication may happen because employees simply have different communication styles, or it may happen because they choose hostile or unproductive language. An employee may use specific body language to indicate that she can't (or won't) listen to what the other has to say, such as turning her back while the other is speaking, crossing her arms and refusing to make eye contact, or even putting her hands over her ears (yes, that has actually happened!).

- **Failure to see options:** An employee may come to the meeting with only one idea in mind, and it usually involves never having to see or work with the other person again. Mediation meetings work best when a plethora of ideas are on the table; a narrow view of solutions certainly slows down the progress.

- **Overconfidence/moral high ground:** If an employee believes, justly or not, that he's in the right and that he has been wronged, he may be overconfident in his position. He may think his position is stronger than it is, because others in the workplace may have sided with him. You'll often hear an employee in this state of mind say that he "just wants to do what's right for the company." Parties who take this stance are reluctant to negotiate because they believe their power comes from being justified in their position.

- **Negative association:** Essentially, an employee may choose not to negotiate or accept offers simply because it's the other person who proposed the solution. A suggestion or offer that would be perfectly reasonable if proffered by anyone else is regarded as not good enough, based entirely on the messenger.

With all the things that can cause folks not to want to negotiate, you may be thinking, how on earth do people ever get past this part? It takes some work and some attention, but you can do a number of things when you reach an impasse. Read on for those ideas.

Exploring the impasse

To help your employees see the conflict that brought them to the table with a new set of eyes, start by asking each of them to describe the stalemate. They may find that they're stuck for very different reasons, and they may discover some workarounds for the areas where they can find commonality.

You may want to ask them to describe each other's position or concerns, which helps them see beyond their own view. Do this carefully, however, as you don't want them to mischaracterize the other's position, or downplay the significance of the other's view.

Creating options

If your employees are stuck repeatedly talking about the details of the problems they face, encourage them to focus on potential solutions instead. This seems like a no-brainer, doesn't it? But don't be surprised when the conversation turns into a rehashing of all the difficulties.

Help them brainstorm answers rather than dwell on problems. You can accomplish this by turning their attention away from the past and focusing instead on the future. Your questions should be future-focused, opening conversations around what *could be* rather than what *has been*. Ask things like:

- ✔ If the issues were solved today and it's three weeks down the road, can you describe how you see the project being completed?

- ✔ What new possibilities might come from working this out?

- ✔ How would each of you like to see the schedule assigned for the next month?

 Encourage both people to attempt a form of detached brainstorming. In other words, get them thinking about what *others* might do in a similar situation, rather than what *they* are doing. This kind of brainstorming isn't limited by what they think they know about each other, so it's easier for them to respond. I often ask the parties to share any ideas they'd give Joe in accounting if he were to describe this conflict to them. Or, when one says, "I don't know" in response to my questions about possible solutions, I ask, "Well, if you *did* know, what would you say?" Works like a charm.

Testing the margins

Create clarity around the boundaries of the situation by asking the parties to give some thought to their other options. Ask if they've considered what happens next if they're unable to reach an agreement. Are they comfortable moving forward without a solution? Your questions should help your employees consider the impact and the implications of not moving forward. (For more tips on troubleshooting problem areas, see Chapter 9.) Similarly, encourage both to describe the best and worst solutions that *could* come out of their meeting. Perhaps they'll be able to find some daylight between the ideal and not-so-ideal agreements.

After they give descriptions of the best and worst outcomes, discuss what they see as the best and worst results of ending the meeting without agreements in place. If they're unable to come up with a solution during the meeting and they choose to walk away, what's next for them? You may know the answer to that question already, but ask it anyway.

Refocusing on values

Mediations rely heavily on dialogue that's centered on the employees' core values and the positions they've taken. Your employees have likely gotten off track, or maybe they're having a difficult time articulating the points that are so important to them. Help by really focusing the conversation on the critical elements.

Ask them to describe what values their proposals address. I like to ask questions such as

- ✔ What does each of your proposals give you? How do they each meet your own needs? How do they meet the other person's needs?
- ✔ How do your proposals satisfy the values that each of you has identified as important?

If you've gone through this exercise and still find that they're struggling, ask them to mentally step away from the negotiation and to describe the qualities of a good agreement instead. Whatever their answers, ask if any of the ideas they've thrown out so far match the good agreement criteria. If the answer is no, encourage them to create new proposals that include the qualities that each of them just described.

Interrupting negative behaviors

Don't be surprised if the parties have difficulty working within the boundaries of behavior you've set out for them (see Chapter 7). Meetings like these can create a lot of anxiety and tension, and in the face of difficult conflict, even the most levelheaded person can lose his cool. However, you don't want those moments to impede your discussion, so address them when you see them.

If someone is continually using language that isn't helpful, you can ask him to

- ✔ Use different words
- ✔ Reframe his statements in more neutral terms
- ✔ Speak in "I-statements" (see Chapter 17)
- ✔ Summarize in terms that the other person can more easily understand

Some topics and conversations cause physical reactions like clenched jaws and rolling eyes. If this happens, call it out when you see it. When it catches my attention, I sometimes say, "I notice that when John said xyz, you had a reaction. Tell me about that."

Don't be afraid to address negative behavior. If it's affecting your conversation, it won't likely go away without assistance. And if you've noticed it, you can bet big money that the other party has noticed it as well.

Another option is to take a break and meet with each of your employees separately. Such a meeting may do a lot to break the negative behavior pattern, and it allows you to do some reality testing and proposal building without the influence of the other employee affecting the flow of your conversation. Check out the upcoming "Meeting Privately with Each Individual" section for the ins and outs of a successful confidential discussion.

Trying one last time to overcome resistance

A time may come when you realize that, no matter how hard you've tried, your employees are unable to resolve their problems with you as the facilitator. When this happens, your participants probably already know it and are prepared to move on to the next step, whatever that may be. But you may not be finished just yet. Many of the mediations I've conducted have found solutions and closure in the last few moments. Your employees may attempt to make a last-ditch effort to solve the problem if they know you've reached the end of your line. So as you're wrapping up, ask whether they have any last (or even best) offers before you end the discussion. This gives them an opportunity to share any last-minute goodies they may have been holding onto, and it can be exactly what you need to finally get the breakthrough you've been looking for.

If, after you ask for any additional thoughts or offers, you hear crickets or stone-cold silence, it's okay to adjourn, regroup, and try something else. Chapter 13 showcases a number of resources within your company to investigate, and Chapter 14 walks you through what you can expect from outside experts.

Meeting Privately with Each Individual

At some point in the mediation meeting, you may get the sense that one of the parties would like an opportunity to brainstorm with you without fear of reprisal. Or perhaps she needs to test some assumptions that she has been making. When I'm mediating, I often get a gut feeling about the elephant in the room, or that something isn't quite right about the story I'm hearing. Maybe the emotions that both employees have been expressing are threatening to overtake the process, or maybe the employees simply need a breather.

Whatever the case, a private meeting, or caucus, is an excellent opportunity for you to provide a different venue for participants to discuss the conflict on a different level. If you opt to call a caucus, you have some choices to make. You need to decide how to break, whom to meet with first, and what kind of approach to take in the private meeting. I cover all these topics in the following sections.

Be sure your employees understand that they aren't in trouble and that you haven't given up on the conversation. Explain that you think this is a good opportunity to take a quick break and try something new. Framing this meeting as a positive step in your process helps you manage your employees' reactions.

Choosing who goes first

No hard and fast rule exists about how to decide whom to meet with first. You know your employees, and you're the best person to make an assessment about what to do, but here are some determining factors that can help you:

- ✔ **Assess emotions:** Is one of the people decidedly more emotional than the other? Or is one struggling more because of the emotional climate? Decide whether meeting with this person first is an opportunity to help her vent and process, or if letting her relax alone for a few minutes while you meet with the other person is the best use of time.

✔ **Assess power:** For this conversation to be successful, you want power to be roughly in balance between your participants. An employee who says she doesn't care, is too overwhelmed to speak, or can't act in her own best interests may be telling you that she feels disempowered. Meeting first with an employee who feels powerless will probably be more effective than trying to squelch or minimize the other employee's power.

✔ **Assess behavior:** Is one of your employees acting out of character? Do you see a typically soft-spoken employee becoming aggressive and demeaning, or an outspoken employee suddenly not making a peep? If so, it's a sign that something has changed, and you need to check it out.

Whomever you choose to meet with first, be sure to clarify to the other person that he'll have the same opportunity as the first person. Clarify, though, that equal *opportunity* doesn't necessarily mean equal *time*. Let both employees know that because you'll be meeting with both of them, going first doesn't really hold any benefit.

After you make your choice, give the employee that you aren't meeting with first something to do. Assign him a task related to the conversation. I typically ask him to make a note of the agenda items and to brainstorm at least two new options or offers that have yet to be discussed. He may come back in the room and say, "I've got nothing!" but this assignment works more times than not. He'll likely labor to create something that works for both parties and come back with great solutions, and he may take great pride in pointing out the benefits to the other person.

Allowing parties to open up with added confidentiality

When you send one of your employees out of the room so you can continue your conversation with the other, make a quick statement clarifying that during this time, you're applying an additional layer of confidentiality.

What this means, essentially, is that anything she shares with you during this time, you won't bring up with the other employee in his private meeting or during an open session. That means you won't do so *even if she asks you to*. This is an important convention, because it

✔ Requires employees to take ownership of any solutions they generate and reinforces your role as a facilitator, rather than an adjudicator.

✔ Allows employees the freedom to create and explore without fear of reprisal from the other party.

✔ Gives employees the opportunity to save face if they need to discuss items that are uncomfortable or potentially embarrassing.

✔ Allows you to discuss topics in such a way that prepares the employee to handle how to share information with the other employee when both return to open session.

Venting and exploring

One of the most vital things you do during a private meeting is create a safe and open environment for your employee. You may likely see this as an opportunity to get down to the bottom of things, but you won't be able to accomplish that unless your employee trusts that this is a safe place to have that conversation.

Begin the conversation in the same way for each participant by asking, "How is this going for you?" Inquire about his experiences, thoughts, and ideas, and encourage him to share any of his reactions to the process. Don't spend any time trying to address specific conflict business yet, because he probably isn't ready to go there. Initially, spend some time reflecting emotions, validating concerns, and summarizing positions. For more information on these skills, refer to Chapter 7.

As your conversation develops, keep these concepts in mind:

✔ **Explore values:** Identify and discuss the values that you've discussed in open session when you were all together. Ask him to describe not only his own values, but what he believes the other employee values as well (this is key for him to see the other person's point of view!). Ask him to explain how the values play out in the workplace and in his relationship with the other party. Doing this helps him generate proposals that are based in values, which are the most satisfying in the long run.

✔ **Identify common ground:** Anytime you can encourage an employee to identify what he has in common with a co-worker, you're helping him create opportunities for solutions. Common ground bridges the gap between different experiences, perspectives, values, and ideas.

✔ **Ask about the other person:** When you hear the employee make negative comments about the other person — and you will — ask questions that move him from thinking about his own perspective to that of the other person's. For example, if Roger says Jeanne owes him an apology, this is the perfect time to ask, "What do you think is preventing her from offering an apology? Is there anything you think she might need to hear from you in order to get that?"

✔ **Brainstorm options:** Encourage him to think about creative solutions. You may go so far as to encourage him to create solutions that assume you have no limits. You'll be able to reality test later, but by giving him license to think outside the box, he may find solutions that he never imagined possible.

✔ **Develop proposals:** Asking future-oriented and other brainstorming questions will help him develop potential offers and solutions. Especially when he seems stuck in what he doesn't like or want, encourage him to speak about what he'd like or want instead. Then you can help him turn his responses into proposals.

✔ **Conduct a reality test:** After you have a few proposals developed, help him sort through and test each one for any potential problems. You may also need to reality test with employees who are unable to come up with solutions. By addressing what will happen if he leaves without a solution, you may help him find inspiration and language to create proposals.

Preparing an employee to return to the open session

Forming proposals privately is really only half the battle. Now your employee needs to ask his co-worker to accept the proposal, which may be difficult, considering that they've struggled with their communication in the past.

You can help him by letting him practice the proposal, with you acting as the co-worker. But instead of commenting on whether the proposal sounds good or bad, ask him some specific feedback questions:

✔ How did that sound to you?

✔ How do you think [the other employee] will respond to it?

✔ If you were [the co-worker], how would you like to hear such a proposal offered?

✔ Is there any other way that you think you could frame your idea?

Get a commitment from him that he will, in fact, make these proposals when both parties return to the open session with you. It does you no good to have spent the time in your private session if he has no intention of making the offer or asking for things he wants. Ask him if he's comfortable sharing his proposals, and if so, ask him to jot them down before he leaves the room.

Back in open session, it's not unusual for employees to forget what they wanted to say (and you can't help because you've promised confidentiality), so having it in front of them gives a visual cue and keeps the conversation going.

Chapter 9

Offering Proposals and Crafting Agreements

. . . .

In This Chapter

▶ Reconvening a mediation session

▶ Creating settlements

▶ Closing the meeting on a positive note

. . . .

*I*t's time to continue your open session discussion with the two employees engaged in this conflict. Your hope is that the continued discussion will lead to proposed solutions and an agreement that settles the conflict. (For information about starting a mediation meeting, negotiation tips, and meeting privately with each party, see Chapter 8.) If you met privately with your employees, you helped both parties create and formulate proposals. That means you likely have a good idea of the offers that could be made. Keep your promise of confidentiality, though, as you bring the parties back into the room together for an open session.

In this chapter, I show you how to make room for quality communication, acknowledge new perspectives, and encourage your employees to have a positive outlook on their future working relationship — which inevitably will include some conflict. You also find tips on how to give your staff the hope they need beyond the meeting to know they can address future problems and not just solve this one issue in a vacuum. Finally, I tell you the six nonnegotiable attributes of a solid agreement.

Continuing Negotiations

As you prepare to continue negotiations, know that your employees' communication improving is more important than coming to consensus right away. As their manager, you may be itching for them to give each other some sort of agreement that you can document, but at this point, you just have to trust that good agreements will come from good communication.

An agreement that's forced rarely holds up over time anyway.

In this section, I tell you how to start this part of the conflict resolution process, and I tell you what to listen for as your employees continue their discussion.

Proceeding with the meeting

If you met privately with each employee engaged in this conflict (see Chapter 8 for details), continue the negotiations by bringing them back to the room in which you first met (see Chapter 7 for more about the initial meeting). Start this part of the mediation process off right: Commend your participants for the work they've done so far.

This process can be challenging and tax even the most energetic person's reserves. A quick observation from you that their hard work is recognized can go a long way toward reenergizing your employees — and it may even give them just enough oomph to get over the hump. In fact, it's a good idea to praise good work and progress at any stage of the meeting.

Remind the parties that your private meetings were confidential and that you won't bring up anything they shared with you during those meetings. Encourage your employees to think back to their private meetings and decide if they discussed anything that either of them would like to share — this strategy reinforces the responsibility that each employee has for speaking on his own behalf, and puts each employee firmly in the driver's seat.

I always say, "Thank you for meeting with me individually. I hope you found the discussions productive. As a reminder, I won't share what either of you had to say, but if anyone has anything they'd like to ask for, share, or comment on, this would be a great time to do that." Then I push myself away from the table and wait — and sometimes wait and wait! This approach always works for me, and I recommend you try it yourself.

Don't be surprised if you see some hesitation. Your employees may go through a brief period of "I don't want to be the first to speak." Especially when they feel uncertain or distrustful, they may want to wait to hear what the other is thinking before they're willing to give voice to their own thoughts. The important thing to remember is *not* to rescue them from this uncertainty.

You may be tempted to think that silence between your employees is a sign that things aren't working well, but try seeing silence as a tool you can use to your (and their) benefit. Silence is a void that wants to be filled. The more patient you are, and the more comfortable you appear in it, the more likely one of them is to fill that void. Lean back in your seat, or pull away from the table as an indication that you won't be filling that gap. Sooner or later, one of your employees will start talking.

One caveat: You'll likely know from your private meetings whether offers or proposals are forthcoming. If that's the case, allow some time for these offers to come to the surface. If offers aren't forthcoming, long periods of silence may only make matters worse. As long as your employees appear to be considering their options or weighing their proposals, give them the time and space to create them. If they aren't engaged in the process, remind them of any proposals that were on the table, remind them of items left on the agenda, recap common ground, or ask whether either of them wants to revisit any points you discussed earlier.

Listening for the good stuff

Pay attention to what each employee is saying because a lot of good work happens after your private meetings, but it's not always going to be couched in really good language. So listen for it yourself.

If your employees come back from their private meetings, and they're doing well and negotiating, stay out of their way. Let them do the work, and make note of the things you're hearing, so you can start transitioning them into the "settlement" phase of your conversation when the time is right. (See the later section "Developing Solutions and Agreements during Open Session" for more details on the settlement phase of negotiations.)

But if one party is saying something worth noting, help him out by stopping the conversation and pointing it out to the other person so she can acknowledge it or respond. Be sure that none of the important points is lost along the way. Do some summarizing any time you hear any of the following.

New information

Often, the conflict that your employees have been experiencing hinges on information that one party may not have had full access to. And in many cases, when this new information comes to light, your employees may need a moment to consider what's being shared. This new information may change their perspective on the other person, may shed new light on decisions that were made, and may even affect offers on the table (or proposals that have yet to be made!).

Whenever I see that one person has said something new, I like to give the participants a chance to digest what they've heard, but I also ask them to speak to what they're considering. For example, I may say, "Ron, I can see that the information Anita provided us about the amount of time she's spent on this project outside of work is new information to you. Can you tell us what you think about that?"

Acknowledgments

Sometimes, an employee may make observations or statements of genuine appreciation for the other person, or acknowledge something important to him. However, because of the nature of these conversations, acknowledgments can be either glossed over or completely lost in the mix.

You're in a good position to make sure that important points *don't* get missed. When you hear a game changer that gets lost along the way, jump in and clarify it for your parties. For example, you may say, "Shannon, I just heard you say that though the two of you disagree about the conclusions drawn from your data, you were, in fact, impressed with Sarah's writing on her quarterly report. Sarah, did you hear that as well?"

Changes in perspective or tone

When an employee has a chance to vent with you privately and explore new ideas and possibilities, he may return to negotiations with a renewed sense of purpose and a new commitment to solving problems. A lot of good work can get done in these situations, so be sure to make a note of this change when you see it! Your employees will appreciate the pat on the back, but your encouragement also helps cement this new way of solving problems.

Note changes in communication patterns, posture, willingness to give each other the benefit of the doubt, and any number of things that may be different from their initial attitudes toward each other. I make note of these in the following way: "Wow, Zach and Heather, I notice a real change from earlier in this meeting. I think the two of you are working really well together. I just wanted to note that the way you're communicating now seems different from when we started, and I commend you for that. Keep up the good work."

Apologies

Some of the best moments in mediation take place in the form of sincere apologies. It doesn't always happen, and a lack of apologies doesn't say anything about your skill as a mediator, but when it does happen, an apology can literally change everything.

If you know someone wants to apologize because he shared that information with you privately (see Chapter 8 for tips on productive private meetings), coach him to deliver a three-part apology that includes:

- ✔ I-statements, as in, "I'm sorry that I . . . ," not "I'm sorry that you . . ."
- ✔ An assurance that it won't happen again
- ✔ A sincere request for instruction on how to make up for it

Without all three parts (and the right tone of voice and eye contact, of course), it's difficult for people to receive an apology as the conclusion of an act or event. Putting the three together sounds like this, "I'm sorry I approached you about the reports in front of everyone in the meeting. You have my word that it won't happen again. What can I do to make up for my poor behavior?" It doesn't sound like this, "I'm sorry you took what I did the wrong way and got so mad. You know I didn't mean it, so let's just get past this thing, okay?"

Apologies can get lost in the mix of a conflict conversation. A participant can easily tuck an apology into the middle of another statement he's making, minimizing the impact. Or he may share it in an awkward way, trying to save face. Or it could simply be that the apology isn't framed in a way that's easily heard by the other person.

Whatever the reason, if you hear an apology shared, and it's missed by the other party, make sure you draw attention to it: "Becky, before you move on, I just want to make sure that this doesn't get missed. I think I heard Denise apologize for the way you were treated when you visited the shipping department. Did you hear that as well?"

Unfortunately, sometimes when apologies are expressed, they're understood but not accepted. If the other party doesn't accept an apology that's been offered, it doesn't have to be the end of your conversation, but it may require some work on your part. Acknowledge both parties and summarize their feelings about the apology itself. Ask some questions about whether the apology could be accepted at another time, and if so, what it would take to get to that place: "Anne, I want to acknowledge that you've offered an apology to Quinn. And Quinn, for you, I hear that at this time you're unable to accept it. I'm wondering if you can imagine a time when you might be able to accept such an apology and what it might take for you to be able to do that?"

When sincere apologies are made and accepted, the air in the room changes. Your employees' body language will open up, they'll sit up straighter, and the tense muscles in their faces and necks will soften. These are signs you're on the right track.

Proposals

Often, by the time you reach this part of a mediation, your employees are ready to start making proposals to one another. Offers come in different forms, however, and some may be easier to pick up on than others. Consider the following:

- **Proposals may be clear and concise and offer little ambiguity as to the intent.** For example, one of your employees may say, "I'd be willing to provide you a copy of the meeting notes on the days when you're unable to attend because of your other responsibilities."

  If the other party continues to talk and doesn't respond, say: "Maggie just made a specific proposal to you, Frank, to provide a copy of the meeting notes on the days when you're unable to attend. Does that work for you?"

✔ **Proposals may be more of a tit-for-tat where one employee is only willing to offer something if he's able to receive something as well.** For example, an employee may say, "I'd be happy to support the project plan among the rest of the team, but only if you send an e-mail to the team first saying it was my idea and that we're working on it together."

If the other person doesn't automatically accept, say: "Let's untangle Michael's proposal and approach one piece at a time. Gloria, how do you feel about sharing the collaboration efforts between you and Michael with the team?"

✔ **Proposals may be offered tentatively, or in such a way that you may not be sure if they are, in fact, an offer at all.** For example, an employee may say, "Well, I guess I could take a look at restructuring the shift schedule, but I'm not sure if I'll be able to give you the times you're looking for."

Clarify proposals like this by saying, "Brandon, are you proposing to William that you could take a look at restructuring the shift schedule? Could you tell him more about what you're thinking could happen with that so he can respond to a specific proposal?"

If your employees are doing well in this process, making offers and counteroffers, and if they seem to understand one another's perspectives and requests, take a more passive role. However, when you need to step in and summarize or follow up with clarifying questions, use clear language. Specifically, if you see your employees struggling to frame a proposal, step in and summarize what you've heard. Here are a couple of examples:

Tony, it sounds as if you're willing to do some research on additional training options, but you're unsure whether that will answer April's request to broaden the scope of her job responsibilities. Did I get that right?

Christina, I've heard you say that you'd like Ryan to work harder when it's his day to stock the shelves. What does "work harder" look like to you? What, specifically, would you like to propose he do?

Developing Solutions and Agreements during Open Session

As your employees' proposals begin to turn into agreements, you may be tempted to think that it's all downhill from here.

The truth is, even though you've spent a good amount of time and energy facilitating this conversation, and even though you and your employees are probably pretty exhausted because of the energy it takes to have this kind of meeting, you still have some work to do. In this section, I tell you how to pay attention to the details of proposals (ideas the parties have agreed to commit to) so you can reduce the probability that your employees will be back to mediate the exact same issue.

Recognizing the nonnegotiable elements of a good settlement

If you hear any proposed agreements, be sure to probe, prod, and tweak them to make sure they're the best they can be. Good, solid agreements that satisfy everyone's needs and hold up over time don't just fall out of the sky. They have specific qualities that are important for you to look for in each of the proposals you discuss. Think of this part of the mediated meeting as a litmus test to identify these particular attributes. If one of the following elements is missing, you increase the chances of the agreement falling apart and adding to the frustration of those involved. Give these elements proper consideration and you'll send the parties away with the greatest chance for success.

Doable

Agreements have to actually fit with reality. This attribute may sound obvious, but it's surprising how quickly unrealistic agreements can become part of a plan that sounds good on the surface but inevitably falls apart. When your employees begin to make agreements on the heels of a lengthy or difficult conflict, a lot of good energy can be generated. This is a good thing, and you want to tap into that energy, but don't be surprised when employees begin to agree to things that aren't doable because the two are on a roll or they're ready to agree to anything. Agreeing to something because it feels right in the moment can cause additional problems.

I once mediated a case between two employees who had been struggling with creating a mutually agreeable floor plan for an upcoming relocation of their department. As they began to make agreements, I noticed that one of the employees in the department was unaccounted for in the floor plan. When I pointed this out, the two parties looked at each other and said to me, "Well, let's not worry about that. This is the only thing we've been able to agree on for months. We'll just deal with it later." Dealing with it later would've meant that I'd have to be brought back in for another mediation when the agreement fell apart and the conflict continued. Needless to say, we opted to deal with it right then and there.

You know your organization, so you should be able to gauge what you consider doable. If an agreement includes one party coming in on a Saturday to complete his part of a project and the job site is shut down on weekends, the doable attribute can't be met.

Support the parties wherever you can but don't set them up for failure by allowing a creative solution you know won't fly with the rest of the company.

Specific

Clearly outline what each employee is agreeing to do. Additionally, ensure that agreements describe the steps that each person will take in order to accomplish tasks, in a way that leaves no ambiguity as to the expectations each has of the other.

Imagine two employees who decide that the best way to make sure that all the tasks assigned to them are getting fulfilled is to meet once a month for half an hour to discuss the workload. You can write it like this: "Matt and Kate agree to meet once a month to discuss the workload."

At the moment, Matt and Kate may think they have the exact same understanding of this meeting. But do they know when they're meeting? Are there certain days or times that are better or worse for the discussion? For how long will they meet? And where will this meeting take place? How will they be sure that what needs to be discussed will get addressed? A better agreement looks more like this:

> Matt and Kate agree to meet at 10:30 a.m. on the first Wednesday of every month, beginning next month, for a half-hour discussion in Conference Room A. This conversation will focus on making sure all the goals assigned to the training team are being met. Kate will bring a copy of the team's goal statement and a calendar to make a note of project deadlines. Matt will use the information to update the online team calendar by close of business that same day.

Durable

Although some agreements may only be intended to be short term or even one-time actions, agreements relating to ongoing relationships, processes, and procedures should have a reasonably long shelf life.

If Bryan agrees to stay late every Wednesday to tally the store receipts and you know he's going to start a night-school course in a few weeks, will he be able to keep this agreement? Ask more questions and probe further if an agreement includes actions by either party that have the potential to cause an inconvenience or become tiring. Give both people permission to "be real" about what they can commit to and ask them not to sign up for anything they feel they won't be able to sustain. Ask them to consider personal commitments, calendar commitments (like holidays), unpredictable factors (like traffic), and any possible organizational changes in the works.

Of course, you can't predict every unforeseen situation or event that could derail an agreement, but the more questions you ask — and have them answer — the more durable the agreement becomes. Give your staff permission to rework the agreement if it warrants a change down the road, and ask them to add language about any "what ifs" they can foresee.

Balanced

Balanced agreements are not necessarily ones in which employees split their resources 50/50, or agree to do exactly half the work on a project they're assigned. Instead, balanced agreements show that both parties are willing to *give* something and *receive* something.

Even where one of your employees has decided to take the lion's share of the responsibility for resolving the problems at hand, look for ways to include the other employee in the process. This can be as simple as one employee agreeing to do a task, and the other employee agreeing to acknowledge him for it.

Balance in agreements goes hand in hand with the quality of *durability* (see the preceding section for more on durability). This becomes evident after you've reached settlement and your parties have moved into implementing their agreements. If one employee looks back over the agreement down the road and feels as if there was imbalance in the outcome, she may be less likely to honor her end of the arrangement, or she may even revisit the conflict anew.

Complete

Has everything of importance to the conflict been addressed by the agreements? If something was important to either party, address it in the agreement — even if the arrangement is to discuss it at a later date. Cover all the agenda items. (Check out the tips for building an effective meeting agenda in Chapter 7.) If it's on the agenda, make sure that you've addressed the issue in some way — either by documenting a solution, or by coming to some verbal agreement regarding how the parties intend to deal with it. If you don't make it through the list, note in the agreement that the parties didn't have a chance to discuss the item or were unable to come to agreement on it. This item will be a good starting point for any follow-up meetings.

Dot the *i*'s and cross the *t*'s. If either party starts to resist pinning down exact details, coach him by letting him know they'll both have a better chance at success if they take care of these details with you as a facilitator instead of walking away with a new misunderstanding to an old conflict.

Satisfying

Often, in the midst of conflict, employees express a concern that their agreements be *fair*. Let me encourage you instead, however, to support the idea that agreements be *satisfying*.

Look back on the rest of the meeting and note any values or interests that an employee shared with you, and ask him if the agreement meets those values. (For information on identifying values, see Chapter 2.) For example, if Curtis talked about his need for autonomy, and the agreement doesn't mention anything that delivers that to him on some level, it isn't satisfying.

Troubleshooting problem areas

A number of factors can contribute to problems when you're facilitating the solution/agreement portion of your mediation. Be aware of these factors and pay attention to how they can affect the overall quality of your process.

Vague language

Although using open-ended language is a good idea, when it's time to write up agreements, be as clear and specific as you can be. Avoid language that can be interpreted differently by the parties, such as the following:

- ✔ As soon as possible
- ✔ If necessary
- ✔ Wherever appropriate
- ✔ When convenient
- ✔ More or less

Use language that almost feels like it's bordering on nitpicking. Be specific! Use language such as the following:

- ✔ By (date and time)
- ✔ No later than
- ✔ Completed on
- ✔ Via company e-mail

Settlement by attrition

Sometimes parties can begin to make agreements that they don't necessarily intend to live up to. They may feel as if their important issues haven't been addressed, or they as if they lack the power or the authority to effect a change. Don't let this happen!

When you hear language like "I don't care — write down whatever you want" or "Let's just get it over with so we can move on" pay attention. Your employee is telling you something. Explore what's happening for him when you hear this kind of language.

No settlement is better than a *bad* settlement. If a settlement is going to fall apart, better that it happen in the meeting where you can address the situation than after they've left and returned to the workplace. Bad agreements can undermine trust in your process and support from your employees.

Fatigue

Fatigue can greatly complicate a settlement. If employees are tired or worn down, they may be more likely to settle for an agreement that's incomplete or unrealistic, which places the likelihood of lasting satisfaction in jeopardy. Watch for signs that the participants are settling because they're exhausted and just want the process to come to an end. Don't let impatience move you too quickly through this part of the process. Take a break if necessary, but do make sure to take the time required to craft your agreements thoroughly.

I usually don't let mediations go for more than three hours before some sort of settlement writing begins, or I get an agreement to call a break with the intention of resuming the next day. You always have the option to schedule another meeting, so there's no need to continue this one if the energy level is so low that productivity has waned.

Uncooperative behavior

You're thinking that you're an amazing mediator because you've been able to guide your employees through a tough conversation that resulted in a list of agreements. Suddenly, one of your employees says he doesn't like the arrangements and starts talking in circles again. What just happened?! Truth is, this situation happens more times than I'd like, and here's why:

- ✓ **The employee never intended to come to agreement.** It's not unusual for an employee to come to a mediated meeting because he thinks he has to "for the record." He went through the motions, did what he suspected you wanted him to do, but didn't really negotiate in good faith. Try calling a private meeting to discuss the situation with him frankly and honestly. Create an atmosphere in which he feels comfortable telling you the truth.

- ✓ **The employee's needs haven't been met.** In one way or another, the agreement isn't meeting his needs or delivering what's most important to him. Hear him out a bit more, ask open-ended questions, and see whether you can help identify what's missing or has yet to be discussed.

- ✓ **Another plan is in play.** Sometimes, one of the people you're meeting with has something else in the works and isn't ready to spill the beans just yet. Maybe he's leaving the company, looking for a transfer to another department, or seeking the advice of a third party. You may not be able to find out what's going on, but calling a private meeting for a candid conversation could help.

✔ **The employee just isn't ready.** Your employees will process conflict at different rates. Often, one of the employees isn't ready to let go of a grudge or doesn't yet trust that the future could be any different from the past. That's okay. Do what you can to let him talk, share his perspective with you, and identify the issues. Consider arranging another meeting after he's had time to process a bit more.

Don't be fooled by a wolf in sheep's clothing! Any one of these explanations for *not* signing an agreement can also be the reason why an employee is ready to agree to and sign anything. Be especially wary of the yes man, who doesn't question, doesn't ask for anything in return, and seems a little too eager to go along with everything his colleague wants. Chances are, either he's not going to sign the agreement or he has no intention of actually doing anything he's agreed to. Get to the bottom of his actions by calling a private meeting and exploring your concerns.

Incomplete contingency plans

Your employees may have the best of intentions and may have created a solid and complete agreement that they fully intend to live up to. However, even the best plans can fall apart if you don't address the "what if" questions. Pay attention to all the possible areas that may cause an agreement to become invalid or would cause it to be renegotiated.

Look for any assumptions or expectations on which your employees are resting their agreements, and test what may happen if those assumptions are incorrect. Having a backup plan may seem redundant, and they may think it's overkill, but it benefits them greatly if and when things don't go according to plan.

Do a quick role-play in your mind: Imagine that two weeks have passed and your employee's agreements have fallen apart. What was the cause? What brought an otherwise solid agreement to a screeching halt? By considering the potential problems in this way, you may uncover some areas that need some additional attention.

One of the most common "what ifs" that adversely affects the success of agreements is the inclusion of third parties. If the person isn't in the room, he probably shouldn't be in the agreement. Agreements that are based on the actions of someone who hasn't had a chance to speak for himself often fall apart when that person is unwilling or unable to deliver on the agreement. Include language that takes the situation into account and makes room for adjustments, such as the following:

Examples of good and bad settlements

I had the opportunity to spend some time with a court commissioner who asked me to tell every mediator I know that, in his opinion, poorly written agreements were the number-one reason people ended up back in court. As he said, "The devil's in the details." Here I give you two sample settlements, one good and one that needs serious work. Note that this first sample (the bad one) is a bit short on details!

> John Hawkins and Lisa Ritchie have participated in a mediation session and they agree as follows:

✓ John agrees to communicate respectfully with Lisa.

✓ Lisa agrees to provide budget numbers to John.

✓ John and Lisa agree to go to their staff together to talk about the coming changes.

✓ John and Lisa will review performance evaluations and determine who will be moved to which department.

Now take a look at an agreement that includes specific details that leave little room for interpretation:

> John Hawkins and Lisa Ritchie, having participated in a mediation session on January 15, 2010, and being satisfied that we have reached a fair and reasonable settlement, hereby agree as follows:

1. John and Lisa agree that, though their communication in the past has been difficult, they're united in their desire for respectful and courteous communication with one another from now on. They agree to refrain from using sarcasm and/or a loud tone of voice in the workplace. Additionally, if either feels they have to speak about difficult topics to one another, they agree to do so in private, rather than around the rest of the staff.

2. Lisa agrees to provide John with a monthly report on her department's spending for six months, beginning in February and ending in July. She will e-mail this report to John by no later than the 3rd of each month. If the department does not overspend during that six-month period, John agrees that Lisa will no longer be required to send the reports to him.

3. John and Lisa agree to hold a staff meeting in the large conference room no later than February 1. They agree to co-facilitate this meeting, where they will inform the rest of the staff about the changes to the database and the new policy regarding purchase orders. John will contact all staff members by no later than January 24 to inform them that the meeting will take place. They agree that this meeting will not include any discussion about the transfer of employees to other departments.

4. Lisa and John will meet by no later than February 15 to review employee performance evaluations. The purpose of this meeting will be to determine which employees will remain in their current positions and which employees will be transferred to another department. John will provide input, but agrees that the final decision will fall to Lisa. Additionally, he agrees to support whatever decision Lisa makes.

Both parties sign and date the document and walk away with a copy that serves as a reference document.

Janet will ask Tom, by 5 p.m. on Wednesday the 3rd, if he is able to reset the start date of the marketing launch to the 30th. She will communicate Tom's response to Rich in person at the staff meeting on the 4th. If Tom is unable to reset the start date, both parties agree to discuss the matter at a lunch meeting following the regular staff meeting and develop an alternative plan, which they will convey to the team via e-mail on the 5th. Rich and Janet will write the e-mail together and Rich will send it.

Writing it down

It's been said that even the shortest pencil is more reliable than the longest memory. Although your participants may be communicating well in the moment, and seem to be on the same page when it comes to their expectations, you'll be amazed by how quickly they can come to very different conclusions after they leave the meeting.

Clearly spell out all the agreements in written form — not only to help your employees know that you expect them to honor the agreements they've made, but also to memorialize all the hard work they've done in the session. When writing the agreements, keep the following things in mind.

- **Use plain language.** Avoid using unnecessarily complex or legalistic-sounding jargon. Complex language only complicates your document and contributes to misunderstandings about content and context.

- **Address who, what, when, where, and how.** Make sure that your employees can identify all the details for each of the points of their agreements. Specifically, consider who will be undertaking actions. What actions will they be performing? When and where will they be performed? How will the actions take place?

- **Remember confidentiality.** The intent of mediation is for everything that happens in the room to stay in the room. If others in the workplace know that the mediation is occurring, they may approach you or your participants for information. Encourage your participants to come up with a strategy for handling those requests, and consider including that strategy in the agreement. It may mean agreeing to simple, stock language like "Everything went well and we're happy with the outcome." Encourage your employees to keep the mediation confidential and not include any specifics with co-workers or associates.

Sometimes after covering everything on the agenda, no specific agreements need to be documented. That doesn't mean, however, that you should simply send your employees out the door with a pat on the back. You may still want to make sure that your employees are on the same page and have come to some understanding about their situation.

Capturing the spirit of the agreement

Occasionally you may experience a situation that warrants an agreement but doesn't require specific details such as dates or deadlines. Instead, the parties agree to change the way they speak to one another or are interested in moving forward on a positive note but aren't sure how to quantify that. In those instances, capturing the spirit of a renewed relationship is important, and writing it down gives the parties a tangible understanding for a somewhat intangible agreement. Following are some examples:

Change in communication

We, Chuck and Cathy, have met today and discussed all of the concerns that we had with one another. The mediation was enlightening and we learned new information that will help us build our working relationship as we move forward. We intend to communicate any future concerns directly and early on to cultivate a positive working relationship.

Change in working relationship

Through the mediation process, we, Randy and Barbara, have reached a fuller understanding of how our past actions affected one another. We

both agree it will benefit everyone on our work team if we have a positive working relationship. We intend to see the best in one another. We both believe that, moving forward, we will be able to work together productively and appreciate what each of us brings to the department.

Trust issues

We, Ken and Lou, acknowledge that trust has been broken between us. We believe that showing a united front to the rest of the staff is important. We were able to discuss all matters in mediation that concern us at this time. We acknowledge that trust takes time to rebuild, and it is our intention to work together to do so. One way we'll build trust is not to talk to other co-workers in our department about any frustrations we have with one another.

Safety issues

We, Mary and Tom, are grateful to have had this opportunity to talk to one another. We both feel safe and comfortable working together. We are looking forward to working together to create a positive environment for all employees in the company.

Typically, such agreements are formulated when your employees have had a conversation about something intangible, have cleared up a misunderstanding, or have a new way of approaching their work relationship. As long as you feel there are no details that need to be captured to keep them on track, create a brief summary that they can take with them to remind them of their accomplishments. I include some sample agreements, and their corresponding topics of discussion, in the nearby sidebar, "Capturing the spirit of the agreement."

Concluding the Meeting and Helping Everyone Leave with Optimism

Congratulations! You've reached the end of your meeting. Your employees' relationship with one another has been transformed, and they're in awe of your mediation prowess. Now they can return to work with a new sense of purpose and an all but inexhaustible source of energy and enthusiasm. All is once again right with the world.

Sounds wonderful, doesn't it? It would be nice if all mediations ended on such a triumphant note. And in fact, sometimes they do! You can have a profound impact on your employees and workplace if you give your employees a chance to talk through their difficulties, provide an open atmosphere that encourages dialogue, and are interested in the continued stability and comfort of the work environment.

But not every mediated conversation ends with such pomp and revelry. In this section, I help you come up with a plan for dealing with all the possible outcomes.

Settlement

When things go smoothly, celebrate! And put your employees' efforts at the forefront. Let them know that you

- ✔ Appreciate their hard work
- ✔ Applaud their efforts
- ✔ Hope that their agreements will yield a stronger work dynamic for themselves and those they interact with on a daily basis

These conversations can dramatically change relationships. And when one relationship in your workplace changes for the better, it has the ability to radiate to the rest of the group.

Even when settlement doesn't produce a ticker-tape parade of good feelings, at the very least it can provide closure and a sense of relief. So, capitalize on whatever goodwill the settlements generate, and let your employees hear your appreciation. Wherever you can, offer your sincere praise of their work, and remind each person of the value and benefit in following through with his agreements. Tell both people that you want to assist them in following through with their agreements, and that if you can do anything to help them be more successful, you're available. Knowing they have you as a support in their ongoing work can help normalize and stabilize their commitment to making this agreement work.

Interim agreements

Not all agreements are fully realized and ready to become full-blown written settlements. In fact, sometimes writing a full agreement may be premature and can become a potential problem down the road. This is where interim agreements shine. Interim agreements are temporary in nature, such as trying out a new communication model for a period of time, or adopting a new policy in the workplace and testing to see its effects.

When you help employees construct such an agreement, both people should understand that it's for a *specific amount of time*. Be sure that they're clear about how long this agreement will last, how they'll know it's time to reevaluate, and when they'll address the outcomes of the interim agreement.

Taking one step at a time with agreements is not a negative reflection of your abilities as a facilitator or manager. You want to set up your staff for success, so let them try things on for a while, discover what works and what doesn't work, and then retool the agreement. Let them know that it's better to have something that works for both parties than a promise neither of them can keep.

No settlement

No matter how hard they try, your employees may be unable to come to a solution. Impasse happens even when employees have the best of intentions and you're relying on a strong process and skill set. Your employees (and even you) may leave frustrated and disheartened.

As long as you've stuck to the process, asked good questions, and encouraged the co-workers to talk with one another, you've done all that you can. The process belongs to you, but the solution belongs to your employees. Yet, it's frustrating to know that you've done everything in your power, and still found a roadblock at the end of the trail.

As you bring your process to a close, try the following to help bring closure to the discussion:

✔ **End on a positive note.** Even though they may not have reached any agreements, look for anything that you can highlight as a positive outcome. Even something as simple as validating that each employee shared his perspective — and heard what the other had to say — can help them feel as if the meeting wasn't a waste.

✔ **Discuss next steps.** Clearly outline what their options are after they (or you) have decided that mediation isn't going to be a good solution for them. Helping your parties have a clear picture of other avenues for resolving this issue can help them leave with some sense of closure. This may be where you offer to bring in an outside mediator or talk about what other resources are available in the company, like those I discuss in Chapters 13 and 14. Feel free to ask them what they feel their next steps are. That question often brings out important details for both to consider and may bring them back to the table for another discussion.

✔ **Don't close the door.** While closing up shop, mention that this is not their one and only chance at a solution. Inform them that, although now may not be the best time for mediation, they're always welcome to return if they want to give it another shot. One of the employees may have a change of heart after he's had time to consider something that you or his co-worker said in the meeting.

Chapter 10

Adapting a Conflict Meeting for the Entire Team

*W*hen a conflict gets to the point that it's affecting an entire team or department, it's often necessary, and even beneficial, to include as many people as possible in resolution efforts. This chapter helps you refine your role as a meeting facilitator, walks you through organizing a meeting, and focuses on the art of working with a large group.

Acting as Facilitator

Even if employees have viewed you as the problem solver or go-to person in the past, when you're in a group meeting to address conflict, you take on a different function — that of neutral facilitator. So this isn't the time to gather the troops so you can deliver a lecture, stifle comments or questions, and then send them back to work with their tail between their legs. Rather, you want to create an environment in which the attendees work through problems and build their own solutions. You're the (somewhat) objective guide at this point.

As facilitator, it's important to communicate that the meeting is a safe and positive place where the team is allowed to communicate openly, share perspectives, and work through ideas together. Focus your efforts in two areas: the process (how), and the content (what).

✔ **Process:** The process is key to the group's progress. It's the infrastructure that creates an atmosphere in which participants effectively work together, knowing that each person has a reasonable chance to express her views and that these views won't be ignored or tossed aside. Process elements include

- Involving participants

- Managing communication

- Building trust

- Giving support to group members

- Generating ideas and evaluation strategies

- Administering procedures for decision making, taking action, and moving to next steps

✔ **Content:** The content is everything from what group members are discussing to the quality and quantity of the ideas they're sharing. Before the meeting, use content to form a plan. Afterward, use it to move forward with resolution, to determine whether additional meetings are necessary, and to decide whether to tap new resources. Examples of content include

- The ideas being generated

- The issues to be discussed

- The decisions being made

- The plan being developed

- The steps taken to carry out the plan

- The progress to be reviewed

Gathering Information from the Group

If you're considering a team meeting to address a conflict, chances are you realize that a problem exists. Even if you feel comfortable with your current knowledge about the conflict, continue gathering more details. Build on what you already know so that you can assess and understand the needs and status of the group more fully.

In this section, I discuss a variety of techniques you can use to gather information from as many of the team members as possible, because the more you know, the better your meeting will be.

Recognizing what you know

Before you jump in and start exploring the situation with other people, spend some time contemplating a few things on your own. Ask yourself:

- ✔ What are my observations of the team dynamics at this point?
- ✔ What issues have been brought to my attention?
- ✔ Can I identify themes from these concerns and complaints?
- ✔ Is the intensity between team members increasing?

Use what you know as a jumping off point to find out what you don't know. For example, if you've determined that the intensity in the group is increasing but that only a handful of issues have been brought to your attention, you can then craft questions that will uncover additional issues and perhaps expose communication problems within the team.

Crafting questions to find out more

Formulating good questions helps you gain more than the basic information. Good questions are open-ended, yet still have some structure. Consider these two questions:

> Example #1: How do you feel?
>
> Example #2: How has this incident affected you?

Example #1 is too open and lacks connection to the subject. Example #2 links the question to the situation at hand and allows the participant to answer with how she feels and what she thinks. Your goal is to allow the participants to feel free to share what's most important to them in a way that provides solid, valuable information that you can work from.

Another way to ask questions is to order them in a past-present-future structure. This allows people to move along a natural path from what has occurred to what's happening now to what the situation could be moving forward. I often use questions like these:

- ✔ Past:
    - • When did the conflict begin for you?
    - • What incidents have occurred?
    - • What impact has this conflict had on you?
    - • What steps have you taken to resolve the conflict?
    - • What effect, if any, did those steps have?

✔ Present:

- What would you like to see changed?

- What ideas do you have?

- How do you feel about attending a meeting to discuss group concerns?

- Are you aware of any external pressures that are affecting the group?

✔ Future:

- What do you want to see happen?

- What would be the best outcome for the team?

- What will you need so that you can work well in the future?

After you ask questions about the conflict, make sure to include some other questions that help people focus on the positive qualities of the group and set the tone for a productive team conversation. Consider these:

✔ What do you feel are the strengths of this group?

✔ What have been some of the group's greatest successes?

✔ What are you most proud of in this group?

✔ What is your vision of what this group can be in the future?

For other tips on asking good questions, see Chapter 7.

Using interviews and surveys

You can use multiple methods for gathering information from a group. Whether you choose to use individual interviews, group interviews, or surveys depends on the group's size, the need for personal connection, the conflict's intensity, and time constraints. If you have a large group with varying job responsibilities like accounting, facilities, information technology, and marketing, interview each department to gather team and individual feedback on how a change will impact these groups as a whole. If you have a time constraint that doesn't allow for multiple group discussions, and you trust that one person can speak for many, interview a representative from each group.

Interviews

If you have a group of ten or fewer, take the time to speak to each party privately by personal interview or phone conversation. One-on-one conversations build trust and help each person feel comfortable when it's time to move into the larger group discussion. Private interviews also give you an opportunity to coach participants on how to share their perspective and insight with others.

Schedule all the appointments prior to starting. This gives everyone a chance to prepare and gives you time between interviews to summarize the information you elicit so that you don't lose sight of important facts. Make sure to schedule each interview for the same duration — about 30 minutes — but realize that some will run short and others will run long.

Surveys

Gathering feedback by way of a written survey — or questionnaire — is an effective choice when the group is large, when safety and anonymity are desired, or when people are in distant locations.

You get more truthful answers when you allow survey participants to respond to questions anonymously. Be upfront about the purpose and use of the survey and whether it will be kept confidential.

Good questionnaires have well-defined goals with clear and concise sentences. Questions should be simple and to the point to reduce misunderstanding. Customize your survey to provide as much information as you need to feel comfortable evaluating the issues, but be succinct. No one wants to spend hours on these things!

Give your survey a short but meaningful title, such as "Questions for the March 5th Team Meeting," or "Team Strengths and Areas for Development," or "What's Affecting Our Ability to Meet Deadlines?"

If you'd rather not tackle putting your own questionnaire together, a number of online services can help you. Many of these services are free, though most offer advanced options for a one-time fee or a subscription-based payment schedule. These services allow you to customize professionally designed templates with your own questions that you can e-mail to your participants, or link to a Web site that administers the survey for you.

Creating a timeline

Create a timeline of events or incidents with the information you gather. Creating a timeline helps you understand more completely what key events happened, when they took place, and their impact on specific employees. This information allows you to build an agenda for the group meeting that addresses both broad perspectives and specific issues.

As an example, suppose a manager created a team to work on a new project. At the first team meeting, she assigned individual duties. At the second meeting, she added additional team members and redefined duties. At the third meeting, she created small groups to work from that point on.

The groups had obvious tension with each other, and the manager began to ask questions via interviews. Team members shared concerns about the way work was delegated. Many members had worked hard on the tasks they were assigned in the first meeting and were resentful over sharing the fruits of their labor. Many had hoped for individual recognition and felt that the creation of small groups minimized personal input and took away any chance for personal rewards. Over time, communication and sharing in the small groups became nonexistent, which undermined the project.

By creating a timeline and conducting interviews to pinpoint the beginning and middle of the conflict, the manager was later able to build a group meeting agenda that focused on the exact moments that teamwork fractured, which made for a much more productive discussion.

Assessing the Intensity of a Conflict

Assessing the intensity and level of emotion in a conflict helps you determine how and when to proceed. If tension is growing and people are beginning to take sides, or if conversations that were occurring in private are now flowing into public areas, then the intensity is increasing and you need to act. (For more information on emotional intensity and when to respond, see Chapter 2.)

Table 10-1 includes information on how to address the conflict after you've pinpointed the team's intensity level. Identify your situation in Table 10-1 to see where your team is at the moment. Some of the solutions in this chart refer to a goal statement, which you find out about in the later section "Determining the goal of your meeting."

If the team members are having disagreements but are still using language that includes the word "we," and they're open to brainstorming solutions, the group meeting would include the group's participation in identifying problem areas and issues as well as ownership in the solutions. If, on the other end of the scale, full-blown warfare has erupted, consider a series of shorter meetings in which you solely identify the goal for the discussion and draw out what team members believe they need to discuss in a longer meeting. For example, if a team is experiencing a complex problem, you may call one meeting to focus only on administrative policies, a second that looks at customer service, and a third for communication options. By having these brief, focused meetings where only topics are discussed (without getting into the details behind the topics), your team becomes aware of what the issues are for everyone involved. Shedding new light on a problem and expanding individual perspectives helps people see the issue in a whole new way.

Table 10-1   **Intensity of Conflict Chart**

	Issues	Emotion	Communication	Behavior	Resolution	How to Work with the Team
Low	Disagreement over goals, values, needs	Frustration, controlled	Open dialogue, "we" dialogue	Willing, forgiving	Collaboration, peace	Team identifies the problem, generates ideas, creates solution
	Argument over values, needs, personalities	Confused, cautious, distrusting	Tentative, holding back, "I" language	Watchful, protective, separate	Compromise, acceptable agreement	You present the goal statement; team stays in large group and works through issues
to	Battle for needs, safety, stability	Distressed, hopeless, struggling	Evasive "she" or "they" language, criticism	Resistance, coalition-building, preparing for the worst	Looking for help, hoping someone will intercede	You present the goal statement; start with large group, then use small groups to create safety and bring out concerns
High	Warfare, destruction	Fear, anger, rage, uncontrolled	Closed to listening, aggressive and negative language	Compelled to act, confrontation, destruction	Appealing to a higher authority	You present the goal statement; immediate small group work — short frequent meetings to build new team dynamics

Formulating a Meeting Plan

When you're facing a group conflict, you can toss everyone into a room and wing it, or you can put some thought into it. The more upfront planning you do, the better your odds are for a fruitful outcome, so set yourself up for success. Prior to the meeting, do the following:

- ✔ Create a goal statement.
- ✔ Set an agenda.
- ✔ Engineer ground rules.
- ✔ Plan meeting logistics (time, place).
- ✔ Assign tasks if you plan to use additional facilitators.
- ✔ Identify and collect data, exhibits, maps, charts, reports, and so on.
- ✔ Clarify time constraints and deadlines as necessary.
- ✔ Distribute meeting details to participants.
- ✔ Gather needed equipment and materials.
- ✔ Determine how you'll use breakout groups.

While you're working out the tactical details of your meeting — like reserving a room large enough to hold the group, getting your hands on the pertinent documents, or ensuring the participants clear their calendars to avoid interruptions — give some thought to the meeting's content. The following sections provide more information on setting goals and approaching your meeting with a strategy for success.

Determining the goal of your meeting

A clear goal statement gives purpose and focus to a meeting. More important, it serves as the criterion by which to consider all ideas and solutions. Be a strong facilitator and determine the goal of the first meeting; then assist the team in setting the goal statement for any additional meetings.

Here are some broad suggestions to get you started:

- ✔ Clarify roles and responsibilities within a project or a team.
- ✔ Discuss behaviors that are affecting the team.
- ✔ Change or retool processes that aren't working.
- ✔ Create harmony and renew relationships.

Start with a broad idea of what you'd like to tackle, and then get specific before you communicate the goal of the meeting to the attendees. How you state the goal makes a difference in the attendees' attitude and expectations. For example, a goal statement like, "The purpose of this meeting is to determine who is responsible for the breakdown in service" would result in a group of defensive participants full of accusations and ready to point fingers. In contrast, "The purpose of this meeting is to determine proactive ways to limit the breakdown in services" sets the tone for a positive, productive discussion in which people's ideas and creative thinking are appreciated. It acknowledges the problem but doesn't dwell on the past or make accusations. Your goal statement should do the same.

Creating an agenda

The agenda serves as a guide for the entire group to follow during the meeting. As people move from large group work to small group work and back again, they can always look to the agenda to know where they are in the process. The best work is often done when time is limited, so keep the meeting moving forward as much as possible. A good agenda includes:

- ✔ Exact start and end times
- ✔ Participation requirements (including ground rules)
- ✔ Breaks
- ✔ Points when the facilitator has the floor
- ✔ Details, details, details

Proposing ground rules

Ground rules allow group members to share information in a respectful manner, creating an environment where ideas are heard and validated. Suggest ground rules that help accomplish the meeting goal, and then give the group the opportunity to create a set of guidelines (or add to an existing set) that everyone can agree to work with. Use them to keep the group on task and to lessen your need to intervene as the meeting progresses. Start with these:

- ✔ Everyone is invited to participate.
- ✔ All ideas are valid.
- ✔ Speak for yourself — avoid "we" language.
- ✔ Speak respectfully — without monopolizing or interrupting.

✔ Stay on topic and work to solve the issue.

✔ Ask questions instead of making assumptions.

✔ Honor each person's right to pass.

✔ Follow time limits.

✔ Avoid interrupting.

✔ Be present by turning off phones and computers.

Display the final ground rules so everyone can see them — they're a good visual reminder of the group's first agreement!

Considering breakout groups

When designing the meeting process, consider making time for small group work. Breakouts can be a welcome change from the large group dynamic and allow people to share more perspectives (they also keep people awake and on point!). For more on the logistics of working with breakout groups, see the section "Breaking into small groups" later in this chapter.

If emotions are running high and trust is low, consider breaking into small group work right away to avoid the angry mob mentality taking over from the start. If the team conflict hasn't reached a critical point, start as a large group and use small group work later in the meeting.

Adding breakout groups to your meeting plan has many benefits. Breakout groups

✔ Give individuals more airtime

✔ Provide a more comfortable forum for reticent people to speak

✔ Allow for efficient, simultaneous work on multiple topics or tasks

✔ Provide anonymity and greater safety when issues are difficult or emotional

✔ Furnish a space for problem solving and proposals that the larger group can refine and approve

✔ Deter soapbox speeches from negatively affecting the whole group

Before you jump in with a plan laden with small group assignments, consider the limitations. Breakout groups

✔ Take up valuable meeting time — from deciding how to divide to settling down to reconvening

✔ Create more tactical work on your part in the preparation phase

✔ May instill resistance in participants who are suspicious of breaking up the larger group

✔ May get competitive, leading people to become territorial and go overboard protecting their ideas

✔ May make individuals feel that they don't need to participate in the large group work

Kicking Off the Group Meeting

Because you called the meeting to discuss a conflict, rest assured that everyone will be watching your every move. Employees will scrutinize everything from how the room is set up to how you describe your role. Be prepared, be present, and be ready to listen as you facilitate the discussion.

Setting the tone

Welcome all the participants to the team meeting. Be confident and clear, maintain eye contact, and don't forget to smile! Your comfort in front of the group will help people relax and will create the open and inviting environment you're shooting for.

Introduce yourself and describe your role as a facilitator. Explain how you'll be assisting the group in the discussions and goals for the day. If you have guests or assistants, introduce them and describe their roles as well.

Read the goal statement for the meeting. Ask for questions and allow time — five minutes at the most — for the participants to understand clearly the task for the day.

Presenting the agenda and finalizing the ground rules

Describe the details of what you're asking of the group and the time frame for the meeting. Help the team understand what the large and small group goals are. Remember that your agenda should include time to ask questions and have a short discussion.

Present the ground rules you created beforehand (refer to the earlier section "Proposing ground rules"), and ask the attendees to add any additional ground rules that are necessary for them to work together (add no more than one or two requests). The entire group must agree (a quick show of hands should do it) to all ground rules before you begin, because you'll use the rules as your moral compass, so to speak, when things get heated or the meeting starts to derail.

Because you can't be everywhere at once, create a version of the guidelines to post at small group stations to remind everyone of how they agreed to participate in this process.

Hearing from the participants

It's imperative to provide individuals with an opportunity to share their point of view. The goal in a large group setting is to do so in a way that has structure and isn't a free-for-all. People can share their perspective in the large group or in smaller breakout groups, but take into account how intense the feelings may be and how vocal the group could get. Whatever you choose, consider the following technique.

Provide a framework for people to follow when it's their turn to speak so that they can acknowledge the past but quickly move to the future with solid ideas and a willingness to create something new. Your guidelines for input should include four parts:

- **Incident:** Simply describe what happened (the details).
- **Impact:** How has the incident affected you personally?
- **Change:** What do you feel needs to change?
- **Ideas:** What ideas do you have to move forward?

Using intervention strategies

Members of a group often have differing expectations, assumptions, and needs. Some members need individual time and attention, and if they don't get it, they may create interruptions. An important part of your job as facilitator is to handle such distractions with appropriate responses so you can move the discussion forward.

Moving around the room can curb disruptions before they occur. Maintaining eye contact with the group — not just the individual speaking — lets others know you care about what they're thinking and feeling.

It's important to your audience that the participation feel balanced, so when someone talks out of turn, makes too many jokes, or challenges your authority, address the disruption by being clear and assertive and by using a confident tone of voice.

Addressing interruptions doesn't mean you have to use a sledgehammer at the first sign of trouble. Always start with low-level, subtle, least threatening responses. You don't want to alienate the disruptive person, and you don't want the others to see you as an ineffectual meeting facilitator.

Here are some of the more common disruptive behaviors and tips for responding to them:

- **Challenging the facilitator:** If someone's undermining your agenda, or is agitated and confused about what you're doing and why you're in charge, or is making personal attacks, then she's challenging you. Interventions are:

  - **Low level:** Remain calm; ask the speaker to repeat the concern for the whole group.

  - **Mid level:** Validate the concern; ask what the speaker needs to know and what information would be helpful to the group.

  - **High level:** Tell the speaker you'll have a private conversation with her during the break, and then chat with her later to quickly hear her out and ask for her cooperation. Let her know you may have to excuse her from the meeting if the behavior continues.

- **Having side conversations:** Side chatter is distracting, disruptive, and disrespectful. It also makes people paranoid! If you ignore it, you run the risk of failing to adhere to your guidelines for the meeting, and you show bias for the chatty person's status in the group by allowing her to undermine your efforts. Interventions are:

  - **Low level:** Walk over next to the disruptive culprit so she becomes aware the group is focusing on her.

  - **Mid level:** Ask her if she has a question or concern that needs to be addressed, and remind everyone of the ground rules (side conversations are a form of interrupting).

  - **High level:** Speak privately with the individual about the disruptions, and ask her for a commitment to change her behavior.

✔ **Being overly enthusiastic:** Some people love to share and share and share. They may think they have great ideas, or they may talk when they're anxious, or maybe they just like to hear the sound of their own voice. Either way, their over-participation discourages others from engaging in the conversation. Interventions are:

   • **Low level:** Thank the individual for her input and ask if anyone else has a point of view to share.

   • **Mid level:** Remind the speaker that you need to follow the timeline in the agenda, and ask her to state the point she feels is the most important.

   • **High level:** In private, confront her about the amount of time she's taking to put forth her views at the expense of other people's opinions. Ask her for a commitment to change her behavior, and offer to provide additional ways she might share her ideas, such as by e-mail or memos.

✔ **Dropping out:** Some people are uncomfortable speaking in public, but if you think a team member isn't sharing for another reason, she may be intimidated by you or others, or she may be waiting for a chance to enter the conversation, or maybe she's just not interested. Interventions are:

   • **Low level:** Ask for input or questions from those who haven't shared.

   • **Mid level:** Share the importance of each person assessing what she might have to add to the group.

   • **High level:** Break into small groups with a specific output expected, such as a list that includes one suggestion from each of the group's members for ways to improve the customer service experience, or privately ask for the opinion of those who aren't sharing and then ask them to share their response with the group.

✔ **Joking around:** You know the joker types — they're always the first with a witty remark. They may want attention from the group, or they may just use humor to get through tough situations. They often have great ideas if you can break through the silliness. Interventions are:

   • **Low level:** Be upfront and clear that you acknowledge the speaker's sense of humor; ask for realistic ideas as well.

   • **Mid level:** Inform the speaker that the humor is getting in the way of hearing other people state what's important to them.

   • **High level:** Remind the speaker of the goal for the day and ask the speaker to hold off on the humor until the team completes the goal.

✔ **Exiting:** Yikes! When someone walks out, she's either not interested or highly emotional. Either way, a public exit is a distraction to the group; in fact, distracting the group just may be the motivation behind her grand exit. Interventions are:

- **Low level:** Ask the person if she's willing to stay and share what's happening.

- **Mid level:** Give the person permission to go. Acknowledge the walkout to the group and allow them to discuss it briefly if they feel the need.

- **High level:** Contact the person after the meeting to discuss the issues.

✔ **Showing a skeptical attitude:** Skeptics are unhappy and troubled no matter what happens. They can sour a meeting without a word. They may have valid reasons to complain, but heckling and using aggressive body language aren't positive ways to handle tough situations. Interventions are:

- **Low level:** Ask the speaker to express her idea or concerns by describing what she'd like to see happen rather than making it clear what she doesn't want.

- **Mid level:** Ask what it would take for her to believe and trust that things can be different.

- **High level:** Ask her to hold her comments about the past, and explain to her that the group is now focusing on future solutions and ideas. Talk to her privately about the group's need for her support, and consider giving her a leadership role in a smaller group.

Breaking into small groups

You can divide any large group into smaller ones in a number of ways: by counting off, using birth month, or pulling names out of a hat. However, in a meeting focused on resolving a conflict, do a little strategic thinking and assign people based on your desired outcome.

Hearing from all perspectives in conflict discussions is important, so diversify the groups by job, rank, or departments so that different sides are represented. This approach breaks down cliques and creates an even playing field. Individuals who are resistant to discussing the situation may be more willing to consider the opposing point of view if they have the opportunity to discuss it in a small group setting.

Size matters! Use smaller groups for sharing personal information, developing ideas, and brainstorming solutions.

- ✔ Groups of two or three are great for more open sharing. They work well when people are new to the team, or when emotions are running high, or when people feel a need for safety.

- ✔ Groups of four or five are good when you want more energy for defining problems and generating ideas.

- ✔ Groups of six or more are useful for team-building. In a group this size, people have to wait longer before they can speak, creating patience in some and encouraging leadership in others.

Creating specific assignments

Small group work requires focus; a group without focus will be unproductive and could end up creating a new conflict. Be sure that your instructions are clear and concise — everyone should know what your expectations are. Allow for questions in the large group before you break out to smaller groups or you'll spend too much time reiterating your expectations to each small group.

Assigning roles minimizes cliques, provides for a freer exchange of views, and allows you to place troublemakers or uninterested parties in positions where they must engage in the discussion. Each group needs a scribe to write down ideas, a reporter to convey those ideas to the larger group, and a facilitator to manage the conversation.

Keeping groups on task

As the main group facilitator, you're responsible for keeping time for the whole group. Set a time limit for the small group work and ask the groups to be prepared to report back to the large group. Their presentation should focus on highlights of the group discussion, key topics, conclusions, and recommendations.

Even knowing the time limit for their work, small groups can have a tendency to focus on the past. Each small group facilitator should be sensitive to the need for people to express their opinions but also be aware of moving the group forward. Give small group leaders permission to use language like, "I can see how difficult this has been for you. What ideas do you have to resolve the issue?"

Small group work can include prioritizing a list generated by the larger group, finding weak spots in current systems, identifying potential snags in suggested solutions, or brainstorming on any number of issues. Regardless of the assignment, consider these guidelines:

✔ Provide focus and be clear about your expectations. For example, if a group is brainstorming, remind the members that they shouldn't also be evaluating or prioritizing ideas. Help groups by posting what the task is at each station: "Remember, your task is to brainstorm ideas only."

✔ Circulate around the room, moving from group to group to answer questions and intervening if flare-ups occur or if groups lose focus. Be careful to allow people the privacy and confidentiality they need — having a manager overhear the conversation could inhibit them.

✔ Prepare small groups for reentry to the large group by calling an end to the task and giving them five minutes or so to clarify their findings. Give them a break before rejoining the large group to settle any last-minute confusion.

Coming back to the larger group

Each group needs a chance to share new insights and highlights. The process you choose depends on the goal for the meeting and the number of participants in attendance. If the group is large, you need someone to capture and record the ideas shared by the small group reporters.

The goal of coming back together is to get all the ideas in a central location, write them down on a whiteboard or flip chart, and then have the group decide which items are the most important. Follow these steps:

1. **Have each reporter share the ideas from the small groups.**

   It's normal for some ideas to overlap, so clarify whether each idea is truly different from what has already been noted.

2. **Before each reporter sits down, ask group members if they have any additional thoughts.**

3. **After you list all the ideas, lead the large group in an exercise to prioritize the topics.**

   Which ideas do they think are most important to the group's efforts to move forward? I often let everyone share their two cents by giving them two votes that they can place anywhere on the list. This is an efficient way for everyone to have a voice but doesn't drag out voting and campaigning for certain ideas. It also demonstrates, in a very real way, the ownership the group has in the solution.

Devising a Team Plan for Follow-up

Summarize the work the team accomplished at the meeting and take some time for the group to celebrate what has been done while you look forward together.

Help the group determine a purpose or goal statement for any future work. This establishes a clear direction, keeping them moving forward with a task, goal, and focus in mind. Discuss how the team will keep communication open and what they need for future meetings. Facilitate a discussion on how they'll handle difficulties or unanticipated issues that come up, and how everyone will have access to new information.

Assigning next steps

When you have a focus for the future, assign concrete tasks and actions that meet the team's goal or purpose statement. This action plan is a document that group members can look to when they have questions. Action plans include

- **What** the tasks are
- **Who** is responsible for what
- **When** assignments are due
- **How** the follow-up will be done

Creating benchmarks

Groups thrive when they can brainstorm ideas, problem solve, develop alternatives, and take action together. By setting benchmarks, the group can easily identify its progress and successes. For example, measuring employee satisfaction and setting a benchmark to increase the current average by two points shows the team that things are getting better when the goal is met. Similarly, if a conflict concerns the glitches in a company process, creating a benchmark to sell more widgets or spend less time filling out forms gives individuals something concrete to work toward.

Report progress to all team members through a newsletter, by e-mail, or by reconvening the group. Consistent information assures members that progress is continuing.

Finally, subtly assess and observe your team to determine if employees are using new skills or tools to resolve problems, or taking personal responsibility for resolving issues on their own, or communicating well during the follow-up time. These are all points of reference that your work is paying off.

Chapter 11

Monitoring Agreements and Progress

....

In This Chapter

▶ Watching for changes in relationships

▶ Following up on agreements

▶ Staying involved and addressing relapse

▶ Supporting and maintaining progress

....

After you address a conflict (see Chapters 6 through 10), you probably feel pretty good. The discussion went well, issues were addressed, and everyone left feeling optimistic. Now it's time for your staff to get back to work — and for you to monitor the agreements they made and keep track of whether they're able to improve their working relationship. You may be holding your breath to see what'll happen — will the peace hold or will things fall apart?

Right after a conflict meeting, relationships between employees often are fragile. The parties involved are typically happy with the results and see the agreement as an opportunity to start rebuilding trust, but they aren't 100 percent certain that the changes are going to stick. They're at a crucial stage — and your watchful eye will be key to providing assistance if and when it's needed.

In this chapter, I offer tips on how to oversee a post-mediation working relationship. I highlight positive and negative behaviors you should be on the lookout for, tell you how and when to step back in, and show you how to use follow-up meetings effectively.

Keeping an Eye on the Environment

The most important action you can take after a conflict meeting is simply to pay attention. This isn't the time to assume that everything's a-okay and head to Cabo for two weeks! Be alert for the positive *and* negative changes in the environment as you keep your finger on the pulse of the workplace.

You can monitor the situation without being obtrusive. Here's how:

✔ **Keep your eyes and ears open.** You don't have to hold a drinking glass against the wall to catch your employees' private conversations — you aren't a spy, and you shouldn't act like one. Instead, watch how your employees interact with each other and listen carefully to their language (see the later section "Tuning In to Changes in Communication"). If tension still exists, it'll stand out — and that's your cue that additional coaching or mediated conversations are necessary.

✔ **Look at the quantity and quality of work being done.** One indication that previously feuding co-workers are back on track is an increase in the amount and value of work they now generate and a decrease in errors. As an employee becomes less distracted by conflict, you'll notice a tangible improvement in his work because he's more focused on the tasks at hand.

✔ **When you're in a one-on-one situation with an employee, ask him how things are going.** This question is a quick, unassuming one that opens the door for a more in-depth conversation. If he gives you a one-word answer, like, "Fine," continue to ask open-ended questions such as, "I'm curious how you think the agreements are shaping up — can you tell me about that?" or "How do you think your colleague would describe your working relationship since the meeting?"

✔ **Check for a reduction in sick leave and absenteeism as your staff settles back into routines.** If you notice that an employee is still calling in sick or missing in action, that's a good indicator that he isn't completely satisfied with the outcome of the meeting. Check in to see where the sticking points are and find out whether he's willing to keep working on finding a solution. If not, you may need to consider corrective action. Chapter 13 provides information on resources you can turn to for help.

✔ **If you have a system in place that allows employees to give feedback, check to see if any new information has come in.** Address negative comments or lingering concerns either with the individual specifically or with the whole group. Make sure to handle the comment constructively by maintaining a positive outlook and working to solve the problem. (For examples of feedback loops as well as hints on what to do when the complaint isn't something you can fix, see Chapter 12.)

Rebuilding trust after a conflict takes time, so don't be discouraged if you see some residual tension and frustration. Workplace mediations commonly take two to three sessions before everyone on the team is feeling better about the work atmosphere. Monitor the overall environment and step in when you can to maintain the progress that has been made. Be willing to come back together and fine-tune as needed. (For more on signs that you need to intervene, see "Knowing when you're needed" later in this chapter.)

Looking for decreased tension

Tension is one of the most significant indicators of how a group is doing after a conflict meeting. Obviously, if all the employees look happy and comfortable, and they're able to carry on lighthearted conversations with each other, that's a good sign. Conversely, if co-workers are avoiding each other or making angry, snarky comments, it goes without saying that you still have more work to do.

Monitoring tension in your workplace requires you to be alert to different levels and nuances. For example, after a meeting, the participants may be hesitant or careful in their interactions with each other. Although this tendency to walk on eggshells can increase tension among the staff as a whole, it probably will have a minor effect and should go away quickly.

You can judge the level of tension in the office by doing the following:

✔ **Considering how long it has been since the conflict meeting:** Much like the doctor dressing a wound tells his patient, "It's going to get worse before it gets better," the days following mediations may not be as calm as you'd like. After the employees have had time to process the meeting, they begin to remember comments that now sting or appear contradictory, causing one or both to be on edge for a while.

Don't overreact and jump in with rescue techniques too soon post-mediation — the tension will likely subside on its own. Give your employees some time to be uncertain and cautious. If the behaviors continue longer than a few days or are disruptive, consider stepping in.

✔ **Noticing who's around when tensions are high:** You may detect patterns of problematic behavior between certain employees, some of whom may not have even been involved in the mediation (yikes!). Patterns can indicate who's still having problems and provide insight into how other employees could be feeding the beast.

As uncomfortable as it may be, don't forget to include yourself in the equation. You may be inadvertently causing the conflict to continue by ignoring poor behavior, unwittingly pitting the employees against each other, or making public comments that show your bias. (To ferret out other ways you may be keeping a conflict going, turn to Chapter 4.)

✔ **Acknowledging how the workload and/or a specific type of work may be adding fuel to the fire:** The tension you're sensing may not be caused by anything related to the conflict meeting itself. For example, if it's the holiday season and you work in a toy factory, it's probably a safe bet that the workload could be a large contributor to the tension in the air. Beyond the obvious cyclical workload contributors, ask if any of the systems in place create tensions — for example, maybe they duplicate efforts, are out of sync, or inadvertently create a competitive climate.

✔ **Observing tension changes in the individual participants:** You worked with these particular employees before the meeting and during the meeting, and now you're observing them after the meeting, so you probably know how they usually react in certain situations. Notice whether the participants are back to normal or still functioning at a higher stress level, regardless of their surroundings or outside influences.

✔ **Identifying any agreement details that could be causing a sudden increase in tension:** Sometimes an agreement turns out to be just the wrong solution, even though it came from the right place. And sometimes, an agreement actually backfires — it solves an old problem but causes a new one in its place. Call another meeting to talk about the remedies, and allow for additional ideas to adjust as necessary.

Watching for positive changes in working relationships

Employee relationships run the gamut from the even keel to the herky-jerky roller coaster ride. So it may be unrealistic to expect that, just because your employees mediated a conflict, you'll find them in the break room exchanging casserole recipes if they didn't do that before.

Watch for changes that help you gauge how current behaviors match pre-mediation interactions. You may see changes with specific individuals or within the group as a whole. Behaviors like the following indicate progress:

✔ **Open and relaxed interactions between staff members:** Smiling and cordial behavior goes a long way toward rebuilding relationships. Are the employees taking the time to greet each other? Something as simple as saying "good morning" fosters contentment and goodwill among staff.

Try jumpstarting a more relaxed atmosphere by modeling the behavior you'd like to see the previously conflicted employees display.

✔ **The reduction of cliques and isolated groups:** If the facilitation that took place was with a larger group, look to see if the members of the team are interacting more freely. If you're on the right track, you should notice a decrease in separation and isolation along with outward efforts to include others where they were previously excluded.

✔ **More cooperation:** Look for an increased willingness from co-workers to interact and collaborate. A new or renewed interest in taking on projects that require teamwork is a huge step (as opposed to an employee saying he'll just do it all himself).

✔ **More positive attitudes toward each other:** After a difficult situation is resolved, your employees may be more likely to give each other the benefit of the doubt instead of jumping to conclusions and being quick to take offense at a poorly worded or ill-timed comment.

Any behavior that indicates employees are more open, positive, and understanding with each other helps the team function better. When possible, encourage interactions and give co-workers a chance to improve working relationships by

✔ **Assigning projects to a different mix of employees:** Depending on how specialized an employee's skills are and the nature of the task at hand, create tasks that can build on renewed relationships.

✔ **Creating a task force or committee that makes sense for the business but allows for relationship building:** One company created a committee comprised of one representative from each department to plan a monthly luncheon. The cost of the lunch was a minimal investment in building positive cross-departmental relationships.

✔ **Looking for opportunities to get your staff out of the workplace and focused on a different project:** Some organizations have volunteer opportunities or community enhancement projects that provide opportunities for co-workers who may not get to interact on a daily basis to pair up and get to know each other a little better.

Don't push employees together if they aren't ready. If tensions are still high, you could do more harm than good by forcing folks to work together on a joint project. Timing is everything, so wait for things to calm down before deciding to pair up previously combative staff. The last thing you want is for your newly formed Employee Satisfaction Committee to make its first order of business a detailed discussion about how to throw you under the bus!

Tuning In to Changes in Communication

Without a doubt, one of the most common topics in mediation is the breakdown of communication. Such a breakdown may be the root of a conflict itself or a byproduct of it, but, in either case, if you notice deterioration in the way your employees are communicating, step in and help repair it.

On the flip side, after a mediation, you should see improvements in communication — and by "improved communication," I don't just mean using polite language. Take into account all the levels of communication covered in the following sections: words, tone of voice, and body language, as well as frequency and consistency of conversations.

Paying attention to content

Pay attention to the specific language employees use after a conflict meeting. Small changes like using "we" and "us" instead of "you" or "they" can be easy to miss, but the subtle change provides a powerful example of a shift in perspective from isolated and separated individuals to a cohesive team. Amending word choices can also indicate an increase in respect, awareness of others, and humility.

How an employee speaks about a prior conflict may determine whether future problems are imminent. Is he wallowing in everything that went wrong, or is he optimistic that things are now on the right path? There's a huge difference between "I'll believe it when I see it" and "I'm hopeful we're moving in the right direction."

When you hear negative language, talk to the employee about the impact his words have on his environment. Ask him to be proactive by sharing possible solutions to the problem rather than complaining about the things that bother him. Help him look to future solutions rather than focus on past problems.

Distinguishing tone of voice

How a message is delivered is just as important as the words an employee chooses. Shifts in tone of voice can speak volumes about how well people are getting along. A moderate tone, rather than loud or demanding voices or snide comments mumbled under a co-worker's breath indicate a reduction in the conflict's intensity. Pay attention to whether employees are comfortable speaking freely and sharing ideas with each other, as opposed to avoiding or withdrawing from communication because of harsh or condescending tones.

The front office staff in a doctor's office used all the right words with the patients; "thank you," "May I help you?" and "I'll take care of that" were phrases the physician insisted they use when tending to patients. However, a few staff members used a tone of voice that made the phrases sound snotty, bored, and bothered. When asked about it in a group facilitation, each employee insisted he was following instructions to the letter! Content *and* tone matter.

Observing body language

You may have an employee who tends to express himself more in actions and movements than he does with words. Whether it's eye rolling, crossing his arms, or stomping down the hall, these actions speak loud and clear about how he's feeling. He may be doing it on purpose, to prove a point, or he could be completely oblivious to his actions. Regardless of his awareness, rest assured that his colleagues have noticed!

If you observe postures that are aggressive and intimidating to other co-workers, coach the employee on body language.

I mediated a case in which a project leader would lean across the table and dig his feet in when the topic of his project was raised. His co-workers would get wide-eyed and shut down. It surprised even *me* when I saw it for the first time. I talked to him on a break about his posturing and asked what he noticed in his co-workers when he talked to them in that stance. He had absolutely no idea that he was doing it, so he wasn't making the connection that his body language was the reason his cohorts shut down and isolated him. When we rejoined the group, he leaned back and asked for ideas. Big difference! For more information on communicating with body language, see Chapter 2.

Watching reactions to difficult conversations

Gauge how respectful the communication really is. On the surface, everything may seem fine, but if you dig a little deeper, you may notice that problems still exist. Pay special attention to the way employees handle themselves in difficult conversations. Are they able to state what's important with respect and tact, or do they resort to previous methods like force and rudeness?

For example, when an employee is giving feedback to a peer, is he doing so in a way that makes it easy for the other person to hear, or is he being negative and critical? Does the colleague receiving the feedback seem open and responsive, or is she angry and defensive? Peer feedback is a particularly sensitive manner of communication, so if you notice your employees are doing it well, that's a great sign that communication has improved. If it's going poorly, that may be your cue to do one-on-one coaching or call another session to uncover what's still unresolved for one or both of the parties.

Monitoring gossip levels

Gossip is a clear sign of continued conflict. Listen for it and note whether it's decreased in frequency, stayed the same, or gotten worse since the mediation.

Gossip and rumors are a serious red flag that the root of the conflict hasn't been successfully addressed. One or more of the employees who participated in the conflict meeting having hushed conversations with co-workers may be a sign of residual frustrations.

I once mediated with a group of co-workers who were angry with a store manager they thought wasn't properly representing them to headquarters. Collectively, they were upset, but they individually reacted based on their personal histories with the manager and their unique value systems. After a mediation to resolve the issues, each employee cautiously worked at moving forward. The first few days, the staff tried to make small talk and even cracked a few jokes about the situation. Within a week or two, the manager reported back to me that everything was going swimmingly. He noticed that a few of the more vocal cashiers seemed to be more positive. What he didn't notice were the conversations taking place in the back room while the clerks were on break, and the sideways glances they gave each other at the cash registers whenever the manager's name was mentioned. Just checking in on one aspect of his environment and relying too much on the attitudes of a few people didn't give the supervisor an accurate read on the situation. A couple of well-placed questions and a broader view of the situation helped him gain a better understanding of how things were progressing.

Looking for Examples of Personal Responsibility

Going through a mediation or facilitation can be stressful and exhausting. Each participant exerts energy to work through the issues, which results in a sense of personal investment in the outcome. Look for that same level of investment in the weeks ahead. After a resolution meeting, observe how the participants are adjusting personally. Look to see whether an employee is keeping his word and making changes that begin with the man in the mirror.

Keeping agreements

One of the easiest ways to tell if someone is taking personal responsibility is to see whether he's keeping his agreements. If a solution was found in the mediation, it probably involved both participants agreeing to do or not do something. If commitments are completed as specified, on time and by the right person, that's a good sign the solutions are working and the employees are on their way to an improved working relationship.

Conversely, if agreements aren't being followed or aren't working as well as you had hoped, consider it an indication that you have a continued conflict on your hands. Prepare to talk with each employee, either separately or together in a follow-up meeting, about the reasons the agreements aren't being followed (see the later section "Leading Productive Follow-Up Meetings" for more on post-mediation meetings). Here are some possible reasons:

- ✔ **The employees have different expectations for the agreements.** It's possible that the parties have two different understandings regarding their agreements. They may have left the meeting thinking they were on the same page only to discover that they're reading from different books.

- ✔ **Circumstances have changed.** Look for anything that has changed between the original meeting and now, including the possibility that a new conflict has arisen.

- ✔ **The system has a problem.** A systemic issue with workplace policies or procedures may be making it difficult or impossible for an employee to make good on his promises. Maybe he left the meeting with the best of intentions but was unable to follow through because of a workplace policy. If so, ask your employees to work together to find a work-around solution, or help them make a change in the system.

- ✔ **An outside influence is prolonging the conflict.** Is something or someone keeping the conflict going? You may have to investigate a systemic cause or look for a co-worker who may be stirring the pot. If it turns out the influencer was a previously uninvolved individual, meet with him separately or include him in future meetings and agreements as a way to get to the bottom of the issues.

- ✔ **The solution wasn't right.** If you know that, technically, everyone did everything right, but there's still a problem, maybe the solutions didn't accurately address the problem. Or maybe the problem looks different now that the employees have started to work on it, and the original answers aren't fitting the bill. If so, reassess with a follow-up meeting.

✔ **The solution is beyond an employee's capacity.** An employee may agree to a solution with the best of intentions, but when it comes right down to it, what he agreed to may not be something he's capable of doing. He may not be ready to admit publically that his skill set or knowledge is lacking, so help him out by asking direct yet empathetic questions such as, "How are the agreements from the meeting working for you? Are there any current roadblocks to the agreements that I or anyone else could help you with?" Create a safe place for him to concede that he needs additional help.

✔ **The participants never invested in the process or the outcomes.** As difficult as it is to admit, there's always the possibility that one of the employees isn't really interested in resolving the problem. He may already be looking to greener pastures and doesn't care how his misery affects you or his co-workers. Your time hasn't been wasted, though, because you now have a better understanding of the overall situation, even if the employee leaves on his own (or with your guidance).

Showing an increased willingness to handle new problems

Conflicts and disagreements will surely rise again, which is actually a good thing! Discord gets a bad rap, because when it isn't handled properly, it causes a lot of negative consequences. But when it's addressed well, conflict has great benefits like stronger working relationships, increases in creative and innovative work product, and more durable solutions to future problems.

So, take a deep breath and relax when a new disagreement crops up, and watch how your team handles the new dispute. What you want to see are employees using good conflict-resolution skills, including adept communication, respectful listening, the sharing of ideas, and open and honest dialogue. Give your employees a chance to work it out in the safety of your presence. If things get too heated, step in as needed and apply some of the mediator tips that I outline in Chapter 7, such as reflecting and reframing. The section "Knowing when you're needed" later in this chapter helps you determine when the time is right to step back in after mediation and help employees continue to work out solutions.

Stepping In to Coach and Encourage

When you observe what's going well and what isn't (refer to the preceding sections for pointers), look for opportunities to step in and help people keep their agreements. The days and weeks following a mediation meeting provide ample opportunities both to reinforce positive behaviors in employees as well as to address relapse and coach through conflict. Look for chances to encourage the positive changes and intercede when negative behaviors arise.

Coaching employees after mediation

You can assist staff in a number of ways as they try on new working relationships. Here are four of the most common strategies:

✔ **Acknowledging progress:** Start any coaching discussion by simply acknowledging an individual's hard work. When he's making an extra effort to improve his situation, recognizing his effort is important. Employees can easily slip back into old, negative patterns of behavior; one way to prevent this is to show that you've noticed his efforts and encourage him to keep up the good work. Be sure to cite specific examples so he's clear on what behaviors he should continue.

✔ **Helping an employee process the outcome:** An employee may have a difficult time adjusting and need an opportunity to talk about his concerns and vent his emotions. In this instance, listen more than problem-solve, focusing your role more on support than on action. If he starts to become overwhelmed or confused and needs some direction, help him identify and work out what he really wants. Then help him create a plan by asking questions like those I outline in Chapter 7 and by focusing on the things he can control, like those I list in Chapter 19.

✔ **Raising the employee's personal awareness:** Another reason for one-on-one coaching is to help bring about awareness. Sometimes raising awareness is as simple as bringing an issue to the attention of a socially awkward or oblivious employee, and sometimes it's a more complicated, ongoing process (for example, to help someone address a more problematic and disruptive issue).

Show sensitivity and tact when approaching these situations because you're essentially holding up a mirror to a behavior or attitude that the person doesn't really want to address. Approach him with genuine curiosity when trying to understand why he chooses the behaviors he does and what his intended outcomes are. An employee may think he's being helpful and isn't aware he's offending others. Or he could be intentionally pushing buttons — in which case, your next move will be to understand his motivation so you can coach him toward better behavior.

Open-ended questions citing specific examples work well. For example, you may say, "If you're aware that Zaniya reacts when you talk over her, like in the staff meeting yesterday, help me understand what was happening for you."

✔ **Preparing everyone for future conversations:** If serious conflicts are still simmering and an additional mediation or conflict conversation is needed, meet with all the participants prior to the mediation to help prepare them for the conversation. Much like a private caucus (see Chapter 8 for more details on confidential meetings), use this time to help the individuals identify what's important to them, consider solutions that they'd like to propose at the next meeting, and help them rehearse how they may word those proposals. Act as their sounding board and help them create a game plan for the next meeting.

Although I list four common methods for you to use, you probably won't use a single approach on its own, separate from the others. Instead, you'll get more mileage out of them if you use a combination of methods. For example, if you need to raise awareness with an employee that his tone of voice needs work, do so by first acknowledging what he's doing well, and then discuss how he can work on bringing the sarcasm down a notch or two.

When you're in a coaching role, your goal is to work one on one to help each person see his own behavior and find his own answers. You're not there to jump in, make a decision, and move on. That approach will only stifle the conflict resolution skills each person gained during the mediation. Instead, ask a lot of questions to draw out an employee's take on things and listen for areas that he needs help improving. Be available to support your employees through this transition, and provide resources as necessary.

Knowing when you're needed

Knowing when to jump in and provide assistance following the first round of mediation can be tricky. You want to give your employees a chance to work it out themselves, but if you wait too long, the dispute could escalate out of control. Step in when

✔ **One of your employees approaches you.** This is an obvious one! When an employee asks for assistance, have a conversation with him about what's happening. Depending on the situation, you can use one or more of the coaching techniques I suggest in the previous section. The important thing is to be available and take his request for help seriously.

✔ **Tension between two or more co-workers is affecting others or is eroding the work.** If time passes and you notice the conflict is no longer contained between the two original parties, it's time to act. You may need to have a private conversation with the individuals (or another mediation) to explore what has yet to be resolved and devise a plan for moving forward. Also, consider that some of the reasons I suggest in the section "Looking for Examples of Personal Responsibility" may be at the heart of the spreading tension, and react appropriately.

✔ **Someone is calling in sick or not showing up to work.** Absenteeism is a giant red flag that conflict is still brewing. Check in with the employee and see what's affecting his ability to be present as expected.

✔ **Behaviors aren't changing.** If participants are stubborn and you're not seeing any improvement, consider meeting with them again or reaching out for some additional assistance. You certainly don't want relationships to reach a point of permanent damage, so consider which resource may be available within your company (see Chapter 13) or outside the company (see Chapter 14). Doing nothing isn't an option.

✔ **The issues continue to be the topic of conversation at the water cooler.** If it feels like the dead horse you thought had been beaten to death is still taking some serious blows, investigate what's happening for those who continue to talk about the conflict. After mediations or facilitated discussions, people often need to process for a few more days. That's okay and no need for you to be alarmed. However, if it goes beyond a few days and you observe that, at every turn, an employee is bringing up the conflict, something remains unresolved for him. Gently pull him aside and ask open-ended questions centering on the behaviors you've seen. Position an opening to the conversation by saying something like, "It's been a week since you and Brittany met. I noticed that the issues continue to be discussed with the rest of the team, and I'm curious about that. Help me understand what's going on for you."

Leading Productive Follow-Up Meetings

If the mediation or group facilitation agreement you're monitoring calls for follow-up meetings, make sure that the events make their way to the participants' calendars and that they're seen as a priority. Conversely, if the outcome of the mediation makes no mention of debriefings but you've observed behaviors and attitudes that lead you to believe the employees could benefit from coming back together, arrange a conversation on their behalf.

Post-mediation discussions are often held to readdress issues, discuss new problems, or work through any glitches that are surfacing because of specific agreements made in previous meetings. The follow-up meeting can be between you and the employees together, you and each of the employees separately, or between two employees without your assistance. Regardless of the attendees, the goals are always the same: to give the participants a chance to share how they think things are going and to create an opportunity for each person to address any new conflicts or concerns.

Setting up the meeting

Provide enough time between the mediation and a follow-up discussion for agreements to work or not. You know your employees, so you know what a reasonable amount of time is, but keep in mind that an employee needs a chance to try out a new method of speaking or implement a different process before you rush in to declare it's just not working. By hanging back a little and monitoring the situation, you and the employees involved can gather fresh information to share as concrete examples in the coming meeting.

You're not trying to give your staff just enough rope to hang themselves, though. What you *are* doing is akin to teaching them how to ride a bike. Let them wobble a bit and see if they can catch themselves before they fall. In essence, let them find their own balance before you start critiquing their behavior and deciding they're not capable of going any further.

Let the participants know you'd like them to meet again by communicating the following:

- ✔ Tell them whether the meeting is mandatory or voluntary.

- ✔ The follow-up isn't a punishment but rather an opportunity for both (or all) to discuss successes and retool what isn't working.

- ✔ The agreement document (if it exists) will be used as the agenda, but the participants can always add to it as needed.

- ✔ Each employee should make notes on what is and isn't working and come prepared with new proposals and an open mind.

- ✔ You're eager and available to help if, when, and where needed.

- ✔ The participants are free to make adjustments to previous agreements. Feeling locked into agreements that aren't working can result in resistance to attending a follow-up discussion and may create a situation in which an employee is hesitant to put anything else in writing. If an employee knows ahead of time that he's able to fine-tune a previous commitment, he may come to the meeting with a few new creative solutions to the same old problems.

- ✔ Let the parties know that you're paying attention and holding them accountable for follow-through. If you've observed major resistance or outright defiance toward the agreements, clearly state your expectations regarding accountability.

For other considerations, like selecting a neutral location, preparing yourself and the participants, and creating a comfortable meeting environment, see Chapter 6.

Holding the meeting

Post-mediation meetings (I use the plural because you shouldn't be surprised if a series of discussions are needed) are different from formal mediations or group facilitations. For starters, there should be less tension in the room. The participants have already seen the value of the mediated process, and although things may not be going exactly as planned, there should be more common ground to discuss and perhaps even a few successes to celebrate.

Manage a successful post-mediation meeting by following these steps:

1. **Deliver a more casual and abbreviated opening statement than the formal statements you used in the first mediation (which you can find in Chapter 7).**

   When you bring employees back for a second or third time, keep your opening brief and positive. Give a quick reminder of the ground rules (like not interrupting each other), and state that the goal of the meeting is to check in to see what's worked and what still needs a little fine-tuning.

2. **Start the discussion with what's working.**

   Tell them that this meeting is an opportunity to build on the successes you see, and then recap the positive outcomes you've observed.

3. **Create an agenda that starts with the previous meeting's agreement document (or participants' recollection of the agreements) and anything new that needs to be added.**

   For pointers on building agendas during mediation meetings, which are different from the typical agenda you may be used to, see Chapter 7.

4. **Use the agenda as a road map while you open the conversation up to the participants as a time for each of them to share what his experience has been since the first meeting.**

   Ask them to speak both generally and specifically to each line item. What a participant says and how he says it should give you a good indication of what, if anything, needs to be discussed further.

5. **Explore whether the co-workers are getting what they had hoped for by asking open-ended questions.**

   For example, you may ask: What about this agreement is (and is not) working for you? What about this agreement do you think meets both your needs, and where do you think it falls short?

6. **Keep an eye on their interaction but remain at a distance until needed.**

   Be less of a facilitator the second time around and give the employees the room to discuss and work things out. But feel free to take back the reins if conversations take a destructive turn. (Prepare for resistance by turning to Chapter 8.)

7. **Schedule another meeting with an eye on the future.**

   Even if all parties believe this is the last discussion needed, put a date on the calendar for a follow-up. If, at a later date, *all* parties (not just one!) communicate that the issues have been addressed and you can see for yourself that the team is working cohesively, you can always cancel it.

   There's no hard and fast rule about the number of meetings needed, so it's up to all involved to consider what's in the best interest of the participants and the working environment as a whole.

Part III
Using Additional Resources to Resolve the Conflict

The 5th Wave   By Rich Tennant

©RICHTENNANT

RECEPTION

"So, you're the mediation expert, huh? So, what does that make you, a big deal or something?"

In this part . . .

Vou're not alone when it comes to resolving conflict! In this part I explain the actions you can take to keep the waters calm while you investigate your options for calling in additional help. I guide you through the steps to find a trusted source within your organization, and I provide a list of criteria to consider when hiring a professional to help you resolve a conflict.

Chapter 12

Keeping a Team Focused During a Conflict

When a workplace experiences serious conflict, your goal is to do all you can to limit the impact of a situation that very well may be beyond your control and help your team collectively move through a difficult time. In addition to dealing directly with the conflict, your employees will want you to address issues, keep them on track, and help them feel supported.

In this chapter, I walk you through what you can do to keep a team focused and productive during conflict. I give you pointers on how to share information without adding fuel to the fire and discuss how to set up communication channels for staff concerns and feedback. Finally, I offer insight into how you can demonstrate that you're a trusted, strong leader who strategizes rather than reacts.

Addressing Safety or Legal Issues

When conflicts arise, your first priority is to protect employees and the company at large. Depending on the conflict and the people involved, you may notice certain red flags regarding security, such as

> ✔ Threats of harm to person or property, including theft or sexual harassment
>
> ✔ Mental health issues from angry or disgruntled employees

✔ Suspicions of violence

✔ Work safety

✔ Drug or alcohol issues

✔ Any behaviors that lead you to believe a situation "isn't quite right"

Act on any of these issues by following company protocol and dealing with them immediately. Document any legal concerns and report them to your superiors and/or Human Resources personnel. You should report anything that negatively affects employees or is an actionable offense — such as harassment of any kind, bullying, emotional abuse, safety concerns, discrimination, or retaliation — as soon as you're aware that it's happening.

Dealing with issues that require the involvement of HR or other authorities often results in employees who aren't directly involved in the behavior needing a place to vent and asking for clear instruction on how to deal with co-workers. Provide information as appropriate. Act as a sounding board to minimize the impact and help employees focus on their work, but be careful not to overstep your boundaries by sharing too much information.

Limiting Chatter

Intelligence officers listen for chatter over the airwaves as a means to determine if and when actions will take place. In very basic terms, the more they hear and the louder the chatter becomes, the more likely an event is about to occur. Although this analogy is a bit dramatic, the idea translates to the workplace. When conflict is happening, employees will talk . . . and talk and talk. Talk turns into gossip, conjecture, and, sometimes, outright hostility.

Chatter breeds discontent because it stems from uncertainty. If everyone knows that something's going on but they don't have accurate information, they fill in the blanks and chatter begins to escalate. Individuals take up the banner, spread rumors, exaggerate information, or fabricate stories.

What your employees are trying to do when they participate in the noise is address the uncertainty they feel about a conflict. As much as possible, work to limit the buzz because it

✔ **Distracts employees:** Last time I checked, I couldn't find any organizations that set out to pay employees to make hallway conjecture. If conversations are taking place around every corner, it interferes with the ability to focus on the work employees are actually being paid to do.

✔ **Increases stress:** Each person has a right to process his perspective, but if employees are constantly forced to discuss the situation over and over, it can be overwhelming. Sick days and time away from the office may provide the only relief from the constant recycling of information.

✔ **Increases confusion:** As employees share their perspectives and add individual spins on the situation, conflict takes on a life of its own and can morph into something much bigger than it actually is.

✔ **Heightens emotion:** Chatter in the form of whispers and information fed bits at a time often causes a slow burn that can easily ignite with one wrong word or phrase.

Acknowledge employees' need to process information and talk through any problems. Hoping that employees aren't going to talk about a conflict is unrealistic, but you can ask them to limit conflict-related conversations with each other and, instead, share their concerns using other avenues, like those listed in the upcoming section "Creating ways to voice concern." This strategy not only helps reduce gossip and misinformation, but also ensures that you and other managers know what the concerns are so you can deliver consistent responses. Even though you may not be able to squelch the rumor mill completely, you can take steps to minimize the buzz that can drag down the team.

Being upfront and consistent

Consistency is one of your greatest tools during a conflict. Communicating on a regular basis allows employees to develop trust in you. If they can count on you as the main source for accurate, up-to-date information, they likely won't feel the need to go to each other with rumors and speculation.

If you feel that you need to protect your staff from certain details, or if you know confidential information, that's okay. But don't use those circumstances as an excuse not to tell them anything. If decisions or changes from outside the group are the root of a conflict, tell your team what you can when you can. Be as open as possible and avoid any appearance that you're hiding something. Perceived secrecy tends to make angry people paranoid!

Demonstrate that you're as in touch with the state of affairs as you can be by

✔ Assuring the team that you're looking out for the their best interests

✔ Stating that you're committed to sharing as much information as possible when possible

✔ Informing employees that when you can't share certain details, you'll at least share the process

✔ Letting your team know exactly when they can count on you to communicate updates or changes

How you disseminate information depends on your unique environment, so establish a forum that fits your workplace. This could mean that you disseminate all information at staff meetings or that you give updates in writing. Regardless of the delivery method, be clear, consistent, and accurate with *all* your employees. Telling one person one thing and another person something else is a surefire way to cause a major squall. People talk!

Finding the time and place to address conflict

Obviously, if a conflict is between just two people and you feel you can successfully mediate their issue, you don't need to address their business with the entire team. (In Chapter 5, I give you insight about when to address conflict, and in Chapters 6 through 9, I tell you how to facilitate such a discussion.) However, if a conflict is affecting everyone, call a meeting for a day and time when most employees can attend. Be sure to include staff who work off-site, are assigned to different shifts, or have positions that require them to be on the phones.

If meeting in a central location allows for more people to attend at one time, consider somewhere other than headquarters. Arranging for an off-site meeting can create a more neutral and confidential environment, especially if the conflict has anything to do with other groups or departments. The location you choose should put privacy first and keep interruptions to a minimum.

Allow enough time during the discussion for people to ask questions and for you to respond appropriately to the issues. If you have a large staff and you want to facilitate a group meeting so everyone can share their perspectives, take a look at Chapter 10 for ideas on how to put together such a conversation to get the most out of it.

If your conditions don't allow for everyone on your team to be present at one time and you're having multiple meetings with different participants attending separate discussions, be diligent in tracking what's been asked and answered. Take notes and use an outline so that you discuss as close to the same information as possible with each group of people. If a question arises in one group be sure to communicate the question and answer with the other employees. This method prevents misinformation from being discussed after the meetings when employees are comparing notes.

The first few meetings you call may take longer because people will be processing new information and sharing concerns. Don't be too anxious about that — as things calm down, you should be able to devote subsequent discussions to delivering succinct updates. You can also save time by reminding everyone of any other avenues you have in place to voice their concerns (see "Creating ways to voice concern" later in this chapter for details on methods for gathering information).

Limiting closed-door meetings

Throughout an ongoing conflict, you may have sensitive information that not everyone needs to learn about in an open forum. Maintaining privacy is important, but try to make closed-door conversations the exception rather than the rule. Limiting closed-door meetings is a good way to cut down on chatter and worry.

Be aware of what your actions communicate. If an employee constantly sees one closed-door meeting after another, she may begin to draw uninformed conclusions, and paranoia can set in. If your staff is left to guess about what's happening behind a closed door, you can be certain that gossip based on false information will ensue.

Regular, open-forum meetings can be a useful outlet for some employees, but you may need to close the door if some people in your group need individual attention because they're less comfortable sharing in a group setting. Closed-door meetings may also be appropriate when you need to share a strategy with mid-level supervisors. Talk things over with them, but be discreet. This approach keeps other employees from feeling like they're the last to know. It also reduces the appearance of favoritism during a time when people may already be feeling insecure.

After information leaves your lips, you have no control over how an employee hears it and certainly no control over how she chooses to repeat it. It's better to speak with one voice to the whole group than to have numerous stories circulating about what you said to whom and when.

Creating ways to voice concern

Implement multiple avenues for employees to offer their perspectives. Productively communicating concerns gives your staff a constructive way to ask questions or vent. And by communicating that an employee's ideas and concerns are important to you, you increase the likelihood that he'll use one of the methods you establish rather than keep the rumors going.

Use as many communication systems as possible because the more avenues you make available the more likely employees are to find one or two they're comfortable using. The goal is to help staff bring ideas and concerns forward and help you gain a better understanding of the causes and impact. Some avenues for employee feedback include the following:

- ✔ **Set up an anonymous e-mail address or toll-free phone number.** Your company can administer these resources directly, or an independent agency can compile the data for you. Be sure to post the e-mail address or telephone number where employees can access it easily. The information gathered will probably be more in line with short notes or comments — sort of like the essay questions on a test rather than the multiple choice or ranking questions you find on surveys.

- ✔ **Provide locked suggestion boxes and encourage people to use them.** Place the boxes in an area that's easily accessible to all employees. You don't want people to feel like they have to sneak past the principal's office to drop in a suggestion. Let employees know how often, and by whom, the comments will be addressed.

- ✔ **Conduct regular anonymous surveys to give your employees a chance to share concerns and ideas.** Anonymity is vital to the success of this strategy. Numerous companies provide free and inexpensive options for collecting information through surveys, so even if you're tempted to conduct surveys in-house, look externally as well before you make a final decision. If employees know that only a compiled list of answers is being sent to the administrator and that there's no way for the company to know who reported what, they're more apt to answer honestly.

- ✔ **Develop an ombudsman office.** An ombudsman is an employee, or group of employees, who are trained in various conflict resolution techniques and are available as a confidential resource for resolving disputes at the lowest level possible. See Chapter 13 for more information about an ombudsman office.

After you have a system in place, create a communiqué to notify employees what the various options are and how to use them. The memo should set the expectation that you (or the company) won't act on every request, but that you're interested in looking at patterns or learning something new. Asking employees to help brainstorm a new or different way to address recurring issues is a great way to broaden the ideas for a long-term resolution.

No matter which feedback loop you create, be sure to communicate to your employees how and when you'll respond. Even when a change you make is small or the question asked is minor, responding demonstrates that everyone has a chance to be part of a solution.

Whatever you do, if it's within your power, don't ask for opinions and then do nothing about them. Asking and then ignoring leads to employees who are no longer willing to tell you the truth. Your staff would much rather have you acknowledge the complaint and explain your reasons for not changing it than see you sweep the concern under the rug but keep asking whether there's anything you can do to make their working environment better.

Sticking to Business as Usual

In times of conflict and uncertainty, do what you can to keep the working environment running smoothly. Daily upheaval is both distracting and overwhelming so any time you have the opportunity to address issues and follow up with ways your staff can still feel good about their work, do it.

Motivating your employees

A major contributor to keeping the work going is accessing your team's motivation. If that motivation still exists, this task may be as simple as you reminding them what's important about what they do and helping them recapture why they come to work every day. Your team may need your help to see how their jobs contribute to the organization's mission, contribute to their own personal goals, or benefit the clientele.

If a conflict has destroyed or severely diminished your team members' core motivation, help them find another reason or goal to work toward. Coming up with other ways to motivate your team in an otherwise hopeless environment can be tricky, but start by being creative and working within your means. Ask yourself a few questions to get the brainstorming started:

- ✔ What has motivated your team in the past?
- ✔ Who might you call on for ideas?
- ✔ What is within your power to change or offer as a new motivation?

For example, if receiving commissions is the main motivation for a team of salespeople and the commission program getting axed has caused some angry reactions, find new ways to motivate them. I use that example because if you were to ask the salespeople what they want, they'd probably respond by saying, "We want our commission structure back." But you probably couldn't accommodate them because you don't have the power to undo what higher-ups have changed. In that case, you'd need to find something else that can calm the situation. Perhaps there isn't enough money in the budget for everyone to receive a bonus, but a quarterly contest with one or two winners may get folks back on track. Or reorganizing accounts so the reps get home by 5 p.m. every day may be the answer. Include the team in the realistic brainstorming session, but come up with a few ideas to get them started.

Keeping your team members focused on what they can control

Some conflicts can cause uncertainty in the actual work you and your team are trying to accomplish. Confusion in job responsibilities is not only unsettling to employees but also devastating to productivity and employee effectiveness. In these situations, provide as much structure as you can. Be clear about job tasks and work objectives, even if you can only speak to those things on a day-to-day basis. If you don't know what's going to happen tomorrow, at least encourage your employees to move forward on what they can do today. Specifically, prioritize projects that need attention and that you know will need to be completed regardless of the outcome of the conflict.

Consider breaking work into smaller increments to help employees see their contributions and feel a sense of success in an otherwise dreary setting. Set specific goals and benchmarks within a detailed plan for how and when those items will be completed. Having a plan will allow employees to stay more focused and feel less hopeless about the situation.

An employee may be not able to control her workload, but she can certainly make a choice about how much energy she's willing to invest in the ongoing problems. Share with your team the information I give in Chapter 19 concerning what you can control in a conflict.

Having regular work meetings

If your team is having a tough time focusing on the job at hand, consider frequent and brief meetings focused on work topics. Depending on the needs of your group, *frequent* could mean daily, biweekly, or weekly check-ins that keep everyone moving forward. A few staff members may grumble about the frequency, but if you explain their importance, they should come around.

Having more frequent, shorter meetings keeps the discussion task-focused and helps staff keep their attention on projects and deadlines. If members of your team aren't getting along, encouraging them to speak to each other in small increments about work topics begins to demonstrate their ability to communicate on some level and sets the stage for discussing the tough issues.

Building a Reputation as a Leader

How you handle yourself during a conflict speaks volumes and influences how you team will handle conflicts in the future. You're definitely leading by example, so model the behaviors you expect from your staff. I can't tell you everything you need to know about being a leader — that's a subject for a whole separate book (it's called *Leadership For Dummies,* by Marshall Loeb and Stephen Kindel [Wiley]) — but what I can tell you are a few core components of leadership that have worked for successful managers I know:

- **Be invested in the people.** Your team needs to know they can trust you and that you have their best interests in mind. As a manager, you can easily get a reputation that you're only beholden to the company, but what is a company without the people who work there? Show your employees respect and consideration, and they'll do the same for you.

- **Have a good track record (and I don't mean your time in the 100-yard dash).** Employees look up to managers who have been able to provide consistency in creating stable, positive, and productive work environments. Your ability to get things done motivates others to look to you for leadership. Quickly address the issues over which you have direct control. Showing your team that you're responsive to the small stuff sets the stage for when larger issues loom.

- **Show that you can provide support.** Employees in a conflict environment need someone they can turn to and trust. Show that you're able to provide support by listening and clearly capturing their concerns. Then let your team know that you're voicing their concerns to the right people in the appropriate venues.

- **Show up every day with confidence and optimism.** Coming to work with something good to say, in some cases, can mean the difference between loyalty and revolt! Have a physical presence — even if you're at a loss as to what to say to make an employee feel better. Sure, some days will challenge your resolve, but your employees need to know that it isn't all doom and gloom. Prepare yourself for difficult days by doing what you can to help yourself stay calm. If you're walking into a battlefield each day, find a way to center yourself before forging ahead. Showing up to work nervous and frazzled sends a message to your team that something's up and they need to worry.

- **Maintain trust.** Trust is a key ingredient in leadership. Your team won't look to you for advice or go along with your directives if they don't trust you. And because most people need to see a pattern of experiences and actions before they're willing to trust someone, it may take time to build a trusting relationship with your group. For starters, be consistent in your words and actions.

Setting unrealistic expectations leads to trouble, so be clear about your role in the situation. Are you a direct player that can influence the outcome? Or are you also waiting to see what answers will be handed down from the top? Don't overstate or understate your role in the problems. Instead, let your team know what is within your control and what you plan to do. Be honest with the team and you'll maintain their trust, even if you're not able to get them what they want.

✔ **Take care of yourself.** Simply put, being a leader isn't easy. Take some time to tap into a good support system and take care of yourself so you can take care of others. Make sure you have someone you can talk to and lean on. No one can handle the behaviors and emotions of a group in conflict alone, so don't be afraid to ask for help. Consider confiding in family, friends, a colleague, a mental health professional, or a spiritual leader. Confidential venting not only releases your emotions and frustrations, but also frees your mind to think creatively.

Be careful, though, when you're venting to make sure that you're not sharing with someone who'll only support your views and add fuel to the fire. Process your emotions with someone who can listen, be honest with his observations, and then help you look for creative options.

Do things you enjoy that give you renewed energy, and give those activities some priority in your life. Work takes a lot of your time and energy, but you need to make sure it doesn't consume your life. You and your team will benefit if you can focus on yourself once in a while.

Encouraging Team Building

Though misery loves company, asking employees to find positive ways to stay connected is a better use of your time than trying to fend off a mutiny. When stress is high because of a conflict, it's normal for a group to start to fracture. Efforts to build up the team can help. Plus, encouraging staff to support each other through the conflict takes some of the pressure off you to be everything to everyone.

Highlighting common interests and creating positive shared experiences

Team members build stronger bonds when they have common ground, through either shared interests or similar experiences. Two people can bond over simple things, like loving the same baseball team or finding out they're both the youngest in a family of five siblings. Anything that helps co-workers relate to one another is useful in team building, so use what you can to create shared experiences that may lessen the impact of problems in the future.

A good, proactive way to get employees to create and maintain relationships is to provide opportunities for them to interact on both professional and personal levels. Often the most successful team-building exercises involve everyone learning something new about themselves and their co-workers. Learning something new can shed a fresh light on how people view each other and, ultimately, how they interact with each other.

There are plenty of team-building exercises out there, and a quick Internet search will provide a long list of possibilities. As you're researching ideas, consider the personalities and characteristics of your team as a whole and pick something appropriate for them. If you have a team who loves physical activity and being outside, consider a ropes course or similar activities. If your group likes reading, maybe you start a book club. Or if your group likes movies or sports events, look for ways to incorporate those into a group activity. Be creative — nothing is worse than forcing your team to participate in an activity they hate. You don't want their dislike of the activity to be the only thing they have in common!

When planning team-building exercises, take into account that you probably have a variety of likes and dislikes on the team and make a few compromises to accommodate the group as a whole. A ropes course may not be the best idea for an employee who has a fear of heights, but you can arrange for her to cheer the rest of the group on and participate in the team-building exercises that take place on the ground.

I once participated in a tournament day with a team of golf fanatics with a little fear and trepidation because I knew that I had never picked up a club in my life. To my surprise, the manager had arranged for a handful of us to receive a lesson from the pro during the morning, and we joined up with the rest of the group at lunch. We all bonded over sharing what each group had done that day, and those of us who received a lesson had gained enough knowledge of the sport to participate in future water cooler discussions.

Lightening the mood

Even something as simple as a delicious snack in the break room can help people feel a little better about their day. (I know I'm a sucker for a gooey doughnut!) Spend a little time thinking about how you can create spontaneous opportunities for lighthearted conversations or activities.

If you have the opportunity to offer an activity during business hours, consider getting everyone out for a few hours for something like a brunch, lunch, or bowling excursion. A client once told me that the best thing his boss did during a stressful time was treat everyone to a movie in the middle of the afternoon. The team had a great time, went directly home from the theater, and came in the next day with a common topic to discuss that had nothing to do with the conflict they were facing. Whew!

Be careful about requesting off-hours time from your employees. Planning a group event like a weekend picnic or a night out can give the employees a non-work-related task to collaborate on, but it can also demonstrate how "management" has no clue about the demands they place on staff and their families.

Lightening the mood doesn't have to cost a thing. For example, some employees on a small team were trying to work through a conflict that was caused by changes outside the group. They were becoming increasingly uneasy on the job most days. The manager knew they shared an interest in card games, so he invited them to get together to play a few hands in the break room. The game had nothing to do with work, but it served as a great distraction and made for some friendly banter in an otherwise tension-filled day. After the initial game, people would spontaneously get the group together at lunch and play cards. It was the team's way of empowering themselves to stay connected during a stressful time and have a little fun, regardless of external issues.

Chapter 13

Determining How Your Company Can Help

*E*ven if you work in the smallest of companies, you may not be completely on your own when the inevitable conflict arises. Companies that recognize the cost of unresolved conflicts will offer various resources to help employees resolve issues early on. And those companies that haven't invested in large-scale conflict resolution strategies usually offer at least a few basic services.

This chapter takes a look at the most common conflict resolution resources, describes what each can and can't do, and helps you determine which option will best meet the needs of your current circumstance. It also looks at how you can help design a conflict resolution system for your organization — one that addresses current and future dispute resolution goals.

Working with Human Resources

The Human Resources (HR) department is a valuable resource to anyone in the organization. Most employees see HR as a compliance office — the place that makes sure everyone is following the rules and regulations. But that's not all HR does. It ensures that your company is implementing policies that protect the organization, helps managers realize the liability they carry through their actions, and sees to it that employees are meeting company expectations. HR receives a complaint, investigates the situation, and determines a course of action to protect everyone involved.

HR experts work hard at balancing efforts between employees, the company, and the law. Take advantage of their objective viewpoint when you need more information or want coaching on how to handle a problem.

Partnering with you to tailor your approach

In times of conflict, think of your HR department as a partner that can help you create an action plan. HR professionals know what conflicts can cost a company. Although HR staff members definitely have an eye on compliance, they often work beyond documentation to coach an employee through conflict and direct him toward resources that educate and reduce similar situations in the future.

After HR has taken any required steps to document a situation and protect the company, it can also

- ✔ **Provide an employee the opportunity to save face and build confidence.** No one likes to be reprimanded. Giving an employee the chance to share his perspective and ask for what he needs in the future helps that person feel better about the overall situation. Being a part of creating a solution builds confidence in the employee instead of being seen as a problem that needs to be "handled."

- ✔ **Provide insights into your management style.** HR can look at how you manage employees and help you identify your strengths and weaknesses — what is or isn't working. They can provide tips on working with staff in a manner that you may never have considered.

- ✔ **Help you manage your employee on an individual level.** You've probably found a management style that works for you and *most* of your employees. But no matter how foolproof your style is, you're bound to have an employee who isn't as comfortable with your approach. HR can help you tailor your approach to that individual to reduce conflict and help you get the most out of your employee.

Letting you know when action is required

Although you'll have many opportunities to use the skills in this book to resolve conflict, sometimes you shouldn't take action on your own. If you have any concerns that you or your company may be liable because of something you say or do, ask the HR department for help.

HR professionals can advise you when

✔ Sexual harassment complaints surface against you or another employee.

✔ You're concerned about any act that could be considered discrimination or you've received direct complaints of discrimination.

✔ You've received reports that an individual in the company has bullied another person or group of people.

✔ There's any indication, threat, or act of violence.

✔ You feel that there may be potential security threats.

If you're unsure whether a scenario should be presented to HR, err on the side of caution. HR offices often have access to in-house counsel or an employee relations attorney who can help guide you when situations are tricky.

Providing training resources

HR can be a wealth of knowledge when it comes to providing in-house training or arranging for contracts with outside professionals. Trainings can be arranged for everything from workplace safety to harassment prevention and from diversity awareness to conflict resolution skill building.

HR staff should be familiar with all the trainings offered through the company's EAP (see the later section "Identifying employee assistance program options"), so be sure to ask for a comprehensive list. They also have local HR support chapters that often offer free training as well. Ask them to research what's available and help you find the right training to meet the needs for your situation.

Accessing employees' work histories

The HR department has probably worked with most employees from the beginning of their careers with the company. They write job descriptions, interview potential candidates, and help hire the right person for the job. These folks protect the company by keeping detailed records on each employee, so if you're having difficulty with an employee, HR can help by looking into the employee's history to determine if this is a one-time incident or a behavior pattern. They should have a record of what strategies have been taken with the employee and can reference previous performance evaluations that include areas that the employee needs to improve, helping you determine your next course of action. For example, if tardiness has only been a problem for an employee recently, a quick chat and schedule adjustment prior to a major discipline action makes sense. But if you find that the employee has had many documented warnings about tardiness, a more formal approach with documented objectives and consequences may be the best course of action.

If you ask HR to look into an employee file, be sure to check for any information regarding special accommodations that he's legally entitled to.

A new manager shared a story with me about his first few months on the job in a lumber mill. He'd inherited a group of employees who were disgruntled with a co-worker who was taking longer lunches than the rest of the crew. When the manager called HR to talk about disciplinary actions, he learned that special accommodations had been made for the employee to receive treatment for a medical condition during his lunch break. The manager was relieved that he had decided to seek HR's advice. They saved him from embarrassing himself and the employee. Instead of recommending disciplinary action, HR was able to coach the manager regarding the medical condition and helped with language he could use with the other employees while still complying with the law.

Identifying employee assistance program options

Employee assistance programs (EAPs) are a great resource if you feel that outside stressors are contributing to workplace conflict. These programs are often underutilized and provide a confidential outlet in which to work through many situations that may be out of your control as an employee's manager. EAP benefits are a packaged resource available to all employees in an organization to help with various transitions or difficulties in life. Contact the person in your organization in charge of employee benefits to investigate EAP options; they may be a part of your health insurance plan or provided by an independent vendor or broker.

EAP resources vary depending on the package your organization has purchased, but they usually include free counseling sessions to help staff through a hard time. If an employee needs someone confidential to talk with, an EAP can match him with a professional who specializes in a particular area of difficulty, such as:

- ✔ Addiction issues
- ✔ Family care needs
- ✔ Legal referrals
- ✔ Relationship/family dynamics
- ✔ Mental health matters

Investigating Neutral Dispute Resolution Services

There's no one cookie-cutter standard for workplace dispute resolution options, so do a little investigating to see what's available in your company. All the services may be found in one central location, or you may have to check out different areas and departments for specific resources.

Talking openly and honestly about conflict resolution options helps your staff feel positive about the subject rather than feeling like the bad kids who have been sent to the principal's office for schoolyard fisticuffs. Familiarize yourself with what's available and how people can access it, so you can use the resources and encourage employees to access services on their own. Proactively presenting them to your team as valuable tools that you support encourages their use.

Mediation program

In a typical *mediation program,* the parties involved are assigned a mediator or they can choose a mediator they both agree on. The process is confidential and allows employees the opportunity to return with an agreement that they can share or keep to themselves.

If your company has a mediation program, it may be accessed through any number of avenues (such as HR, an EAP, or the ombudsman office), or it could be its own independent department. Generally, a mediation program has trained or certified mediators who can facilitate a discussion between you and another person, or you can refer employees to the service. If you prefer, you can take on the task of mediating a meeting between two employees (see Chapters 6 through 9) or an entire team (see Chapter 10).

Keep in mind that mediation is *not* a tool to use only when a problem escalates beyond what you can comfortably handle. Use it early on to prevent a problem from getting out of control.

I mediated a case referred to me by HR between an executive and a shift manager at a resort. Both people were nervous going into the process, but within a few minutes, the two were talking productively and they barely noticed I was in the room. Within 20 minutes, they realized that they had received different information from their employees and immediately committed to having regular meetings to communicate directly about the resort's business. Having early access to mediation allowed them to resolve the situation before their relationship broke down to the point of no return.

Shared neutrals program

A *shared neutrals program* is made up of various individuals in the company who have been trained as mediators. They're selected from different departments and have different levels of authority within the organization, with the goal of creating diversity in the group. Shared neutrals programs are more common in large corporations, universities, and government agencies, though the concept is catching on and is often implemented in other establishments that are open to applying a little creativity to conflicts.

Some organizations partner with a similar agency or business as a way to create an extra layer of confidentiality. These organizations contract with each other to share their trained neutrals. It's an effective way for a company to bring in mediators from another company who are unknown to its employees, allowing for anonymity in their facilitated discussions.

I know of a group of construction companies that have a shared neutrals program that provides experts in construction. Though I firmly believe that a skilled mediator can facilitate a workplace conflict regardless of her familiarity with a particular industry, it can sometimes be helpful to have a mediator from a shared neutrals program onboard who understands the jargon and the way industry-specific nuances may affect the situation.

Ombudsman

An *ombudsman* is a person who is trained in various conflict resolution techniques and who's available to everyone in your establishment as a confidential resource for resolving disputes at the lowest level possible. What does that mean? It means that if you or an employee needs a safe place to talk, vent, troubleshoot, or brainstorm any topic, an ombudsman can hear you out and help you choose the best path for you and your unique situation.

An ombudsman office is founded in confidentiality. In fact, it's often said that the greatest piece of equipment in an ombudsman office is the shredder! Unlike other company resources, an ombudsman isn't required to keep records of meetings or details. In fact, when you're concerned about sensitive topics, he can be a great sounding board to help you consider all your options and get you started on a plan of action.

The ombudsman will keep confidential the information you discuss with the office. Be aware, though, that certain scenarios are *not* protected. Threats of physical harm to oneself or others and any threats to property or possessions aren't protected by confidentiality and will be reported.

If you decide to talk to your ombudsman, know that you're always in control, so don't worry about the conversation getting away from you. An effective ombudsman shouldn't force you to take a particular path, and it's likely that merely having a discussion with him will make you, or any employee, feel better. If, however, you decide that more needs to be done, you can always return to the ombudsman later to get coaching on how to approach specific individuals or situations. You can also ask him to contact the other person so that the two of you can sit down together to discuss the problems you're having. Often just knowing that the situation won't be documented is enough for the other employee to be willing to come to the table and open up.

I knew an employee who was feeling sexually harassed by his supervisor. He was uncomfortable filing a formal complaint, so he chose to talk with the ombudsman before doing anything else. The ombudsman listened and helped him talk through all the options available, including filing a complaint with HR. After the conversation, the employee was armed with an awareness of all his options to resolve the matter and chose to tell his supervisor specifically what behavior needed to stop. The supervisor was temporarily embarrassed and apologized, but the issue didn't damage her career.

Tapping into Unions

Take the time to build a relationship with the union and its leadership, and you may find them to be a great resource in resolving conflicts early and cost-effectively. Talking to the organization about your mutual conflict resolution goals and brainstorming what you both can do to work toward those goals can benefit both sides.

Extending an offer to work together goes a long way in creating a strong working relationship that produces effective results.

Tap into the power of unions by

- ✔ **Identifying the conflict resolution framework:** During the *collaborative bargaining process,* employees organize together to negotiate their working conditions with their employer. Everything from salary to how disputes are resolved is on the bargaining table to be negotiated. Many management teams and unions develop mediation programs during this time as well as beyond collective bargaining agreements to allow an employee to request mediation as a means to resolving workplace issues.

- ✔ **Harnessing the strengths of the union:** Unions have hired staff that are experts in dispute resolution and are available to come to the workplace to help address issues or conduct trainings. Some even contract with outside experts for training and mediation to resolve disputes for their members. Typically, a union grievance procedure specifically refers to the use of mediation as an optional or mandatory step prior to labor arbitration. Ask the union in your workplace what resources they can contribute to address your particular situation.

If you're in the middle of a multiyear collective bargaining agreement, consider speaking to the union representative about drafting a side agreement or memo of understanding that outlines a workable dispute resolution process. See what steps you can take now, instead of waiting for regular contract negotiations to begin.

Proactively Designing a Conflict Resolution Plan

Conflict is inevitable, but it doesn't have to affect you negatively. Instead, look at conflict as an occasion to hear what's most important to others, so you can draw out ideas that strengthen your company, making it more resilient for the future and allowing it to be at its best today. It may be counterintuitive to see conflict as an opportunity rather than a problem, but think about it in terms of what you can do now and what you could do in the future to strategically place dispute resolution in a forward-focused business plan.

Designing a conflict resolution plan means giving several members of the organization the skills they need to resolve conflicts early, as well as providing a variety of avenues for them to seek support in resolving conflicts. The greater the number of alternatives, the more likely it is your people will be proactive in resolving their own conflicts. Having an array of options available allows people to choose a resource they're most comfortable with and increases the likelihood that they'll resolve conflict before it escalates.

What you can do

You may not be in a position to change the overall culture of your entire company, but you can change the culture of those who work directly for you and share your successes with those up the ladder. If you're not entirely comfortable requesting that the organization develop a formal conflict resolution plan but want to lead by example, you can consider taking the steps outlined in the following section.

Offering training

Providing training in conflict resolution helps employees become aware of the behaviors that affect others. It also gives them the skills to begin addressing those behaviors and conflicts on their own. Schedule trainings that start with communication basics, demonstrate active listening skills, identify conflict styles for each person, and teach how to approach a co-worker when conflict arises. Have the team receive the same training (together or at separate courses) so they have a common framework that everyone works from.

Cultivating inside mediators

Training a select number of employees as mediators can be a great way to supplement the company-wide training. Be sure to have a diverse group of mediators so that employees are able to choose someone they're comfortable with. If your work group is small, start with yourself and add others later.

Providing outside mediators and facilitators

Identify resources outside the company that provide conflict resolution services. Having an idea of where you can turn if a conflict escalates beyond your skill set is a smart, proactive move that keeps you from having to scramble in the heat of the moment. Plus, outside mediators provide another layer of confidentiality that's an important factor for most employees. (For more information on hiring a contracted mediator, see Chapter 14.)

Giving employees multiple ways to access resources

Be sure your employees know everything that's available to them (trained mediators, EAP, ombudsman, HR, and so on), so they can choose what's most comfortable. If they're limited to contacting only one person for help, they may be less apt to approach conflict from a solutions-oriented perspective.

I mediated a case in which a conflict had been going on for two years because the employee had a bad relationship with his union representative and wouldn't ask her for help! The employee called me on his own dime, and the conflict was resolved in a few weeks.

Make information available in multiple formats and locations so your staff doesn't have to spend hours searching through employee handbooks to find what they're looking for. The easier it is for an employee to access the resource, the more likely it is he'll use it.

Always leaving the door open

No matter how far a conflict escalates, always create an opportunity for parties to come back to the table to resolve it. Even if you're on the verge of a lawsuit, the climate may still be ripe for settling a case. Be open to any requests to settle while you still have some control over the outcome.

One company's plan for resolving conflict

Prior to being promoted to the top of her division, Lois was aware that a number of departments were struggling within the company. She had previous training as a mediator, so she knew she wanted to use her new position as a vehicle to create a culture of resolving conflicts early on.

Lois decided that the HR department would be a valuable partner. Her first step was to ask the HR director, Sydney, to go through basic mediation training so the two could have a common conflict resolution framework to work from. Together, they began listening to what was being said *behind* employees' words. They used their professional mediation skills to determine what employees valued, and they asked great questions to draw out employees' concerns.

Lois and Sydney developed an education program that included internal and contracted training sessions on topics such as communication styles, personality types, and conflict resolution. The courses provided insight into work styles and a foundation for everyone to work through disagreements before asking for assistance from upper management.

Although Lois and Sydney had been able to resolve most employee concerns internally, they realized there were still some situations that required additional assistance. On occasion, they called in professional mediators to help. HR would prepare the employees for the mediation process, helping the parties identify what was most valuable to them and to view the mediation as an opportunity to ask for what they wanted from their workplace, their co-workers, and their managers. The coaching helped employees view the mediation as a positive opportunity to be a part of the solution rather than a disciplinary action.

A variety of mediations were held, including one that helped the customer service department realize how easily voices travel in the common workspace and how the noise level affected everyone's ability to work effectively with customers. Another mediation helped move a long-term employee who was struggling in his current position to a job that better utilized his strengths, retaining a valuable employee and saving the company the cost of hiring and retraining a new staff member.

Beyond the specifics of particular cases, the proactive work Lois and Sydney did had the following results:

✔ Employees used language and techniques from the trainings and mediations when working through problems.

✔ Employees became more loyal because they knew they could be part of the solution.

✔ Employees brought ideas forward and respectfully used the chain of command to share ideas that reduced frustrations and had the potential to limit conflict in the future.

✔ Employees proactively resolved issues early on and tried more than one technique instead of complaining with no ideas for solutions.

The company is now committed to continuing its investment in resolving conflicts early on and has set aside money in the annual budget to cover mediation training for all its managers. HR has developed a strong conflict resolution policy and created a new employee handbook that includes all the options employees have available to them as they work through tough situations. By building on what they already had in place, Lois and Sydney effectively partnered to change the company's perspective on conflict — one resource at a time.

What your company can do

Having support from the top down is absolutely necessary for a successful conflict resolution plan to work, so consider who else in the organization would be interested in adding to and improving your existing resources. If you're currently in the middle of a conflict, now may not be the best time to take on a company-wide initiative, but if you're interested in working with like-minded people to build a system that creates opportunity out of conflict, consider the options covered in the following sections.

Expanding the role of HR

Spreading resources throughout the company is a strategic approach to conflict resolution. An HR department that's trained in conflict resolution (instead of simply stating policy or documenting issues) could provide added coaching and resources to employees facing difficulties. They can bridge the gap between a company that says it values conflict resolution tools and a company that actually uses resources through a well-written, and actionable, dispute resolution policy. Limiting the role of HR limits the possibilities.

Creating a peer review panel

When employees go through a formal grievance procedure to resolve a conflict, it can be costly on a number of levels. (Chapter 5 describes some of the hard and soft costs of conflict, as well as the cost of doing nothing.) One way to limit the damage is to set up a confidential peer review panel that allows an employee to appeal a company decision to a group of his associates. The panel reviews a decision and reports back in a hearing format whether it believes the company has made a fair and just decision. Hearing from one's peers that the decision was the right one reduces the likelihood that a person will continue to fight the outcome. Similarly, if the company is found in error, an opportunity for learning and adjusting is created.

Developing additional agreements with the union

Take a look at what currently exists and assess areas for improvement or expansion. Pay special attention to whether the agreement provides a viable conflict resolution plan.

Early detection of issues is a good thing.

Involve as many voices as possible to create a representative perspective. Having buy-in from the union membership early on allows you to avoid unnecessary surprises down the line. Use the union's strength to benefit all sides.

Research what conflict resolution initiatives have been created by comparable companies and their unions. Oftentimes, a union will turn out to be an excellent resource in knowing what's working in other companies; it may have access to the union locals' conflict resolution contract language.

Finally, joint labor-management conflict resolution trainings can go a long way in assuring that both sides are speaking the same language when working through conflict. Plus, they can keep the costs low by sharing expenses.

Revising the employee handbook

Employee handbooks typically have a dispute resolution section. If yours only has a few steps before you're required to document behaviors in an employee's file, you're possibly setting up employees to fail from the get-go. Emotions that may have been manageable with a different method can spiral out of control when permanent records are involved, so find ways to include steps and language that give employees a chance to make things right.

Choosing a starting point

Creating your own company-wide plan for resolving conflict can seem overwhelming and expensive. But you don't have to spend a ton of money all at once to reap the benefits of creating an organizational culture that resolves conflict early on — there's more than one approach for getting it right. So be open-minded while you figure out what's best for your company. Here are some things to consider as you get started:

- ✔ **Determine what conflict is costing the company by checking out the line items in Chapter 5.** Having an idea of what you're currently spending on conflict (or what you're spending by ignoring conflict) helps make a case for setting aside money to build a conflict resolution plan. What executive doesn't understand return on investment? So approach any budget requests from that perspective.

- ✔ **Look at some of the ideas in the sections "What you can do" and "What your company can do," earlier in this chapter, to assess what you're doing well and where you can improve.** Some of the suggestions cost very little to get started, such as peer panels and modifying existing training seminars.

- ✔ **Identify key players in your organization.** Who else may be interested in resolving conflict early on? Are there others who are already trained as mediators? Ask your HR department what skills they use in resolving conflict before it escalates. Keep sharing resources and include as many people from different areas to build on what exists. Work with the union to see how mediation can expand beyond the current processes.

✔ **Research what resources are available in your community.** Is there a dispute resolution center or community mediation center you can access? Most centers are nonprofit and use highly trained mediators to resolve a variety of issues including workplace disputes at a relatively low cost.

✔ **Start small and track your success.** It's okay if your company is only able to afford to train one person in conflict resolution or the budget only allows for a one-day training for middle managers. However you start, track any noticeable changes as a way to show tangible results when you go to bat for more dollars. Keep track of whether

- Managers are dealing with complaints better.

- Employees are having fewer conflicts.

- Complaints made to HR and/or the union are decreasing.

- Employee turnover, use of sick leave, and tardiness are declining.

✔ **Commit enough money to support your plan for conflict resolution.** Earmarking even a small amount of money each budget cycle to strengthen conflict resolution can provide a solid return on investment.

Chapter 14

Getting Outside Experts to Facilitate Resolutions

. . . .

In This Chapter

▶ Deciding when a professional is needed

▶ Reviewing available services

▶ Hiring the right person for the job

. . . .

*T*wo or more of your employees are in a conflict and you know an intervention is needed. You may be thinking about stepping in and trying to use the processes outlined in Chapters 6 through 10, or maybe you're looking into the company's internal resources like those in Chapter 13. Or perhaps the option of bringing in a professional conflict resolution specialist is more in line with your needs, especially if you've tried other options and they're just not working.

As you think about the conflict and the needs of your employees, gather as much information as possible to make the best decision for you, your team, and the company.

This chapter provides you with information you need when hiring a conflict resolution consultant. I give you tips on how other managers decide when a professional is needed, lay out criteria to help you zero in on which service best meets your goal, and tell you how to find the right person for the job.

Why Managers Do or Don't Call in Help

Making the decision to call in help can be a slippery slope. Unfortunately, there are no hard-and-fast rules to tell you definitively that, yes, a professional is needed, or no, you can handle this situation yourself. This section helps you research your options, weigh the pros and cons, and consider the best next steps.

I recommend that managers in the process of making these decisions consider their own skill level, the severity of the conflict, the impact of a prolonged conflict, and the benefits and drawbacks to calling in a particular type of professional. In my experience, when managers are on the fence about whether to call someone in, I hear common reasons for hesitation as well as common reasons that ultimately push them into picking up the phone.

Common reasons for delay

Organizations often delay calling in help because they're hesitant to allocate the money. Trainers, mediators, coaches, and consultants usually don't work for free, but don't let the cost dissuade you from considering outside help. You won't know how much an expert costs until you do the research, and you may be surprised by what you find.

If you're personally uncertain about spending the money, or if you need a solid argument to get accounting or upper management to authorize the expenditure, refer to Chapter 5 to assess the cost of doing nothing. The hard and soft costs associated with unresolved conflict can make a convincing argument for even the most fiscally conservative CFO.

Financial analysis aside, you may be hesitating to call in professional help because

- ✔ **You're worried that there's a stigma attached to asking for help.** You want to believe — and, maybe more important, you want to show — that you can handle anything that comes your way. Reputation is important in business as well as in life, and the fear of how others will perceive the situation could lead you to hesitate in taking the next step. By calling in the right person, though, you have the opportunity to build on your reputation as a capable leader.

- ✔ **The idea of hiring a professional is overwhelming or intimidating.** If you've never worked with a conflict resolution specialist before, the uncertainty associated with an unknown service may be daunting. The right person can calm your concerns, as can the rest of this chapter! (The section "Hiring an Expert and Knowing What to Expect" later in this chapter guides you through the process.)

- ✔ **You're holding out hope that the conflict will work itself out if you give it just one more day or another week.** If you're willing to give it a little more time, that's okay. Keep in mind, though, that problems between a few co-workers often affect other employees and can lead to a larger conflict.

✔ **Emotionally, you feel you're giving the troublemakers too much attention, which is what you think they want.** You may see calling in an expert as giving in to bad behavior. What appears to be giving in, though, can be a very strategic move on your part. Working with experts gives you the opportunity to set clear expectations for future behaviors and consequences.

✔ **You just want to fire the culprit.** Starting the formal process of firing an employee may feel easier than giving her one more chance to correct the behavior or trying a different angle. The option of letting the person go is always there, but documenting your efforts to resolve the situation first is rarely a bad idea.

Common reasons experts are called

Each workplace conflict has a number of unique variables that move even the most adept managers to call for help. Some conflicts are easily handled, and others, well, are not so easy. You may want to call in a professional to manage the resolution because

✔ **You've assessed the conflict and it's beyond your abilities.** There's no shame in acknowledging that you're not the right person for the situation; in fact, doing so shows that you're being thoughtful and cautious about the conflict.

✔ **You've tried everything else you can think of, and nothing has produced the desired effect.** Giving it one more try by providing a fresh perspective may be what's needed to calm the situation or to move an employee from his fixed position.

✔ **You want the employees to know that you're serious.** Bringing in a professional can send a message to your staff: You want them to make a change and do things differently, and you're willing to put your money where your mouth is. If you're clearly invested in the process, employees often follow suit and invest in the outcome.

✔ **You can't guarantee neutrality, impartiality, or confidentiality.** Mediating a case in which one of the employees could accuse you of favoritism is a potentially destructive way to spend a few hours. And if the circumstances of the conflict are such that you're not certain you can guarantee personal confidentiality, don't risk your reputation or the trust of your employees by trying to tackle the situation on your own.

✔ **You want to create a personal or professional boundary.** You may not *want* to handle every dispute and disagreement in the office! Create some space by allowing someone else to help out once in a while.

✔ **You believe your employees will be more receptive if they hear the message from a different messenger.** Hearing someone else's voice and learning from someone new may provide a needed breakthrough.

✔ **You anticipate that a disciplinary action will be necessary, and you want to show you've done everything you can.** By bringing in a professional, you make a clear statement to the employee that a change is required. If a change isn't achieved, you can follow up with punitive action.

✔ **You want to be a part of the process, but not as the mediator.** There are times when being a participant alongside your employees in a mediation, training, or group facilitation produces promising results. Taking a supportive role in conflict can create a new dynamic and an atmosphere of team building and problem solving that can last long after the mediation session has ended.

Whether the decision to hire a conflict resolution expert is yours to make alone or you need authorization from someone higher up, be sure you're giving it thoughtful and thorough consideration. Then when you approach your supervisor or Human Resources professional regarding your decision you'll be fully prepared to answer questions. Include a summary of the current situation, how you've already tried to remedy the problem, what (if anything) has been successful, and why a professional is the right choice now.

Considering the Menu of Professional Services

You can use a variety of professional services to solve conflicts. Often these services are referred to as *alternative dispute resolution* (ADR) because they can be used as alternatives to the standard avenue of litigation to resolve conflicts. Each service has benefits and limitations, and you may want to consider using the services on their own or in tandem with each other.

A key element in choosing the right ADR process or combination of services is understanding fully what your conflict resolution goals are — both short term and long term. Short-term goals are more specific to your immediate needs — for example, getting Kathleen and José to stop yelling at each other, or getting Chris to reduce his absenteeism are two immediate short-term goals. Your long-term goals speak to broader ideas like developing respectful communication methods, maintaining a productive work environment, and building team morale.

Customize a plan that meets your specific goals. Carefully assess the situation so that the appropriate services are scheduled with the right people at the right time. Employees will get frustrated if you schedule everyone for a large group facilitation when all you really need to do is have a one-on-one conversation with a single employee. Mediation or conflict specialists can work with you to formulate a comprehensive plan or review yours with you.

Training

One of the most proactive steps you can take as a manager is to make use of conflict resolution trainings for yourself and for your staff. Look for existing trainings to send one or more of your employees to, or look for a trainer who can customize a course specifically for your needs.

Common training topics include but certainly aren't limited to

- ✔ Improving communication skills
- ✔ Working with different personality styles
- ✔ Holding successful one-on-one conflict conversations
- ✔ Holding successful group meetings
- ✔ Dealing with angry co-workers or clients
- ✔ Managing workplace violence

Whenever possible, I recommend that a company invest in training a number of employees at one time to promote a common experience that team members can refer to when they need it.

The benefits of professional training include the following:

- ✔ It builds employee skills.
- ✔ It shows employees that you're invested in learning.
- ✔ It can be a team-building experience.
- ✔ It creates a common language or process to work from.
- ✔ It can help staff see conflict as an opportunity for positive change.
- ✔ It reduces future conflicts.
- ✔ It fits well when coupled with other services.
- ✔ It encourages early problem solving.

Professional training can have drawbacks, however. Some of the more common ones include the following:

- ✔ It takes people away from tasks during work hours.
- ✔ It doesn't usually address a specific, ongoing conflict.

✔ The employee(s) may feel punished for having to attend.

✔ There's no guarantee that an employee will be open to learning new skills.

An employee told me she once sat through all three days of a workplace communications training with her headphones on, avoiding eye contact with the instructors. When I asked what her motivation was for the behavior, she replied that her boss "could make her go to the training but he couldn't make her learn anything."

When negotiating costs with a trainer, remember to ask for a group discount. Costs per student/per day average about $100 to $200; however, a trainer will often consider reducing the rates depending on such variables as the number of students, length of training, and number of trainings she'll be providing for your organization. And remember to ask about travel and per diem costs, too.

Conflict coaching

Bringing in a professional to work one-on-one with individual employees can have a huge impact on the reduction of conflict and tension in the office. *Conflict coaching,* which involves an employee meeting with a conflict coach or mediator, allows the person a chance to work through a particular conflict in a productive manner. Coaching helps her gain a better understanding of the situation and her role in the conflict, as well as the encouragement to brainstorm or consider different courses of action. This approach is also useful in helping the employee learn and test out new ways of reacting and interacting with her co-workers.

Coaching can be used on its own or in combination with training, mediation, or group facilitation. (For examples of how and when you, as a manager, may coach an employee, see Chapter 11.)

Here are some benefits of hiring someone to conduct conflict coaching:

✔ It allows for in-depth one-on-one interactions.

✔ It provides a safe way to address sensitive behavior problems.

✔ It lets the employee practice and rehearse what she may say or do.

✔ It allows the employee time to work through the conflict before addressing (or readdressing) the other person involved.

✔ It helps the employee consider the best and worst alternatives if the problem goes unresolved.

Possible drawbacks to conflict coaching include the following:

- ✔ It can be time consuming and costly if multiple employees need multiple sessions.
- ✔ It may create dependency issues, in which an employee relies solely on the coach for support and decision-making.
- ✔ It's not a substitute for counseling.

Conflict coaches shouldn't be hired to help an employee process intense emotions or address mental health issues. It is, however, a good idea to use a conflict coach in conjunction with mediation and group facilitation. When you have a conflict between a few employees, a conflict coach can work with the employees individually both before and after mediations to create and maintain cooperation.

Because conflict coaching is often paired with mediation and a mediator may provide both services, consider negotiating both when you're hiring an expert. Coaches may offer their services on a per-session or per-hour basis.

Mediation

Mediation is an ever-evolving field of practice in which two or more people in a dispute sit down with an impartial facilitator to discuss a conflict and brainstorm mutually agreeable solutions. Chapters 6 through 9 give a thorough explanation of what the mediation process includes and how to go about conducting a mediation if you're interested in tackling it yourself.

No one wants to see a dispute mutate into a three-headed, fire-breathing beast, so addressing and resolving a conflict early with a mediator can save you and the company a lot of pain, suffering, and money down the line. Here are some other benefits to using outside mediation:

- ✔ **It provides you with an experienced professional who has received specific training in effectively analyzing and resolving conflicts.** Hiring experts who can keep an employee engaged in the process while they peel back the layers of a conflict can be invaluable in helping you find resolution. And experts can act as sounding boards or give you a reality check when you may be too close to the forest to see the trees.
- ✔ **It frees up staff time that otherwise would be spent dealing with the conflict.** You may be better served by putting your energies into what you do best and letting a mediator manage a conflict on your behalf.

✓ **It allows for an additional layer of neutrality and confidentiality for you and your employees.** Mediation is an open forum that allows employees to discuss and problem-solve any issues or concerns they have. It's often easier for employees to discuss and problem-solve when they have a neutral third party in the room to help facilitate the conversation.

Here are some drawbacks to using outside mediation:

✓ **It's not always an instant solution.** Mediation can take a few days to set up; you need to contact the mediator, clear employee schedules, and find a two- to four-hour block of time in which everyone can sit down free from distractions and interruptions. The conflict may continue to brew as calendar issues are worked out.

✓ **It doesn't work as well with larger groups.** Mediations work best if you have fewer than six to ten people. More than ten significantly increases the length of the mediation while decreasing the amount of time each person has to speak and contribute. For groups of ten or more, facilitation is a better option. (See Chapter 10 for information on how to adapt mediation process for a large group.)

Styles of mediation

Not all mediators follow the same process or use the same mediation model. Some professionals adopt a style of mediation that blends different models, while other mediators see their style as "pure." Each mediator also has a distinct combination of instincts, training, and experiences, and this combination influences the way he approaches each case. When you provide the mediator with information about your specific situation, he should be able to tell you if his mediation style is right for you and how he'll apply his expertise to your case.

Here are common mediation models:

✓ **Evaluative:** The evaluative model presupposes that the parties want or need an evaluation of their situation from the mediator in order to solve the problem. Evaluative mediators provide more directed assistance by giving their opinions, assessing the strengths and weaknesses of each position, and suggesting outcomes for settlement. In most cases, the mediator has experience or training in a specific field — law, real estate, labor bargaining, and so on — and reaching a settlement is the goal.

✓ **Facilitative:** The facilitative model contends that the people in the dispute are the ones who can find the most durable and satisfying solutions to the conflict. The clients know their situations better than the mediator does, and they know what solutions would be satisfactory. The mediator doesn't make suggestions on how the issue should be resolved; instead, he focuses on uncovering what's beneath the surface issues, creating better communication between the parties, and helping them brainstorm solutions. The goals of this style are to clarify the issues, enhance communication, and assist the parties in resolution.

✔ **Transformative:** Mediators using the transformative style are likely to delve into the clients' behaviors in the hopes of creating a sustainable change. This model focuses more on the interactions and communication between the parties than on the settlement of the issues. It seeks the empowerment and mutual recognition of the parties involved, rather than resolution of the immediate problem.

✔ **Narrative:** The narrative style lets the participants tell their stories and share their perspectives. There's no one truth to be uncovered or judgment to be made about who's right or who's wrong. In sharing and discussing the stories, the mediator works to find the source of the conflict and helps the clients create a mutually acceptable "alternate" story. Improved communication and mutual understanding are the goals.

Variations on mediation structure

Along with mediation styles, mediation meetings can be structured in a variety of ways. Here are some structures to consider:

✔ **Co-mediation:** As the saying goes, two heads are better than one! In a co-mediation situation, two mediators work in tandem to avoid any appearance of bias, favoritism, or partisanship. They model good communication and create a neutral environment.

✔ **Shuttle mediation:** The structure of a shuttle mediation allows the clients to remain separate from each other for the majority of the meeting. Shuttle mediations are more common in family law or civil cases, but they can be used in workplace situations where the conflict is so intense that the employees can't or won't sit in the same room.

I try to avoid using a shuttle mediation style because keeping employees separated greatly reduces the possibility of rebuilding working relationships. Shuttle mediations also require more time and resources, and the risk of miscommunication is higher.

Group facilitation

Facilitation is a process used with larger groups of employees, usually when the whole team is affected by an event or conflict. The meetings are an opportunity to bring everyone together and address the problems. They allow everyone the chance to define issues, share information, and brainstorm.

The structure of the facilitation and the methods used by the facilitator will vary depending on the professional's experience, his process, and the kind of conflict you need addressed. It could include one or more large-group meetings or a combination of large- and small-group meetings. (You can find specific details about facilitation, as well as guidelines for holding a large group facilitation, in Chapter 10.)

The benefits of handling a conflict or potential conflict in this manner include the following:

- ✔ It provides you with experts who are trained to handle high conflict and volatile group dynamics.
- ✔ It gives you the opportunity to focus your time on co-developing a strategy for the meeting but leaves the details and groundwork for the facilitator to manage.
- ✔ It frees up the team to brainstorm with someone who isn't invested in the day-to-day aspects of the organization.
- ✔ It provides an avenue to gather a more accurate view of the situation. Information can be gathered and reported by neutral, objective experts who have no stake in the outcome.

Here are some drawbacks to hiring group facilitators:

- ✔ Employees who don't like speaking up in front of groups may feel even more uncomfortable with contractors they view as outsiders.
- ✔ Some employees may take advantage of the "substitute teacher" syndrome and choose not to engage.
- ✔ A hired professional doesn't know the individual personality quirks of your group and may require extra time on your part to get up to speed.
- ✔ The facilitators may hold strictly to a group model, which eliminates the opportunity to address a particular participant's concerns or problematic behaviors.

Going to Arbitration

Arbitration is a more formal ADR mechanism, most commonly used if an employee is in dispute with the company rather than with a colleague. The arbitration process can be voluntary (where an employee and employer consensually agree to participate) or mandatory (if there's a contract or other preestablished arrangement requiring it).

An arbitrator is a neutral third party who operates more like a judge than a facilitator. In arbitration, all participants in a dispute sit down with the arbitrator and each side has the opportunity to present its case. This system is very similar to trials in a courtroom but generally with less adherence to rules of civil procedure. The arbitrator then makes a decision, which may or may not be legally binding for both sides, depending on the terms of the contract that brought the case to arbitration or the terms that the parties agreed to.

Nonbinding arbitration, on the surface, looks similar to evaluative mediation (refer to the earlier section "Styles of mediation" for an explanation). The principle distinction, however, is that an arbitrator will give a determination of liability and a summary opinion on the amount of damages after he's heard evidence from both sides; mediators don't do that.

Many companies use an arbitration system as one step in a multi-step dispute resolution program. Typically, arbitration comes into play after mediation was unsuccessful in settling an employee's claim or grievance. If you work for a company that has a union, you may already have a multi-step dispute resolution program or grievance procedure in your collective bargaining agreement. Binding arbitration is commonly used as the final step in deciding grievance issues; in many states, it's used to make final decisions when labor and management are unable to come to an agreement on their overall collective bargaining contract negotiations.

Arbitration is used over litigation for a variety of reasons:

- ✔ It's significantly less expensive than a formal legal process.
- ✔ It's a relatively speedy process.
- ✔ It's usually confidential, with no public records and no public hearings.
- ✔ It's more informal than court. The more laid-back nature of the process can be a real advantage, especially when an employer is trying to preserve a relationship with an employee.
- ✔ When arbitration is binding, it provides a final solution. Generally, there's no process in which a party can appeal a decision made in binding arbitration.

Like any conflict resolution process, arbitration has its drawbacks. They include the following:

- ✔ When used as a first step, you miss many opportunities to resolve the dispute informally.
- ✔ You lose all decision-making authority, and you could end up with a decision that no one likes or a compromise with two "partial winners."
- ✔ Decisions are final in binding arbitration, and the loser can't appeal.
- ✔ It enforces the belief that others have better answers than the parties do.

Hiring an Expert and Knowing What to Expect

Finding the right expert requires research and planning on your part. Jot down some notes regarding the conflict and what some of your expectations are for a professional. Then as you walk through the process I outline in this section, use your notes as a reference to help you stay on track and find the right person for your unique situation.

Starting with referrals

You can get referrals for outside help from the staff in your HR department who may be members of the Society for Human Resource Management (SHRM) and who often receive information and updates on conflict resolution experts in your area. HR should also be able to tell you if your company already has a mediation benefit through its employee assistance program (for more information about how HR can help resolve conflicts, see Chapter 13).

Other options for referrals are professional associations such as the Alternative Dispute Resolution section of the American Bar Association, dispute resolution centers that are often tied to nonprofit or community resource organizations, professional mediation associations (like the Washington Mediation Association, which keeps a directory you can sort by location, area of expertise, and range of services), and any colleagues you know who may have been down a similar road.

Don't forget to check out the Yellow Pages for local, county, and state dispute resolutions centers that may be court-funded, or tap into the Better Business Bureau and Chamber of Commerce. In the Yellow Pages you may find mediators listed under "legal services," "conflict resolution," "mediation," or "dispute resolution." On the Internet, a search using those phrases and the city in which you work should render a list of possibilities.

Determining qualifications

When you're calling experts, look for certain qualifications and ask some key questions. Conflict resolution professionals operate under a variety of titles — mediator, facilitator, coach, trainer, or consultant — but for the sake of consistency, in this section I'll call them experts.

When contacting experts, provide a general overview of the situation you're experiencing and what outcomes you're looking for. You may have an idea of the service(s) you want, but if you keep it open and tell the expert your goals, he may surprise you with options you haven't considered.

Ask all candidates the following questions:

✔ **What's your experience in the field of conflict resolution?** Pertinent experience can include how and where he was trained, what kind of work he's done, and how long he's been in the field. Ask for any certifications, degrees, or professional memberships he holds.

In my area, a rigorous and lengthy training through a dispute resolution center is available for certification, and not everyone who applies makes it through. In other areas, the criteria may not be as stringent but could require membership in a mediation association. I know competent mediators who aren't certified but hold degrees in law or psychology or are HR professionals. The requirements for certifications and licenses vary from region to region.

✔ **Do you feel that this situation requires a particular set of skills or knowledge?** Discuss his comfort level with your situation and allow him the space to decline. I know mediators who really enjoy working with civil court conflicts but are the first to admit that they don't have the emotional fortitude to mediate family cases. Not every mediator is a fit for every conflict, nor will every expert be a fit for your unique case.

✔ **When and how will you provide me with a statement of work?** Whoever you hire needs to be on the same page with you regarding what work will be done. Ask him to include start and end dates for the services, as well as an agreement regarding fees (including charges for travel time, preparatory work, and expenses).

✔ **Do you offer follow-up services?** Some experts will provide follow-up meetings with you or a summary of work that was completed. This summary could include

- **Surveys completed by the participants:** Though a mediation meeting between two or a few employees is confidential, most experts offer the participants an opportunity to provide feedback about the mediator and the process, which the expert will make available to you in a form that maintains participant anonymity.

- **A summary of issues identified and work completed:** One of the outcomes you can contract for is a compilation of feedback and concerns gathered from a group facilitation process. The collection may or may not include such insight as prioritizing issues, identifying patterns, and interpreting data.

- **Recommendations for future services:** After developing an understanding of the overall problem, an expert may be able to develop a conflict resolution plan for you that's customized to the current situation and/or take into account future needs.

 Ask for references, but understand that due to confidentiality, an expert may not be able to give you contact information for current clients. He could, however, provide testimonials. He also may be able to refer you to a colleague or third party who can verify his experience and quality of work.

Contracting with a professional

The agreement you make with an external expert can vary from a letter of intent to a statement of work to a formal contract. How you proceed will depend on the professional's standard practice and how prepared he is to match your needs. Each person or organization you consider will be different depending on how prevalent these types of services are in your area; the going rate for such work; and the details of your circumstance, such as the intensity of conflict, the number of individuals involved, and the length of time needed. However, the mediators I know generally offer a small menu of services and charge by the hour, or a package deal that includes their travel time, pre-meeting work, and half-day or full-day mediation sessions. The rates where I live can range from $100 to $300 per hour and about $1,500 to $2,000 for a day package. The professionals also provide draft contracts or agreements for potential clients to review.

Talk with a few conflict resolution specialists to determine the going rate in your area before you start negotiating. When hiring a professional on a long-term basis — for example, a year-long contract — you can negotiate a yearly fee with unlimited services or a per-session, per-service rate. For instance, a large group facilitation expert may charge a corporation on a per employee/per-month basis and offer unlimited conflict resolution services to that company and its employees. Other experts may work on a per-service basis and offer discounts for multiple sessions over a specific period of time.

Understanding the process for intake and gathering information

After you decide which expert will help address your conflict, he'll complete an intake process with you and then conduct another intake process with the participants. Some experts require a significant amount of information beforehand, and others gather only a brief statement from each party because they prefer having the employees hear each other's perspective in a face-to-face meeting.

My preference is somewhere in the middle: I like to have just enough information to know what I'm getting into but not so much that I start making assumptions before I've even had a chance to meet the parties. People often tell me things over the phone that they won't say when they're in the middle of a mediation, or I discover that my initial understanding of the situation is radically different from what's revealed during the meeting.

The intake process with you

The expert will want to know the details of the conflict: who's involved, what you've already tried, and any special requirements you have (such as the desire for agreements to be in writing, that staff participation is mandatory, or that certain behaviors must be addressed by an employee). You can also expect an expert to provide you with a detailed plan of action and talk with you regarding your participation in the process. Are you passing this off and don't need to be contacted until the expert is finished? Do you want to be informed every step of the way? Or maybe you prefer occasional updates throughout the process.

As the initial go-between for the expert and employees, make sure you provide accurate information to everyone so they have the same expectations.

Don't be like the manager who was trying to repair his damaged reputation that he caused by telling his team they were attending a sales skills training when, in fact, they were meeting with a conflict coach to work through problem behaviors. This switcheroo infuriated the employees and made the coaching sessions nearly impossible.

The expert should ask you for the contact information of each participant for the purposes of intake only. Don't let the news of his involvement come as a surprise, though. Let each employee know that an expert will be calling him to have a discussion. As the manager, you're the go-between until the expert contacts the employees directly, so be upfront and honest about what will take place and how it will benefit each person. Say something like, "We've hired an expert to help us with the current situation. He'll be calling you tomorrow to hear what's been going on with you, and I think this is going to be a good opportunity for some creative thinking and a way to find solutions that work for everyone. After you talk to him, he'll schedule a confidential meeting between you and Lee."

The intake process with employees

Often, the person doing the intake and performing the conflict resolution service are the same person. However, sometimes a third party — someone who's schooled in intake or conciliation — will make the initial phone calls or conduct the initial interviews, as well as complete paperwork and keep a confidential file in which the case status is documented.

Because the conciliator is the first line of communication with an employee who's upset, confused, or distressed, the intake specialist should be trained to gently, but effectively, make the disputant feel comfortable about moving forward in the conflict resolution process. Getting a phone call from a complete stranger (planned or not) can be jarring and unsettling.

During intake calls, I have a handful of questions I use for everyone, such as asking what the employee has tried to date, who he thinks needs to be involved in the discussion, and what his perception is of the situation in general. If appropriate, I also use the time to coach him on how he could present some of his concerns (including language choice and tone of voice). The last question I ask usually focuses on something positive, such as asking him to share what *is* working (or has worked) in the relationship, or what the employee enjoys about his job.

Generally, an intake call to an employee goes something like this:

1. **A specific time is set for the intake expert to make the call.**

   The employee should be in a private place where she can speak freely and uninterrupted.

2. **The expert introduces himself and states who has asked him to call, states the purpose of the call, and asks for a few confidential minutes to talk.**

3. **The expert asks the employee to briefly share her perspective about the conflict, and the expert takes notes while reflecting back what he's heard.**

   Questions in this phase may include what the employee has already tried and who she may believe is involved.

4. **The expert asks clarifying questions and asks if the employee has any concerns about meeting.**

   If the employee has concerns, the two brainstorm about how her anxiety may be mitigated.

5. **The expert goes over the mediation process; states the date, time, and location; and then outlines what the employee can expect to happen that day before he ends the call.**

6. **The process is repeated for all participants.**

If a group facilitation is planned, the initial employee contact may be in the form of an introductory letter that outlines the expert's background, qualifications, and scope of work. It should include the purpose of the meeting and outline any requirements for participation. Often, a brief survey will accompany the letter with clear directions on completing the questionnaire, as well as contact information in case the recipient has any questions. If appropriate, the introductory document speaks to any confidentiality instructions and lets the reader know who will be attending.

Part IV
Smoothly Handling Conflict When You're One of the People Involved

The 5th Wave   By Rich Tennant

"You're not going to go into one of your nit-picking, hotheaded, blowgun-hating rants, are you?"

In this part . . .

No one likes to be in hot water. In this part I take you through a one-on-one process for resolving conflict with co-workers and colleagues (psst, it works at home, too!). I also tell you how to tailor your approach to match your audience, from boss to co-worker to subordinate, using techniques that can turn a difficult conversation into a successful one.

Chapter 15

Identifying What Both Sides Want

....

In This Chapter
▶ Taking a close look at what you really want
▶ Considering the other person in the conflict
▶ Using a worksheet to build an action plan

....

You find yourself in a conflict that takes up way too much of your energy. People are starting to talk, the conflict is affecting work, and when you think about your long-term career goals, you know that maintaining the bad feelings and tension isn't a good idea, regardless of the other person's position in the company.

Whether you're a manager, team member, or the head of an entire department, as a party to a current conflict, you may not know what to do. Perhaps you've tried a few tactics that you thought would fix the problem, like going over the other person's head, addressing the issue directly, or ignoring the conflict altogether. Yet the problem remains unresolved. You're now at a point where you want this whole thing behind you, and you need a plan.

But, if your plan involves living out a daydream in which you publically crush your opponent while Queen's rock anthem "We Are the Champions" blasts in the background, this chapter isn't for you. If, instead, you want to develop a strategy that uses a highly successful approach, read on. The information in this chapter helps you gain a better understanding of the real issues in the conflict and build a winning strategy to address the situation at hand, as well as conflicts in the future.

Asking Yourself What You Really Want

When thinking about addressing a conflict, ask yourself, "What's motivating me to have this conversation?" If resolution is your goal, next ask, "Am I emotionally and mentally ready to meet and talk with the other person?" If you're so angry that you can't stand to look at him, be real with yourself and don't schedule a discussion in the next five minutes.

Before you create a list of issues you want the other person to address, take a hard look at yourself and your motivation for staying in the conflict. When you figure out what you value and what you want to achieve from a meeting, you can shift your thinking to reflect on how you truly feel about the problem, and you may be surprised to find that the other person's past behavior affects you less. When you focus on what can be rather than what has been, you can think more creatively about solutions that meet your values.

In addition to helping you discover your values, the following sections help you identify your hot buttons, effectively listen to others, be humble, ask others for help, and recognize your strengths. Doing a little pre-meeting work in these areas helps you have a productive conversation when you do finally meet with the other person.

Figuring out your core values

Be aware: What you *think* you want and what you *really* want likely aren't the same — and to figure out the difference, you need to get in touch with your values. So, what are these values? Sometimes they're called interests or motivators, but basically, your *core values* drive you and influence the way you think and respond to different situations.

People often describe what they want as an action or an outcome instead of the larger value that inspires that desire. For example, if someone asks you what you want out of your retirement, you may respond that you want a million dollars in the bank. If you consider what that money allows you to do in retirement, you're getting closer to understanding values. You want to travel (freedom), you want a cottage on the beach (peace and quiet), and you want to care for your family (security). This example demonstrates how looking at desired outcomes helps you discover the underlying values you find most important. Applying this process to a conflict allows you to state clearly what you want from the other person and work toward doing the same for him. Don't assume he knows what you're looking for — he can't know which values you find most important if you've only just found out yourself. A good way to start recognizing your values is to consider all the issues in a conflict and then ask yourself what's *most* important to you. Keep in mind that connecting the dots from a behavior to an emotion to a core value can sometimes be difficult and time-consuming.

Here's a useful exercise: Reflect on your current conflict, jot down a few words or phrases that explain what's happening, and see if you can match them to one or two core values. This may take some practice before you find it effective, but it's worth the prep time. (If you need additional info on core values, turn to Chapter 2.)

For instance, if you say you're irritated by your boss's micromanagement, you may discover that one of your core values is autonomy, or maybe respect.

Managerially, if you say you want error-free reports turned in on time, the value you're addressing is likely competence or responsibility. If your team works like a well-oiled machine except for one person who says his opinions don't matter, consider that he's looking for acceptance or recognition.

Identifying your hot buttons

During the meeting preparation phase, identify your *hot buttons,* or points that you're most sensitive about, and make a plan to address them when they come up (because they very well may come up). Identify the kind of statements (or actions) that can make you ready to scream or blow your top. Be aware of these sensitive areas, because other people often know what they are and how to take advantage of them.

Your hot buttons are closely tied to your values because anything that can make you that angry is probably something you care deeply about. If you get upset when a co-worker rolls his eyes or talks over you, respect is very important to you, and his behavior is counter to your definition of respect.

Knowing that you're likely to go off if a co-worker touches on one of your hot buttons allows you to prepare a response that doesn't include turning red and slamming your fist down on the table. Instead, you may answer, "You know, it may not really be control I'm after, but I can see where you might think that. I've discovered that respect is really important to me, and I can understand where trying to earn respect might come across as controlling." This kind of answer is sure to deflate *that* balloon!

What dirty dishes can tell you about core values

Values and interests can pop up in even the simplest situations. Consider the following example: Seven employees share a common kitchen area that often has cluttered counters and a sink full of dirty dishes. Employees frequently discuss the messy site at staff meetings. A few of the team members say they don't give it a second thought and wonder why it keeps getting brought up. One employee says it's embarrassing to bring clients past the area, another suggests a chore schedule, and yet another is irritated that grown adults have to be told to clean up after themselves. The issue is the same for everyone — a dirty kitchen — but the values are different for everyone involved. Those who aren't bothered by it may feel that peaceful coexistence is more important than angry discussions about the dishes. Respect may be important to the individual who says he's embarrassed, cooperation may be an interest of the person requesting the chore schedule, and accountability is likely essential to the person who displays irritation. A manager in this situation may have the team brainstorm a solution that takes into consideration the stated values as a means to ending the conflict and getting on with other business.

Preparing a response to hot buttons isn't the same thing as preparing a really good comeback to deflect responsibility, paint the other person in a negative light, or disempower him. A mechanical (or poor) response is one in which you seek to shut down or one-up the other person. You need not agree with his assessment; you only need to demonstrate that you've understood his perspective. Preparation is good and helps anticipate difficulties, but it's no substitute for being open to feedback. Mechanically reciting canned responses to anticipated attacks doesn't demonstrate good listening skills and may limit you when trying to create dialogue.

Considering your ability to listen

Determine how open you are to listening — really listening — to the other person's perspective. If you tend to think of his time to talk as a distraction or an interruption of the significant things you have to say, check that attitude at the door. If you haven't taken the time to show him that you're listening, then he likely won't bother listening to you. Before going into any conversation, be prepared to hear things you disagree with.

You may assume that because you're hearing the words another person is saying that you're actually listening to him, but what would happen if you were asked to summarize what he just said? Be sure you actively listen to his words, take them in, and then respond. For tips on effective restating or reflecting, see Chapter 7.

Silence can be a powerful tool, and showing that you're taking time to consider what's been said can go a long way in demonstrating your willingness to resolve your issues. Prove to the other person that you're trying something new in an effort to change how the two of you may have approached problems in the past.

Think about how others show they're listening to you, and emulate that behavior when preparing to listen to others. This reflection helps you demonstrate that same level of attentiveness toward others. Start by trying the following:

- Make eye contact.
- Maintain open body language.
- Nod once in awhile (even if you disagree!).
- Allow pauses between the other person's time to speak and your time to speak.

If you jump in to respond to or correct the other person right off the bat, even with the intention of clarifying misinformation, you may be doing more harm than good. You want an open and honest dialogue, not a heated argument.

Taking notes may force you to listen, but don't bury your nose in the notes as a way to avoid eye contact. Bring a list of the key items you want to discuss, and set the list aside for when you need it. Let the other person know you'll be taking or reading from brief notes as a way to help you participate better in the conversation — not so you'll have evidence that can be used against the other person in the future. Add a comment about your willingness to shred the notes when the conversation is over.

Doing your best to be humble

Be ready to be humble. If you've had the same conversation over and over, maybe you're not taking ownership or responsibility for your share of the conflict. Even if the devil himself is working in the cubicle next to you and bullies you every minute of every day, you can probably think of at least one behavior you've exhibited that may have made the situation worse or kept it going. Being humble means owning up to your part of the conflict, even if your part was simply to ignore it for too long. And if you can't get yourself to say you've done anything wrong, just think of it as a strategic move that gets you what you want in the long run: a solution to the conflict that has eaten up way too much of your time.

Being humble doesn't mean becoming a sponge for blame, however. If you feel you have some responsibility, by all means take it. But remember the difference between being humble and taking a fall. Overstating your role in a conflict doesn't allow for an authentic conversation.

Dianne was about to be called into the manager's office for a reprimand. In past conversations the store manager would tell her everything she'd done wrong and Dianne would spend too much time defending herself, leaving both parties frustrated. This time, Dianne decided to try something different. She walked in, admitted the error, talked about her plan to avoid it in the future, and said, "Okay, now, let me have it!" Well, this response wasn't much fun for the boss, who was ready for a fight, not a mea culpa. Prepare to accept responsibility for your role right upfront instead of planning a defense.

Asking for help

If self-assessment isn't easy for you, ask for help. Invite a trustworthy person to be brutally honest with you — to give you unbiased information *and* keep your conversation confidential. If you and a colleague have been complaining about a conflict for some time, that confidante may not be a neutral person to approach for feedback, so choose someone else.

Asking for help and gossiping aren't the same things. If you want someone to brainstorm an approach or help you identify interests and emotions, you're on the right track. If you're looking to trash the other person and just want a witness, reconsider. Gossip and trash talk are poison in a workplace.

When looking for advice, people often seek out others whom they know will give them the answers they want and support the positions they've taken. If you just want to vent and blow off steam, this approach is fine, but it doesn't do much to help you conduct an honest self-evaluation. Try to think of this person as someone who can help you prepare for the productive conversation you plan to have.

After you identify your sounding board, ask him the following questions:

- ✓ What do you think I'm doing to keep this conflict going?
- ✓ What am I not seeing on the other side?
- ✓ How might others describe my values?
- ✓ What do you think the other person might gain if I *do* take the time to listen and consider his ideas? What might I gain?

Be open to hearing what he has to say and then act on it. If he tells you that you don't respond well to other people's ideas, consider what impact that may have on others, and then figure out how that behavior lines up with a core value. If he describes you in a way that doesn't resonate, ask more questions. You may have to spend some time processing his observations to see the situation the way he does, but if you're asking him because you trust him, heed his advice.

Recognizing your strengths

Every core value has two sides. In one light, a value has the potential to get in the way of a cohesive team, and in another it can reveal itself as a great asset. If you value control, you may hear others complain about micromanagement, but that same value may be the very thing that gets you promoted! If you value independence, you may bristle at the idea of being paired with a co-worker on a project, but you may also be more likely to be viewed as a self-starter. And if one of your core values is accomplishment, your co-workers may have assigned you the unflattering title of "taskmaster," but your boss sees it as doing what it takes to get the job done right and on time.

Consider the upside and potential pitfalls of your values and recognize the positive aspects of each. Valuing respect allows you to treat others with dignity; regarding competence moves you to create reports your company can trust; and appreciating autonomy makes you a manager who knows how to encourage the people on your team to advance their careers.

It's okay to honestly acknowledge your strengths and be proud of them. Just remember to acknowledge and appreciate the strengths of the other person in the conflict as well (hard as that may be!). Recognizing and validating values gives you a great wealth of insight to pull from when assessing how to address a conflict. As you begin to pay more attention to values, you're able to view behavior, language, and activities that were confusing or frustrating for you through a whole new lens.

Thinking about What the Other Person Wants

The other person in the conflict also has core values that aren't being met, respected, or honored. He's probably ready for the problem to be resolved and is eager for someone to consider his perspective. The main difference between you and him is that you've had the luxury of thinking through a plan that meets *both* of your needs. Keep in mind that he may still be stuck on what he wants and unwilling to bend on certain issues, so you may need to include a strategy to help move him along in your plan for resolving the conflict.

Before you ask to meet with the other person, take a minute and recognize that he isn't *against you,* he's merely *for himself.* As you prepare for a new conversation and begin to consider his point of view, you'll see him less as an enemy and more as a potential ally in solving the difficulty.

Identifying what you know

Consider what you know about your co-worker. Be honest, but be kind. What does his job demand of him? What stress could he be under? Think about what you've noticed when he's most upset. Be clear about what you really know, and separate out secondhand information you may have added to strengthen your initial point of view. Can you tie his words or actions to values? Take the time to jot down a few words that describe his needs from his perspective.

While you're talking to a trusted source about *your* strengths and areas for development (see the earlier section "Asking for help" for more information about talking to trusted sources), be sure to ask him what he knows about the co-worker and why he may respond to you the way he does. This isn't the time to stir the pot, so be careful whom you chat with and when and where you chat. You want to get information that helps you present resolution ideas in an appealing way to your co-worker, not to dig up dirt on the fellow.

Run through a couple of ways to approach the situation. As you prepare, brainstorm some questions that may help you understand what your co-worker's values are. Some possibilities are:

- ✔ "What do you want to see happen here today?"
- ✔ "What about 'x' is important to you?"
- ✔ "I can tell it bothers you when I 'y'; help me understand your reaction."

The most important thing is to be sincere and open with your questions when you meet with him. If your co-worker can tell you what he wants most, the two of you can look for solutions that fit.

Putting the drama aside

When trying to discover the other person's values and what he wants, you may fall into the trap of answering questions with dramatic responses like, "He wants to control everything and take my job, that's what he wants!" Instead, put the histrionics aside and follow these guidelines:

- ✔ **Spend time putting yourself in his shoes.** If someone continues a conflict even after you've tried to address it, chances are his behavior is a symptom of his interests not being met. Thinking objectively about the other person's needs can be difficult, but if it can provide you with tools to manage future conflicts, it's worth it.

- ✔ **Stop thinking in terms of "always" and "never."** These definitive words tend to create more drama than they resolve. They cement you in place rather than help you look at the situation from a new perspective, so put them aside and use language that more clearly states the situation.

Rob and Karen have a pre-staff-meeting conversation where Rob talks about a project he's considering implementing. During the meeting, Karen mentions the idea, and it's well received by the boss. Rob feels as if Karen has hijacked his idea and his accolades. Rob thinks, "You know what? She ALWAYS does that!" Rob calms down and decides to clarify the parts of the situation that bother him. Does he feel that he's not receiving credit for his ideas? Or does it bother him that Karen feels the need to speak for him? Or does he feel that Karen doesn't respect conversations held in confidence? When he figures out that he's most upset by Karen speaking for him, he talks with her and shares that he prefers to brainstorm ideas and present them together. Karen is receptive to his request, and Rob is thankful he didn't act on his first impulse, which was to storm into her office, and let her know that she's NEVER to do that again!

Considering what you don't know

It's impossible to know everything about everyone, so you have to do some guesswork about what the other person in the conflict values. You may be able to assume from someone's behavior and language that he values respect or autonomy, but many of his values remain a mystery to you. Not knowing everything that he values may work to your benefit, though. It may inspire your curiosity and reduce preconceived notions. Look to channel your curiosity about his values into creating a dialogue about understanding.

Start a list of what you think may be important to the other person, and have it with you when you meet. Let him know you've given his values some thought, and ask to hear from him to see whether your list is correct. (See Chapter 16 for more information on setting up a meeting.) Demonstrating curiosity shows a willingness to listen, creates the possibility for commonality, and can open doors that may surprise you.

The other person may have personal, professional, or other difficulties going on in his life. Problems like these may have a significant impact on him and the conflict. Try to remember that personal problems and pressures may be holding him back from being at his best, and give him the benefit of the doubt.

Taking a Look at Both Sides

Now it's time to get to work, take a broader perspective, and consider both sides of your conflict. Gather your lists, do a little considering, and put pencil to paper by filling out the worksheet in Figure 15-1. There's no right or wrong way to fill in the boxes. You can work your way down while only considering yourself before turning your attention to the other person, or you can answer each section for both of you as you consider each topic. I help you get started by walking you through each topic in the upcoming sections.

Issues

Start by filling out the issues section of the worksheet for yourself. In the appropriate box, write down as many issues as you can think of that apply to the conflict from your perspective. Don't think too deeply at this point; just write what comes to mind. Keep asking yourself, "What about this is important to me?" The payoff is a discussion about the primary issues rather than the tangential ones. Having an authentic conversation keeps you from agreeing to solutions that sound good on the surface but don't actually line up with your values.

	You	Them
Issues What are the surface issues?		
Values What are you really trying to satisfy?		
Hot Buttons What words, phrases, or references might cause an emotional response?		
Strengths What does each of you bring to the team?		
Common Ground Where do we agree?		
Proposals What solutions would work for both of us?		

Figure 15-1: Use this worksheet to help you identify what you and your co-worker want.

As an example, suppose you're having a conflict with a store employee about being late to meetings. Perhaps you make entries like these:

1. Shows up late.

2. Doesn't apologize.

3. Disrupts work flow.

4. Doesn't know what's going on.

5. Ignores requests to be on time.

Note every aspect of the conflict you can recall, and put your perspective in the column you've designated for yourself.

Complete the worksheet by filling in what you think the other person would write if he were completing the worksheet. Would he say that you spend too much time watching the clock, or that you micromanage group meetings?

Values

After you've had a chance to identify the issues, think about *why* those issues have impacted you. Take a look at what you've jotted down and spend some time evaluating the deeper reasons that these things have had an impact on you. Underneath the surface issues, what are you both trying to satisfy? Are you looking for respect, cooperation, autonomy, or teamwork? (If you need a refresher or more information on values versus issues, check out Chapter 2.) Really consider what may be most important to the other person, realizing that his values may differ from your own. After you've done some speculating and evaluating, jot down that information on both sides of the worksheet.

Resist placing your own values on the other person. If you carry around the expectation that others should behave according to your value system, you'll be frustrated and disappointed. When you recognize that you may not share the same values as a colleague, you can go into future conversations without being let down by his behavior, making it easier to ask for what you need.

For example, if Cathy wants the corner office because she currently resides next to the copy machine, water cooler, and candy bowl where everyone meets to chat, one of her core values could be peace and quiet. Dave, who was promoted last year but stayed in the same cubicle, may want the corner office because he values recognition. If Cathy and Dave switch the conversation from who gets the office to how to create peace *and* get recognition, they'll end up with solutions they wouldn't have considered before.

Hot buttons

Move on to the hot buttons area and fill in the aspects of the conflict that bother you most. Here you should enter phrases like, "Thinks an apology isn't warranted," or, "Ignores me when I try to bring it up." Identify topics or conversations you've had in the past that have raised the tension in the room. Which specific words or phrases pushed you past a calm demeanor?

As you're creating your list and responses, include potential hot buttons you may inadvertently push with the other person. If you've been tiptoeing around subjects or certain phrases to avoid an emotional response on his part, those subjects or issues are his hot buttons. Complete both sides of the worksheet.

Strengths

Consider the strengths each of you brings to the workplace. The individual who has a difficult time focusing during staff meetings may be the most creative person on the team. The guy who points out the errors in his co-workers' daily receipts may be the person who catches disasters before they happen. Think about what each of you brings to the work group that's unique, valuable, and important. Be generous but realistic. Use the earlier section "Recognizing your strengths" to help fill out this portion of the work-sheet for yourself.

Common ground

As you prepare to complete the common ground section of Figure 15-1, remember that both of you would like improved working conditions and for the problem to go away. At least you agree on something! Beyond those things, you may both be interested in improving a process, fostering team-work, or bringing success to the job site; you may just be working on these issues differently.

Be open to the possibility that you may share goals with the other person, and make note of these goals on the worksheet. The goals are great starting points for ideas and for your conversation in general.

Proposals

When you have the bigger picture in mind, generate some proposals. Now that you have a better understanding of where the two of you stand, think about what you want to ask for and what you can offer the other person. Get creative!

This is a time to be specific about what you'd like to see and what you want to stop. If the other person talks too much in meetings, rather than asking him not to talk, consider proposing he take notes, prioritize his top three issues prior to the meetings, or send suggested agenda items in advance. At this point in your preparation, think beyond fair trade negotiations and get creative about how you may solve the problem. Remember, these are just pro-posals, and you can't know if they'll work until you have an open conversation with the other person. Give the ideas some thought, but don't get too emotion-ally attached to them until you know the other person is onboard.

Ask yourself:

✔ What has already been tried?

✔ What has worked in the past?

✔ How can we be more creative?

✔ What can we do differently?

✔ What solutions or ideas work for both of us?

✔ Who else might help us develop a solution?

✔ What is within our power to change?

✔ Are my proposals realistic and possible? Have I considered all the details?

✔ Do I need all the answers right now?

✔ What am I willing to give to resolve the conflict?

✔ What are my intentions for proposing these ideas?

✔ What would an ideal working relationship look like?

Chapter 16

Asking for a Meeting to Talk about the Conflict

In This Chapter
▶ Figuring out how to approach someone
▶ Dealing with resistance tactics
▶ Considering time and place

The steps I lay out for you in Chapter 15 lead you to a decision about meeting with the person you're in conflict with. (If you haven't read Chapter 15, I suggest you do that now.) You've considered what's most important to you, thought about what may be most important to her, and maybe even asked for a little help to make sure you're looking at the situation with an objective eye. Now it's time to ask for the meeting.

This chapter helps you to do just what the title says; ask for a meeting to talk about the conflict you're having with a co-worker. I help you find the best approach, prepare your responses to resistance and potential rough patches, and then decide on the time and place for the meeting.

Considering the Best Way to Approach the Other Person

Everyone has a different level of comfort with conflict. Some people don't worry about it, and some people obsess over the smallest upset. Keep this in mind as you prepare to approach the person with whom you're having a conflict. Be aware of her stress level, as well as your own. (Chapter 15 can help you determine the underlying issue for both of you, and Chapter 2 tells you more about what kinds of things people bring to conflict.)

If previous attempts at resolution haven't gone well, realize that the other person may see you and want to run the other way. Just because you've decided you'd like to give it another try doesn't mean she'll immediately embrace the idea. Be mindful in the way you introduce the request for a meeting, it will be easier for her to say yes to you. And remember: Conflict can be a good thing! Do a little self-talk to ready yourself for a good approach, and use this opportunity to enact meaningful change.

Remembering that timing and location are everything

Before you attempt to resolve your conflict, consider when and where to approach the other person. Start by deciding what day of the week or time of day will get you the most receptive response. Before your co-worker has had her morning coffee or right at the busiest point in her workday aren't good options. Look for a moment of relative quiet, when the two of you have the ability to focus on your conversation. For example, early afternoon after lunch gives her some time to have settled into her routine while leaving enough time in the day to give you a few minutes to talk.

Additionally, pay attention to where you both are in the emotional cycle. If either of you is likely to raise your voice, completely shut down, or walk away, then by all means let the situation settle down a bit before asking for a meeting. Don't assume that if you're calm, everyone else involved will be calm as well. The best time to talk about a conflict is when both parties have had time to compose themselves. (See Chapter 2 for an explanation about how high emotions make for low reasoning abilities.)

Next, where should you approach the person? Where would she be most comfortable? Consider your location and what resources are available to you. Approaching the person in the hallway in front of someone else and telling her, "It's about time we figured this mess out" will certainly get her attention, but it probably won't set the tone for a productive meeting. It may catch her off guard, embarrass her, or instantly make her defensive. Instead, choose a private location or politely approach her in her own workspace. (For more information about meeting in neutral locations, see Chapter 6.)

The best option is to make a meeting request in person, but if logistics aren't in your favor and you have to make the request via phone or e-mail, take care to choose your words carefully and speak in a sincere manner (see the later section "Selecting the best mode of communication").

Choosing your words wisely

When you address the person to set up a meeting, use language that's respectful, hopeful, and genuine. It's important that your invitation actually be *inviting.* To demonstrate your desire to sincerely resolve the difficulties, what you say should communicate the following:

- ✔ **Confidentiality:** Communicate that this request and any subsequent conversations will be kept in confidence, just between the two of you. Of course, you should also be open to your co-worker's request that another person be made aware of a meeting.

- ✔ **Optimism:** Show that you're hopeful that the two of you can find a solution. It does no good to ask for a meeting if even you don't believe it will solve anything. Keep your language future-focused and constructive.

- ✔ **Sincerity:** Make sure the person knows that you genuinely want to hear what she has to say. You already know you'd like this meeting to be a fresh approach, but she may not. Use language that demonstrates your interest in hearing her perspective as well as sharing your own.

- ✔ **Safety:** Don't try to intimidate or bully the person. You may have the ability (or the desire) to force your co-worker into this discussion, but trust me, hostility or pushiness works against you in the end. Addressing your desire to see the situation resolved in a way that's mutually satisfying shows your co-worker that you don't want to corner or trap her but rather you want to have a real dialogue.

Here's an example of an optimistic and inviting verbal meeting invitation: "I'd like to meet with you to talk about the challenge we're having and to find a way to resolve it that would work for both of us. I think if we work together, we can find a solution. Are you willing?"

It's hard for someone to blurt out that she's *not* willing (who wants to be accused of not being willing to have a chance to find a solution?). This approach, lets her know that you're thinking about all sides, not just your own.

Selecting the best mode of communication

Think about what mode of communication will garner the best response. Communicating in person, on the phone, or in writing are all options. What method do you use most often with the other person? Is that method effective for both of you? Is there a benefit in trying something new? What approach would make the person most comfortable? What are your strengths in each area?

In person

Asking for a meeting in person is always your best chance for a positive response. Privately and politely letting the other person see the authenticity on your face, hear your friendly tone of voice, and witness your open body language speaks volumes about your sincere desire to work things out. It's difficult for a co-worker to rebuff your efforts at mending fences if you're on her turf and demonstrating how you'll behave in the discussion.

On the phone

If you're not able to approach your co-worker in person, or if it would be unsettling for you to show up in a workspace you never visit, the telephone can be an effective tool for requesting a meeting. Before you dial, take a deep breath, make a few notes about what you'd like to say, and above all else, speak with a friendly and approachable tone of voice. Make an effort to speak with the other person directly; leaving a voice mail should be a last resort.

In writing

If you think you may stumble over your words in person or forget what it is you want to suggest, a well crafted e-mail could be in order. Or if geography is preventing you from making your request in person and it's impossible to get your co-worker on the phone, spend some time writing an invitation that discusses your awareness of the difficulty and your interest in hearing her perspective, and ask if she's willing to chat with you in person so the two of you can find a solution that works for both of you.

If you choose to send a note, be careful not to write more than is necessary. Keep it simple and honest, and include your intentions for a positive, productive meeting. Allow the other person enough time to respond before taking further action.

It can be helpful to craft a document, set it aside for a while, and then review it before you send it. Upon review, you may notice something that the other party could misconstrue. You certainly don't want to make matters worse by writing anything that may be misunderstood. It's also really easy to misinterpret tone and intent in written documents, so have a trusted friend look the note over before you send it.

Preparing for Resistance

In a perfect world, asking someone to meet to discuss a conflict is met with an enthusiastic, "Sure, yes, you betcha!" every time. But because workplace difficulties are often fraught with conflicting emotions and deep issues, a request to talk is usually unsuccessful. Therefore, think ahead to how you'll respond if the other person uses one of a handful of common refusals.

In the following sections, I tell you about some of these typical forms of resistance and give you strategies to work through them. But first, here are a few general guidelines to keep in mind:

✔ Be specific and upfront about your intent for the meeting when you approach the person, and then tailor your reaction to her resistance as a way to let her know you're sincere in your attempt to resolve the conflict.

✔ Identify a neutral third party that both of you trust (someone the other person respects who'd be willing to observe the conversations and who wouldn't hinder the flow in any way). You don't have to talk to this third party right now; just be prepared to suggest the idea to the person if she says that she's uncomfortable meeting with you alone.

✔ Try to build trust steadily with the person by having discussions on topics other than the conflict, especially subjects in which you have a common interest. A quick conversation in the hallway in which you ask about her weekend activities, or state your amazement at the last-minute three-pointer that won the game, or ask for her banana bread recipe is a great way for both of you to ease into bigger conversations.

✔ Suggest a series of meetings as a means for the two of you to start building trust and to let her know that you're willing to try something completely new.

If a conflict has been going on for quite some time, or if there are a number of issues involved, she may feel overwhelmed at a request to solve all the problems in one sitting. It may be more palatable to approach the subject of your meeting as addressing one issue at a time. Give your co-worker the option to choose the topic of discussion for the first meeting, and she'll be more apt to agree to (maybe even suggest!) a second one.

Responding to push-back tactics

Pushing back is the most aggressive of the reactions you may get from the other person. People who push back acknowledge the problem but often react defensively. They may see the responsibility for the problem falling predominantly on your shoulders, or they may throw out a variety of roadblocks or preconditions to a meeting.

Comments like the ones in this list are often indicators that you're dealing with push-back tactics:

- ✔ You're the one who let this get out of hand; why should I help you fix it?
- ✔ If we're going to meet, I think our direct supervisor should be there.
- ✔ I don't want to meet with someone who's just going to yell at me.
- ✔ I just don't want to. I don't have to tell you why.
- ✔ You need to show some respect first.
- ✔ If you have a problem with me, take it up with *x*.
- ✔ I'm not meeting with you until you apologize.
- ✔ We don't need to meet; it's not *my* problem.
- ✔ You wanna talk? Okay, buster, you got it!

Be ready to let the person know that you understand how frustrating the situation has been for her. Try sharing some areas of common ground (work through the worksheet in Chapter 15 to help you discover these common ground points) such as, "It's clear we're both interested in the final outcome of the project, so I'd like us to find a way to work together that would work for both of us."

If she wants to escalate the conflict by bringing in a supervisor, the Human Resources department, or the union, show her that you see the benefits in trying to work it out on your own first. Provide examples such as:

- ✔ Both of you having a stake in the process and ownership in the outcomes, as opposed to having a third party make a decision that perhaps neither of you will like.
- ✔ The opportunity to build trust and a relationship that will see you through future disagreements so they don't turn into full-blown conflicts.
- ✔ The chance to create a working relationship based on insight and understanding of the real issues and to grasp fully what each of you requires for a peaceful coexistence.
- ✔ An opportunity to show others your problem-solving capabilities and to avoid negative documentation.

Finally, if she wants an apology for the incident in the staff meeting, address that issue: "You're right; we should talk about that incident." If she insists on an immediate apology, you need to consider whether you're willing to give one. If not, make it a point for discussion: "I'm not saying I won't apologize. What I'm saying is that I'd like to hear how the incident affected you, and I'd like an opportunity to share with you my thoughts on the incident before considering an apology. Are you willing to have that conversation with me?"

Someone who pushes back may want to start the conversation right then and there. Be flexible but proactive, and explain that scheduling a private meeting for another time would be beneficial because it would give you both time to think of possible solutions.

Getting past denial

Some people may not admit that there's a problem. Either the conflict simply isn't a problem for them (they're fine with calling your ideas stupid in the middle of a staff meeting) or they're completely oblivious to what's happening around them. Or maybe they fit into the classic definition of *denial* — they don't want there to be a problem so they've convinced themselves that there isn't one.

Here are some examples of denial language:

- I don't know what you're talking about.
- Problem? What problem?
- I don't even know what we'd talk about.
- Your problem isn't with me; it's with someone else.
- I know we had an issue in the past, but everything's okay now.

It may seem next to impossible to get someone to meet with you about a problem that she says doesn't exist. To combat denial, come prepared with responses to increase your odds of success. Gently point out inconsistencies — words versus actions. For instance, you can reply with, "I hear you saying that you don't think there's a problem, yet I've noticed that whenever I ask about the project, I see you roll your eyes. Help me understand." Replying in this way allows the person to respond to your observations and acknowledge that something may be going on.

Be open to talking about anything, and be prepared to ask whether you can improve the situation by the two of you having a conversation.

You may also want to ask for the person's help as a means to keep the conversation going: "It sounds like you're hesitant to discuss *xyz*. Can you help me understand why?" Tell her that you're willing to listen to what she has to say, and describe the impact that the issue has had on you to see whether she's willing to provide some insight. A good response is, "I'm open to hearing your thoughts. Is there anything that you think would be beneficial for me to know? I'm willing to listen to whatever you have to say."

Addressing avoidance

Some people are masters at avoiding difficult situations. They'll often freely admit that there's a problem, but doing nothing about it feels better to them than having a conversation about it. They may also hope that the problem goes away on its own or think that it's not serious enough to deal with.

When you ask the person to talk, you may hear her say:

- ✔ Now's not a good time.
- ✔ I'm just too busy.
- ✔ Whatever you say — just tell me what you want [and then the person never follows through].
- ✔ Yes, let's talk. Have your people call my people.
- ✔ [Silence, crickets, dead air.]
- ✔ I'd really rather not.
- ✔ It's not a big deal; I'll get over it.

The first step in a response strategy for avoiders is to create safety. Before you approach an avoider, have a plan that includes the possibility of adding a third party: "If you're uncomfortable meeting with me alone, would you like to bring someone else in to help us chat? I think maybe [name] is someone we both trust." This suggestion works well with peers but may be a little awkward if the other person is your boss or someone you manage. In those instances, the third party you suggest may be an ombudsman, someone in HR, an external consultant, or another employee who is your co-worker's equal (not yours).

Be flexible and focus on language that's open and inviting: "If now isn't a good time, I'll meet with you anytime, anywhere — you name the time and place." Concentrate on relationship-building and the employee's importance to the team: "It's important that we work well together and set a good example for the rest of the team." You can be honest about how the situation's affecting you: "Leaving this unsettled has left me feeling uncomfortable. I'd really like to resolve this so we can get back to working as a team. What would you need to make that happen?"

Acknowledge her excuse ("I understand that you're very busy"), find a benefit for her ("I think if we can work through this, it'll free up more of our time in the future"), and make sure she knows that she's being *invited* into a conversation, not ordered ("Are you willing to talk with me? Are you interested in resolving this?").

Finding hope in hopelessness

Some employees may have experienced disappointments that have led them to think there's no hope, the ship's sinking, and there's nothing but rough waters as far as they can see. Although you may come across folks who almost seem to thrive on conflict, at the other end of the spectrum are those who are nearly crippled by it and can't imagine ever finding a way out.

If you approach an employee who feels the situation is hopeless, you may hear:

- ✔ What's the point? It isn't something we can resolve.
- ✔ We've tried this before. You never listen.
- ✔ Why bother? Nothing will change.
- ✔ What's the use, it's not going to work.
- ✔ What say do I have?
- ✔ I don't trust you to have a different conversation than what we've already had.
- ✔ How many times do we have to talk about this? I'm tired of rehashing.

These may be legitimate responses if this isn't the first time the two of you have tried to fix things. So acknowledge that and validate the response! Doing so demonstrates your willingness to see her perspective and empowers her to keep the conversation going.

If you've talked about your problems before and were unsuccessful, recognize where the missteps took place. Let the person know that you've given it a lot of thought, and point out a few areas you think could be different this time. Ask a lot of questions: "What would you need in order to feel as though a conversation about the issue might be a good use of our time?" "What would it take for you to feel I'm really listening to your perspective?" "How could we come up with some fresh ideas to approach this in a new way?"

Give the person hope and let her know that you're interested in change by saying, "I'm hoping we can have a new kind of conversation this time." Address additional concerns and confidentiality issues, and invite her to set the boundaries — time, place, length of meeting, topics to discuss, and potential participants — in hopes of making her more comfortable moving ahead with a meeting.

Setting a Time and a Place for a Productive Discussion

The devil is in the details when it comes to making sound agreements, and the same is true for choosing a time and place for a meeting. Spending time upfront to think through what will make both of you equally comfortable demonstrates your sincere desire to resolve this conflict.

Time considerations

Pick a time when both of you can focus on the conversation. Uninterrupted time is a key element to a successful conversation, so choosing to meet right before the staff meeting — when phones are ringing, last minute e-mails are coming in, and co-workers are knocking on the door — isn't the best move. Ten minutes isn't really enough time to discuss the issues and proposals for solutions, so schedule at least an hour, and make room in the calendar for the meeting to run over so that you don't end up cutting off the other person to get to your next appointment. Politely ask the other person to do the same.

Time of day may also bring food into the equation. Do you or the other person have problems with low blood sugar? Do you get really tired and lethargic late in the afternoon? Let her have a say in setting the time. You want her to know that working together is important to you, so use this as an example of your new perspective and get the meeting started on the right foot.

And while you're at it, give her the benefit of the doubt that she probably does want to meet with you — maybe just not right now. You don't know how much time she may need to prepare for a conversation, so be open to suggesting a compromise. You'll get better results if you can negotiate some middle ground between when *you* think the problem needs to be handled and when *she* may be willing to talk about it.

If you've calmed down and think you can handle the conversation, that's fine, but consider that the other person may not be emotionally ready. That doesn't mean you should let her off the hook and permit her to put the problem off indefinitely. You may have to press the matter later, but for now, be open to creating some space if needed.

People at the height of emotion have the lowest ability to reason. Let yourself and others calm down before attempting to work through a problem.

Geography matters

Think about where to meet before you ask for a conversation. Be prepared to suggest a meeting place that demonstrates you've thought about privacy, safety, and the impact on the team. Impartiality is important to many people, so plan to meet in a space that screams neutral. Take into consideration titles, power, and the desire for a balanced conversation (Chapter 18 tells you more about the importance of the organization chart when resolving conflict).

It's probably not a good idea to choose the glassed-in conference room that everyone refers to as the "fishbowl," or to choose your own office. More than likely, others know about the tension between the two of you, so pulling the other person into your office may make her feel as though she's being reprimanded in front of her peers, even if you have a positive conversation.

Approach the other person with a few options for locations in mind, but don't forget to ask her to provide input on a location that works for her. Asking her to suggest a setting shows that you're open to her opinions and that you won't be making all the decisions. Be prepared for her to suggest her own office or workspace. Consider whether you're comfortable meeting there, and have an alternative to suggest if you're not.

If you think it may be better to meet away from work, like at a coffee shop or restaurant, consider whether the two of you will want to discuss emotional issues or stay as long as you'd like at a restaurant. Will she feel comfortable with interruptions from wait staff and strangers? Will you be able to stay as long as you like at an eatery, or do you run the risk of being herded out in the middle of an important point? You may decide that meeting off-site to have a surface conversation is a good first step in developing rapport between the two of you, but it may not be the most productive environment for a difficult conversation. Also think about how the two of you will get to the location (awkward car ride?) and whether the trip back to the office will be emotional for either of you.

I find that a quiet, out-of-the-way conference room is a great place to set up camp and work through the issues. In large organizations with multiple buildings, you can arrange for a room in another location to ensure privacy. If you work at a location with just a few employees, or if the only conference room is also the communal lunch spot, consider asking for a private booth at a nearby restaurant and spend some time away from curious co-workers.

Chapter 17

Sitting Down to Talk Through the Issues

. . . .

In This Chapter

▶ Balancing the roles of facilitator and participant

▶ Mediating a conflict in which you're involved

▶ Finding solutions and positive alternatives

▶ Putting your words into action

. . . .

You've likely let a lot of little things go between you and the person with whom you're having a conflict. If left unchecked, little things can amount to a bigger problem. A better strategy is to sit down, discuss the situation, and clear the air. But initiating a productive conversation about difficult topics takes courage. Though it may feel uncomfortable and risky to talk about the situation, you can use the tools in this chapter to keep yourself calm and focused and to keep the conversation productive.

Prior to sitting down with the other person, identify both of your needs using the tips and tools I lay out in Chapter 15. Refer to Chapter 16 for some details you need to consider when asking for a meeting, and, if necessary, tailor your approach to fit your audience by looking at how the organization chart may influence some of your decisions (see Chapter 18).

In this chapter, I walk you through how to mediate your own conflict, make your point, and consider the other person's perspective with an open mind. I give you tips on how to keep things on track while the two of you discuss the issues, and I also give you some ideas about what you can do next if you just can't seem to work it out.

Preparing to Mediate Your Own Conflict

You'll wear two hats in this meeting — that of mediator and that of contributor. Granted, you're not acting as an objective third party in this instance, but coming prepared with an understanding of the mediation process gives you an opportunity to step back a bit and make room for both perspectives while following a structured and proven method.

The following sections help you understand your two roles and give you an overview of how to adapt the mediation strategy to fit a one-on-one scenario.

Recognizing your dual role

Your task is complicated because you occupy two distinct roles at the same time, and one shouldn't overshadow the other. In mediation, all parties have the right to ask for what they want, and by keeping the focus of the meeting on both your needs, you reinforce that goal. In other words, by staying true to the role of the facilitator, you reinforce your role as a participant.

- **Facilitator:** This chapter, along with the rest of the book, prepares you to bring a mediation skill set and process to the situation. Knowing this, your responsibility is to use the process for *both* your benefit and the other person's benefit, not just your own.

- **Participant:** You have a right to speak your mind and ask that your needs be met, because this meeting is as much an opportunity for you to ask for what you want as it is for him. Use constructive language and make judicious use of the skills I present *while* striving for solutions that are meaningful and beneficial to you.

Be aware that the very fact that you asked for this meeting holds a certain power. *You* took the first step. *You* extended the olive branch. *You* took proactive measures to make sure that the conflict doesn't get any worse. And most important, *you* are the one who's coming to the table with a specific skill set and process to maximize returns on the conversation. That carries with it a lot of weight and responsibility. Researching mediation skills means you're coming to this meeting to resolve the issue, not outsmart an opponent.

Adapting a mediation process for a one-on-one meeting

Use your own words and be yourself during the meeting to discuss the conflict between you and your colleague. Have a plan, though, or the meeting probably won't result in the outcome you had hoped for. You can use the mediation process I use, but keep in mind that when I use this process, I'm a neutral, objective mediator. You, on the other hand, are required to balance your needs with the needs of your co-worker.

Follow these steps for a productive conversation:

1. **Sincerely greet the other person and briefly acknowledge the conflict and the impact it's had on you.**

2. **Explain that you'll be following a mediation process (because you think the method will help you both focus) but that you're just as much a participant as he is.**

3. **State your goal for a positive, respectful meeting, and that you both should consider this a time to confidentially present your views.**

4. **Ask the other person to share the events and the impact that the situation has had on him.**

5. **Reflect what you've heard, neutralize emotions, and spotlight values.**

6. **Share your perspective and ask your co-worker to reflect back to you what you've presented.**

7. **Build an agenda of topics for the ensuing conversation.**

8. **Collectively address any misunderstandings or assumptions.**

9. **Brainstorm solutions.**

10. **Filter through ideas to find those that best meet what's most important to both of you.**

11. **Finalize agreements, paying special attention to details and what to do if things don't work.**

12. **Share with others any details and results of your discussion *only* as necessary and appropriate.**

The rest of the chapter covers these steps in more detail.

Getting the One-on-One Started

When I mediate I use a structured process (I outline the steps for you in the preceding section) and briefly share the structure with the participants. This part of the meeting is called an opening statement. You should make an opening statement, and like mine, it should take no more than a few minutes.

Putting together a natural-sounding opening statement

Because the start to your meeting is so important, use language that feels natural and comfortable in your opening statement. Both of you will likely be a little anxious and concerned about how the meeting will go. That's normal, and it's okay to acknowledge your nerves at the start of the conversation. Prepare yourself by thinking about what you want to say, how you want to say it, and how it applies to your particular situation. Include all the points I outline for you in this chapter. Just make sure that what you say doesn't come across as rehearsed or phony. Your words should be authentic and come from a genuine desire to resolve your difficulties.

Even as an experienced mediator, I always have a cheat sheet in front of me so I make sure to cover important points. Do the same so you have an opportunity to practice a little beforehand. Use the rest of this chapter as a guide to what to include on your cheat sheet.

Here's an example of what your opening statement may look like. Remember — this is only a sample, and you'll need to tweak it to fit your particular situation.

> Reese, I want to thank you for being willing to take the time to sit down with me to talk about the challenges we've been having lately. This has been a tough couple of weeks for me, and I can imagine for you as well. I'm beginning to see and hear other people starting to talk about our conflict, and I think we have an opportunity to change that. So I'm grateful that we're taking this opportunity today. I've been thinking a lot about the situation, and I'm hopeful that we can put our heads together and have a respectful conversation so we can come up with some ideas on how we can solve things in a way that meets both of our needs. I think if we follow a structure, we should be able to get everything on the table and then work on how to solve our issues. I'd like to propose that we use the same process as mediators use — start by sharing our perspectives, listen to understand each other, and then build an agenda with the topics we'd like to cover, and then go into brainstorming. I also propose that our discussion be confidential and just between us. Does that sound like something that might work?

In the next section I give you more information about the elements of an opening statement so you can craft your own.

Acknowledging the current challenge

Set the right tone for the conversation to come. Consider adding a few words to your opening statement that capture some or all of the following ideas:

- ✔ **A sincere thank-you:** This conversation may be a long time coming, or an uncomfortable one for both of you. A quick (but authentic) thank-you to the other person for being willing to sit down and talk goes a long way toward kicking off your meeting with the right kind of attitude.

- ✔ **A recognition that it has been difficult:** Feel free to share that the conflict has been tough on you. Saying that you've had enough is in no way a sign of weakness. In fact, it may be exactly what the other person needs to hear so he can acknowledge that he's been struggling, too.

- ✔ **An awareness that others are watching:** If you've seen this conflict radiating outwards, say so. It's important to speak to what you see, and if you know that camps are forming or morale is dipping, share that you want to see the problem resolved before it goes any further.

However, don't speak on behalf of others or attempt to interpret how the conflict is affecting them. Your colleague may disagree, so speak about this only in an objective manner:

  - "I notice that there are whispers about how the two of us are inter-acting, and it would benefit both of us to work this out." (Good!)

  - "The accounting department is having a hard time getting anything done, and they want this to stop." (Not so good!)

- ✔ **Your desire to resolve the situation:** Let the other person know that you're committed to resolving the tension between you. Speak about how both of you will benefit from resolving your differences — you'll have less stress, you'll be more productive, and you'll have peace of mind.

- ✔ **A new approach:** If you've tried to have this conversation before but the results have been unsatisfactory, share how this time will be different. What did (or didn't) you do last time that you won't (or will) do this time? Speak about the approach in a hopeful and positive way — a little optimism goes a long way.

Explaining the steps the meeting will follow

When you mediate a conflict that you have a role in, you perform a number of steps in a certain order (see the earlier section "Adapting a mediation process for a one-on-one meeting"). At the start of your meeting, briefly go over what will happen when, sharing just enough about each step so your colleague isn't surprised when you call for a break or transition from one phase to another.

You don't need to reveal specifically how each step contributes to your ability to bring parties to resolution in a neutral and transparent way. It's up to you how much of the process you want to share with the other party. But coming to the table and announcing, "So, I read this chapter in a book about conflict resolution at work, and I'm going to play mediator" may put off a co-worker who's already upset with you.

Conversely, your colleague may get frustrated if you following guidelines he isn't privy to — if he's trying to tell you something, for instance, and you tell him that it's not his turn to talk. A brief explanation that you'd like the two of you to follow a proven mediation method in which you take turns speaking, listen to understand each other, and brainstorm solutions that benefit you both is likely to be viewed positively by the other person.

Committing to a productive meeting

After acknowledging the conflict, explain what you want to get out of the meeting, and what the other person can expect from you. Saying that this is a new and different approach isn't sufficient unless you describe *how* it will be different. Here are some talking points to cover:

- ✔ **Look for answers:** Emphasize that this conversation isn't meant to be a gripe session or a chance for the two of you to hammer away at each other's flaws and prove who's right or wrong. Unite yourselves around idea generation instead of being chained together by negativity.

- ✔ **Be mindful of this opportunity:** Speak about this conversation as an opportunity to build the kind of relationship the two of you want to have and to paint the kind of picture you want to see in the workplace. Suggest that you'll do this by focusing on the things you *can* change rather than those you can't.

- ✔ **Communicate respectfully:** Because this meeting is a step toward changing how you work together, it's important that you speak in a manner that's respectful, professional, and appropriate — and that goes for both of you, of course.

Sharing Perspectives

After your opening statement, answer any questions and then shift the meeting to the step in the process in which you both have an opportunity to speak about what you've been experiencing, to hear what each other has to say, and to understand how each other sees the issues at hand. This step is a very busy point in the process, but an important one, to say the least.

So as you begin this sharing step, consider what you want to know and how you want to present your point of view. When speaking:

1. **Describe specific actions, statements, and events.**

2. **Then describe how they affected you.**

3. **Then make any requests you'd like regarding future incidents, keeping your language focused on what you want rather than what you don't want.**

At this point, don't spend too much time asking a lot of questions. When listening, make a mental note of, or jot down, any questions you'd like to ask in order to understand better. You'll have time to clarify and investigate later, when you get to the brainstorming part of the conversation, but here, all you want to do is be sure that each of you has heard and understood each other.

The following sections show you how to decide who gets to share his perspective first, how to listen for understanding, and how to explain your point of view constructively.

Deciding who will begin

Although each of you will get an opportunity to speak and respond to each other, you have to start *somewhere*. Your specific situation will help determine who goes first.

If both of you are fully aware of the reasons that you're having this meeting, it can benefit you to offer the other person the opportunity to begin. Doing so demonstrates openness and a willingness to hear what he has to say, and it allows you the opportunity to demonstrate how to summarize and highlight what he values before sharing your own point of view. Often in mediations, when I reach the point in the process in which I reflect and reframe a party's perspective, I can actually see a physical transformation from "ready to fight" to "ready to listen." My hope for you is that you witness the same reaction as a testament to your ability to try something new.

In a sense, you've *already* gone first. By setting up the meeting and creating an opening statement, you've already shared to some extent what you're hoping to accomplish and briefly touched on how the conflict has affected you. By giving the other person an opportunity to describe his own experience, you're modeling good behavior by sharing the spotlight with him.

Your invitation for the other person to speak first must be open and genuine, however, and not a challenge or a threat. Nothing shuts down a conversation faster than hearing a disingenuous offer to start the ball rolling. For instance, mull over the following possible invitations:

I'm going to let you start this off. I have my own ideas about this mess, but I'm sure you have your own take, too. So let's hear it — go.

Doesn't sound so good, right? Now try this on for size:

I'd like us to get started, and I'm curious to hear how you see the situation, and what you think we need to do to resolve it. I want you to know that I won't be interrupting you, because I'm interested in your perspective. And when you're done, I'd like to have the opportunity to summarize what I heard so that I can be sure that I have a good understanding of your point of view.

If the person is unaware of your reason for calling the meeting, asking him to start (even using the good example from above) may be unproductive. Also, if you have some insight or information that may be helpful to the exchange, offering to begin isn't a bad thing. Bear in mind, though, that rumors, conjecture, and assumptions are *not* insights or new information. Be sure that the information is pertinent and helpful to your conversation.

Another time when you may offer to begin the sharing phase is when you sense that the other person is resistant or hesitant, and you believe his attitude is related to distrust — either of you or of the mediation meeting in general. Choose appropriate and constructive language that demonstrates your sincerity in resolving the problem and shows that this meeting will be different from what has happened before. Such an offer may sound like this:

I'd like to take a moment, share my perspective, and tell you a little about how this situation has been affecting me. I want to stress, though, that you'll also have the same opportunity when I'm finished, because this conversation isn't just about me. I'm interested in hearing your thoughts as well, because I believe that if we each have better understanding, we'll reach a better solution.

Listening actively

As concerns about the conflict are shared, listen closely to how he describes the situation. How each of you interprets the events gives you insight into how the conflict developed, what's keeping it going, and what approaches you can collectively take that will lead you to solutions.

Bear in mind that even though both of you likely experienced the same incidents, he'll probably describe the impact differently than you do. This isn't a time to question who's right and who's wrong, because both accounts are true. They're two different ways of viewing the same situation and are merely reflective of both of your experiences and perspectives. Keep in mind that you don't need to agree in order to understand.

Show the other person that you're listening by:

✔ **Presenting open body language.** Create an inviting space by assuming a comfortable posture with your arms at your sides or rested on the table. Lean forward a little, but be careful not to invade his personal space.

✔ **Making and maintaining good eye contact.** Connect by looking him in the eye as appropriate (no need to freak him out or stare him down, though!). Checking your e-mail or texting while he's talking may feel like constructive multi-tasking in the moment, but he'll certainly see such actions as a demonstration of your disinterest in his story. Put everything away and give him your full attention.

✔ **Positively reacting to his statements.** A few well-placed nods and subtle verbal responses let him know you're hearing him.

Be careful not to react too much, though. You may hear some surprising things, but keep your poker face! A raised eyebrow, a rolled eye, or a dropped jaw can send a message that you think he's exaggerating, or that you believe he just doesn't know what he's talking about.

✔ **Waiting to correct or clarify.** Honor his time to talk. As tempting as it may be to set the record straight or to speak up when you feel you're being mischaracterized, *don't do it!* Even briefly clearing up minor misunderstandings undermines the integrity of the process, so be patient.

✔ **Taking notes for the facts and more.** Getting the facts straight is important, because missing a date, stating an incorrect dollar amount, or getting a name wrong may give the impression that you're not listening or that you're not as interested in his perspective as you say you are.

As you take notes, make sure you also capture his emotions about the conflict and the values buried beneath his remarks so when it's time for you to reflect, you can speak to those things. A statement such as, "You're always looking over my shoulder at everything I do!" can give you some insight that he's looking for *autonomy* or *trust* in his relationship with you because he values those things in general. Chapter 2 describes a number of common values and how to interpret remarks.

✔ **Looking for ways to neutralize strong language.** As the other person speaks, he may come out with some pretty strong opinions about the situation and anything else he thinks makes sense to throw in. Try to respond by confirming how upset he is but by using language that doesn't inflame him. For example, if he states, "Joe and everybody around him are idiots," you could mentally craft a neutralized response such as, "You're concerned about Joe's ability to get the job done."

Don't expect your colleague to know what he's looking for when he first begins to tell you his point of view. He may say that he wants *x*, *y*, or *z*. He may say that he sees the problem in the simplest of terms and can't understand why you don't see it that way as well. Just let him talk. The more he shares, the more information you'll have when it's time to respond and you can demonstrate then that you understand where he's coming from.

Summarizing what you've heard

Before launching into a response to your colleague's initial remarks, take a moment and contemplate what to say and how to say it. You've been listening for the values and emotions that are important to him; now you want to reflect his emotions and reframe his statements into what he *does want* instead of what he *doesn't want*. Repeating "you want me to stop talking at staff meetings" gets the point across, but reframing the statement to "you'd like me to find a more effective way to communicate my ideas" gives the two of you something to work with when you get to the brainstorming phase. Plus, it frames the conflict as an opportunity to *do* something!

REMEMBER

You don't have to agree with the points you're summarizing — you just need to show that you understand what he said. Doing so may be more challenging when you're the subject of the conversation than when you're facilitating a discussion between other employees, like the process I outline in Chapters 6 through 9. Still, understanding the difference between reactive responses and meaningful summaries is the key to moving the conversation forward.

REAL LIFE

For example, I was coaching two parties through a conversation when an employee informed his manager that he believed he played favorites when assigning shift assignments to the staff. The manager jumped in with:

> I never play favorites, Chris! I work really hard to make sure that the shifts are assigned in a fully transparent and fair way! In fact, I've documented everything and I can even show you how fair I've been.

When you boil it down, this reactive response was a fancy way of saying, "Nu-huh." And all it did was set up the employee quite nicely to answer with his own eloquent response of, "Ya-huh." Not a very useful approach. And the harder one tried to prove his point, the harder the other worked to do the opposite. Imagine instead if the response had been:

> Chris, it sounds as if you're concerned about the way in which the shifts are assigned. You want to make sure they're handed out in a way that's fair and equitable.

Can you imagine how Chris might have responded to this summary of his concern? He certainly couldn't say that his manager was arguing the point, or choosing not to see his perspective, which is how most conflict conversations end up going awry. Instead, the manager would have captured his interest and spoken to his concern without saying that he agreed or disagreed with him.

When you reflect and reframe a co-worker's point in neutral words, you reinforce that you're open and receptive, but you don't sell short your own take. This technique buys you a lot of credibility as the process continues.

Reflecting, reframing, and neutralizing take some practice. Take your time, be mindful of what you'd like to say, and don't worry if it doesn't come out exactly right. You'll see subtle clues that what you're saying resonates with your colleague. You know you're on the right track if you see his eyes light up, if his body language goes from crossed arms to an open posture, or if he's actively nodding. And if you notice that he has a quizzical look or furrowed brow, or that he's shaking his head, feel free to ask for an opportunity to try it again.

Speaking to be understood

When it comes time to chronicle your side of the story, speak in a way that's constructive and clear, modeling the kind of conversation you want to have.

Describe the incident and then the impact

If you have particular concerns, address them specifically. What was the event that you experienced, and how did it affect you? You can think of this in terms of the *incident* and the *impact*.

For instance, if you have a concern about an employee monopolizing the floor during staff meetings, you could say, "Don't monopolize the floor during staff meetings." But this example is non-specific, and it tends to place the other person on the defensive. He probably doesn't see his behavior as "monopolizing time," and he'll likely respond accordingly. Instead, present the incident and what its impact was, like this:

> At our last meeting, many of the other employees were unable to share their concerns. **(Incident)** It's important to me that all employees have time to talk about their programs. **(Impact)** I'd like us to look for ways to give all staff members the opportunity to voice their opinions.

This example differs from the first one in that it doesn't label behavior (or people), and it addresses in objective terms what you see as concerns. Additionally, it sets up the opportunity for you to turn your concerns into a proposal that's open and constructive and that invites cooperation.

Use "I-Messages"

When sharing your perspective, only speak to your own experience. Keep your comments focused on how you perceived an event and how it affected you. Use "I" language to take the sting out of a tough message. Talking about hurt feelings is better when you deliver the information by saying, "I felt confused and hurt when my phone calls weren't returned," even though you may want to say, "What's up with not returning my phone calls?"

Simply starting a sentence with "I" doesn't ensure a positive reaction. If you say, "I'm not the only one who thinks you should return phone calls!" the opportunity to state your perspective in such a way that your co-worker can understand your point of view and not react with defensiveness is lost.

Similarly, using "we" language to strengthen your perspective is intimidating and can make the listener feel like co-workers are joining forces against him, causing him to become defensive or shut down. Avoid speaking on behalf of the group, even if you're in alignment with others.

Avoid using language that places blame, points fingers, or affixes labels to people, because such language raises defensiveness in the other person and derails the conversation. For instance, steer clear of these phrases:

- ✔ You always
- ✔ You never
- ✔ You should
- ✔ You didn't

Imagine if you're the recipient of one of those phrases, like getting into an argument about the cleanliness of your office space when a co-worker says, "You never take out the trash!" The sting is the accusation that "you never." Meanwhile, all you can do is think about every time you've lugged a heavy, smelly bag of trash out to the container on the curb during a downpour, getting drenched in the process. And as you start recalling all your heroic efforts, you're probably thinking about how "no one ever" appreciates all the hard work you do. Think that conversation is going to go anywhere productive?

Be brief and clear

Keep your message short and sweet. Get right to the point. Repeating the same information multiple times doesn't benefit anybody. Enough said.

Reaching across the divide when it feels as big as the Grand Canyon

After sharing your respective points of view, the two of you may feel that the perspectives couldn't be more opposite. Perhaps the talking has stopped, and all you hear are the crickets. That's okay. Try to keep the meeting going by

- ✔ **Describing the stalemate:** Recap the positions in a way that shows you've heard the other person, and yet you still have hope you can come to an agreement. Say something like, "It appears we have very different perspectives. Your position is that you should take the lead on all the projects, and mine is that I should be the lead. Maybe we could each share why being the lead is important to us."

✔ **Looking for common ground:** The two of you have at least one thing in common — you're experiencing a conflict. You probably both want to have it resolved, or you'd appreciate a little peace in the workplace. Say something to the effect of, "I can see right now that we have different points of view. Do you think there's any part of this we can agree on? Is it safe to assume that we probably share a desire to figure this out?"

✔ **Talking about the future:** Just because you're stuck now doesn't mean you have to continue to be stuck. You could offer, "It looks like we have very different viewpoints on this. Maybe it would be more productive to talk about the future rather than what's happening now. How can we work together in a way that shines a positive light on us both?"

For more ideas on what to do if the conversation stalls, see the "Keeping the conversation on track" section later in this chapter.

Creating an Agenda

After you've each told your side of the story, create an agenda for the rest of the meeting. You may be wondering why I'm asking you to create an agenda midway through the meeting. Well, an *agenda* in mediation is *not* a pre-generated list of issues, nor is it a schedule of events and activities for your dialogue. Instead, it's a list of topics the two of you want to talk about that you build together. By generating the list together, you're more likely to see each topic as belonging to both of you.

Use the agenda creation process to clarify and name issues. You can get formal and write them on a whiteboard or easel, or the two of you can create an informal document at the table. The agenda reminds you of the topics you want to discuss, and as you check items off the list, it becomes a visual indicator of your progress. For more information on building neutral, effective agendas, turn to Chapter 7.

Looking for Win/Win Solutions

You've shared your perspectives and built an agenda. Now it's time to start capitalizing on all your hard work by proposing solutions based on the values you've identified and what you've learned from each other. The following sections can help you arrive at a solution.

Spend a few minutes considering (and explaining) that mediating a conflict between the two of you is different from other negotiations. This part of the meeting isn't about making sure you both get two scoops of ice cream, or bartering for the best price at the local flea market. It's about both of you walking away having addressed the values that matter the most. Dividing something in half only works if you both feel you've won because you moved beyond the surface issues and understood what's really behind your conflict.

Proposing positive alternatives

You may be really good at telling others what you *don't* like. But in telling your co-worker what you don't want, you haven't offered any alternatives. Alternatives help him understand what he could be doing. The foreman who tells a worker on a construction site, "Don't stand there," is letting the worker know that where he's standing isn't safe. But without further instruction, the laborer may just move to another spot that's just as dangerous.

The same is true in any work setting. Imagine telling a co-worker, "Stop being so negative, Bob! This project isn't getting any easier with all your doom and gloom. You're dragging us all down with you." The perceived problem is pretty clear, isn't it? But making a statement like this provides no framework for preferred behavior.

Imagine instead using the following language: "Bob, it's important to me that we all speak positively about this project. I recognize that the workload is a challenge, and I need us to stay focused to meet the deadline." This statement makes clear what you want without making a demand, challenging the other person, or putting him down. Instead of telling him to stop being negative, you've asked him to be positive and given him a concrete example of what you mean when you say "be positive." It's a subtle difference, but one that has a tremendous impact on conflict conversations.

Because your co-worker probably doesn't know how to frame his language to state clearly what he *does* want you to do, you'll have to do some of that for him until he catches on.

For instance, if you hear, "You always ask Darren for his opinions first!" don't jump in with a defensive response. Instead, try to help him by summarizing the intentions of his statement to include what you think he would like you to do: "You feel you have valuable contributions that you'd like to share, and you'd appreciate it if I asked for your opinions first."

You've effectively helped him craft a proposal out of what would otherwise be seen as an attack. And you can't do that if you're quick to react, become defensive, or try to prove that he's wrong. Patience and grace go a long way toward helping you get through this part of the meeting. If you feel you're backing down too much or giving in to his demands, think of the situation in terms of applying a strategy that in the end gets you *both* what you want.

While you're speaking about alternatives, give a nod to the values that are inherent in both of your requests. This helps you identify what motivates each of you to find a solution to the problem. (For more on values, see Chapter 2.) For example, consider these contrasting statements:

- ✔ "You're always late to meetings" versus "It's important to me that you arrive at our meetings on time because I want to make sure there's enough time for everyone to provide updates on their projects."

- ✔ "You never bother to proofread your reports" versus "I need to make sure that your reports are accurate and error-free because I take a lot of pride in the team's reputation with other departments."

- ✔ "Your workspace is a disaster!" versus "I'd like our workspace to be organized and tidy so I can find things quickly when asked."

You may already know what you'd like to see based on filling out the worksheet in Chapter 15, or you may need to tailor your request based on what you discover in this meeting. Either way, speak to what each of you wants in order to prevent confusion and increase the likelihood that you'll both follow through with requests.

Keeping the conversation on track

Even in the most structured of conversations, sometimes things start to go haywire. Work through the tough spots first by using the agenda and choosing another item that may be easier to discuss. Then be sure to

- ✔ **Spotlight shared interests:** Look for things that unite you. For instance, although you may not agree on the best way to build morale on a team, you both recognize that it's important to have a satisfied staff. When you can validate that you're operating with the same goals in mind, you may be able to find ways to meet those goals that satisfy both of you.

- ✔ **Underscore progress:** Stay positive. It may be a challenge to look for the silver lining when the two of you seem to be at each other's throat, but remember that changing relationships and building trust takes time. Build on the small victories — they add up in the end.

- ✔ **Focus on what you *can* control:** You can acknowledge if much of the conflict is out of your hands, but don't dwell on it. You won't be able to change some things, but you *can* change plenty of other things. Although you may not be able to control gossip in the workplace, for instance, you can certainly control whether you participate in it.

✔ **Get creative:** Some of the best solutions come when you least expect it. Don't put any limits on your brainstorming or you'll focus all your energy on what *won't* work instead of what *may* work. Sometimes the wackiest ideas lead to the most effective outcomes.

✔ **Remain future-oriented:** After you both share the events that led to the conflict, you gain very little by revisiting and staying invested in the past. Your answers and solutions will come from a more future-focused conversation about what's possible instead of what didn't work.

✔ **Allow for saving face:** This conversation may create vulnerabilities in your co-worker; *never* take advantage of that fact. Don't hold him hostage to the process or use information he shares against him. Instead, allow him the opportunity to test and explore ideas in a safe place. You can point out inconsistencies you hear, but do so from a position of curiosity and inquiry rather than as a means to rub it in his face.

✔ **Take breaks:** Exhaustion is the enemy of constructive dialogue. Take a few minutes to stretch and refocus. And, reaching a satisfying outcome may take multiple sessions, so allow some time between meetings to gather information, test proposals, or just to see how things go.

Making decisions

Look at the proposals you have on the table, and turn them into specific actions that will give you the best outcomes and will likely hold up over time. Consider asking some of the following questions as you both test the boundaries of the proposals:

✔ Does this solution fully address the problem? Make sure that your agreement speaks to the root of the conflict. If it doesn't, you increase your chances of ending up right back in the same situation that led you to this meeting in the first place. (See Chapter 2 for more on satisfying values.)

All the work you do to uncover values in the course of the conversation is for naught if your solutions don't meet those needs. Values should be your primary consideration when filtering through proposals.

✔ Are these agreements realistic? It does you no good to craft an agreement that the two of you are happy with if it violates company policy, doesn't account for time restrictions, costs more money than is available, or (gasp!) is illegal. Be sure that agreements fit within the scope of reality.

✔ Can we both support the decisions? In other words, is your agreement likely to hold up because both of you can get behind the outcome? If your decisions are imbalanced or unsatisfying, one party may end up feeling short-changed and abandoning the agreement.

✔ Are our agreements specific? Make sure that both of you are clear about expectations and the terms of your agreements. You won't do yourselves any favors by ending your conversation with different interpretations of what you intend to do. That's just a new problem in the making.

✔ Do our agreements have the potential to improve our working relationship? By having this conversation, you've been able to address and validate each other's emotions and values. If your agreements are designed with these things in mind, your relationship with your co-worker is much more likely to improve over the long term.

Concluding the Discussion

At the end of your discussion, summarize what you've accomplished and what you intend to do next. If you've reached agreements, be specific about follow-through. If you're at an impasse, consider what both of you can do before coming back together. Either way, end your meeting highlighting the progress the two of you made, and be open to continuing the dialogue if necessary. At a minimum, keep in mind that the fact that you both were willing to talk is progress. Good for you!

The following sections help you move beyond the conflict if you and your co-worker have reached a solution. If you're still at an impasse, the final section offers ideas for what to do next.

Capturing the intent

You may want to take a cue from many of the workplace agreements I've helped craft and include a statement about your collective intentions, followed by specific details, such as one of the following:

✔ We agree that we want our communication to be respectful and courteous. (Details follow.)

✔ Our goal is to leave the past behind and work together to create a positive work environment. (Details follow.)

✔ Our desire is to create a safe and comfortable workplace. (Details follow.)

Focusing on a goal (or intention) can change the way you interact. You may find as time goes by that the details of your agreement are unrealistic, yet both of you are still focused on resolving issues because you have a greater goal in mind and are therefore more apt to come together to work on answers.

Fine-tuning the details

Be specific about what actions are necessary to accomplish the goals you've set. Who will do what? By when? And for how long? Be sure to consider the following:

- ✔ **Third parties:** Your solutions may involve other people. Take into consideration the time required for one or both of you to seek permissions or get buy-in from someone else. If that's the case, have a few alternatives at your disposal rather than relying on a single strategy. If your plan is completely dependent on whether Misha in accounting will allow expense reports to be turned in on the 15th rather than the 10th, you may run into trouble.

- ✔ **Possible conflicts:** Pull out the calendar and look at a significant period of time to determine whether agreements about dates will work. If you agree to meet on the fourth Thursday of every month, what will you do on Thanksgiving? It's better to plan than find yourselves in another disagreement.

- ✔ **Vague language:** Saying, "Oh, we know what that means" may work in the moment, but avoid unnecessary problems by explaining what each other means when you use phrases such as "when time allows" or "as soon as possible."

- ✔ **Attempts versus commitments:** It can be beyond frustrating to hear from a colleague that he'll "try" to make it on time to meetings. Either he's committing to make it on time or he isn't. If he's concerned about traffic, or other projects getting in the way of the meetings, make sure that the agreement contains a contingency plan for such "what if" situations.

- ✔ **Written versus verbal agreements:** Are your agreements straightforward enough to be remembered verbally? Or would it be helpful to jot down the details? My recommendation is to put it in writing as a way to memorialize the spirit and the details. The two of you may think you have an understanding at the time, but memories can (and often do) change over time. A simple e-mail that you write together and send to yourselves may suffice.

Ending without agreements

As hard as you try, you simply may not be able to reach any agreements. Perhaps it's because the dispute is so complex that keeping track of where you are is difficult. Or maybe you've recognized that the two of you are just so far apart in your positions and expectations that you can't see the light at the end of the tunnel.

Whatever the cause, you can do some things to end on a constructive note:

✔ Summarize where you are. Have a quick discussion about your attempt to resolve the situation. Acknowledge that you've hit a rough spot but that you need to discuss what your next steps are.

✔ Agree to return to the conversation after a period of time. Though you may not have been successful in this conversation, don't close the door on the possibility of another. After some time has passed and each of you has had a chance to reconsider the situation, you may both find some benefit in returning to the discussion for another shot at it.

✔ Bring in a professional. You may need some assistance in having this discussion. A neutral third party may be able to shed new light on the situation. For more information on bringing in a professional, see the options I discuss in Chapter 14.

Whatever decisions you end up making about your future, be sure to take a moment and acknowledge each other's efforts. Maybe the two of you haven't seen eye to eye, but at the very least you can thank each other for devoting the time and energy to finding a solution. Doing so also sets the right tone for returning to the work environment while you begin looking forward to whatever next steps you decide to take.

Chapter 18

Tailoring Your Approach to the Organizational Chart

• •

• •

*F*inally resolving a conflict in which you're one of the players may be at the top of your to-do list, but having to actually sit down and address it is probably causing a certain amount of anxiety, especially if the person you're in conflict with is a peer on equal footing or an individual higher up than you on the corporate ladder.

After you decide to tackle a one-on-one conversation using the skills I lay out in Chapters 15 through 17, give some thought to how you'll tailor your approach based upon your audience. Before you jump in with both feet, you need to take into consideration who the other person is in the organization, what title she holds, and what power she has to affect your future. (**Hint:** Everyone has power!)

Who hasn't heard the nightmare story about an employee who treats his co-worker badly only to face her a few years down the road in an interview for his dream job at another company. Ouch! So take care to treat everyone with the same level of professionalism.

In this chapter, I cover the nuances you need to know so you can effectively conduct yourself in a conflict meeting when your role changes from that of manager to peer to subordinate. I discuss how to acknowledge hierarchies and still have productive conversations about conflict. I also break down the possible scenarios into altering your style when you have the power and when you may feel a colleague's title trumps yours.

Resolving Issues with Someone You Supervise

You've probably seen the Hollywood images of the dastardly boss who relishes any chance to destroy his underling. That scene can make for good entertainment, but the truth of the matter is, confronting someone you supervise because the two of you are butting heads is never fun. Yet it's a necessary part of being a manager — and when the subordinate is causing more grief than good, you have no other choice.

Creating a dialogue

If the employee you're approaching has admitted to a grievous action and you're bound by law or company policy to act according to the letter, then do that. But in other cases, you can turn the need for a disciplinary conversation into an opportunity for a new working relationship.

Punitive meetings are usually a *monologue* in which there's no room to negotiate — the boss talks and the employee listens. Facilitating your own conflict discussion should be a *dialogue* in which you and the employee *both* talk and listen to understand the issues and then work to bring about change — together. Being part of a productive dialogue gives your staff member the opportunity to rise to the occasion, maybe even beyond your expectations, instead of operating out of fear or anger.

Keep her focused on what you'd like her to do instead of allowing her to be interested only in what she needs to *stop* doing to get out of trouble.

To expand a corrective discussion from monologue to dialogue, try the following:

✔ **Have a discussion about how long the difficulty has been happening, and express your regret at not having contended with the issues earlier.** This approach gives you the opportunity to demonstrate your desire for something different moving forward and sends the message that just because you didn't address the issue doesn't mean the actions or behaviors are okay with you. It also sets your expectations for what the two of you will do when other issues arise. I'm not suggesting you fall on your sword if you don't feel you've done anything wrong. Merely saying, "The strain between us has been evident for some time and I should have addressed it sooner" is enough.

✔ **Tell your employee that the meeting is a chance for the two of you to come to agreement without having to go through a formal process and without placing documents in his personnel file.** Find language that allows for the spirit of the statement instead of sounding threatening or foreboding. For example, you may say, "I'd really like the two of us to figure this out without having to involve other departments or get formal with anything. I know we have it in us to come up with something that works for everyone."

✔ **Communicate that this is an opening for her to create something new and play a part in her own destiny.** The employee doesn't get to call the shots, but you can open the window for her to undo some wrongs, fix sticky situations, and develop as an employee. In essence, if she has the opportunity for a do-over, is she going to take it or continue on the same path? Allow for a choice.

What the conflicts are usually about

Though I've mediated cases in which managers and staff members have been at each other's throats over how to achieve sales goals, where patient records should be kept, or when to complete the walk-through with a new homeowner, most conflict conversations with subordinates are usually about interpersonal relationships, work styles, or behaviors. Here's a sampling of common points of contention:

✔ **Communication:** An employee's perception of what information should be shared, and when, as well as the way she addresses you can get in the way of healthy supervisor/employee relationship. Tone and body language speak volumes!

✔ **Work habits:** Being out of sync with a subordinate's daily work routine — and she with yours — can create a negative environment pretty quickly.

✔ **Treatment:** Poor conduct in the workplace mimics life on the outside and runs the gamut from bullies to passive-aggressive manipulators. Just because you're the boss doesn't mean you're immune from becoming an employee's target.

✔ **Attitude:** The *way* an employee approaches her work can sometimes be more important than *how* she performs it. And when she snarls, gripes, and blames you for everything that goes wrong, her attitude can be distracting at best and easily lead to damaging consequences.

✔ **Gossip:** Your staff talks about you — you know that. But having an employee who spreads rumors, keeps the gossip mill running at full speed, and speaks on your behalf creates a difficult situation. You have to walk a fine line between giving her comments credence and allowing gossip to spread out of control.

✔ **Honesty:** Realizing that there's a good chance that the conflict you're having with a subordinate boils down to honesty can be devastating and maybe even a little surreal. Addressing someone's truthfulness can be tricky, complex, and daunting. Giving her a chance to come clean is an important step in getting the relationship back on track.

✔ **Insubordination:** Completing disregarding you as a manager, refusing to acknowledge the authority your title holds, or fighting you at every turn may feel like a personal attack — and be one of your greatest challenges as a boss.

Proactively adapting your approach

When you're having a meeting about a conflict you're directly involved in, and that meeting is with one of your subordinates, you need to adapt your approach. Here's how:

✔ **Keep in mind that, even though the person you're addressing is below you on the organizational chart and you may not want to give her concerns credence, the two of you are in this conflict together.** Only you, as a duo, can choose to resolve the conflict in a positive way — a way that reflects well in the eyes of other team members and upper management. It takes two to tango and two to untangle; you need each other.

✔ **Put yourself in your employee's shoes and think about how you'd want your boss to approach you about your communication style or your integrity.** Especially if you were in conflict with your boss and had your own opinions about *her* ability to treat others well or *her* attitude toward staff. You'd probably want to speak in private, in a neutral place, with enough time to allow each of you an opportunity to share your concerns and desires about these touchy subjects. You'd probably also want her to have done a little contemplating before she even asked you for a meeting. You'd want her to consider the situation from your point of view, and figure out exactly what she wants so she doesn't "um" and "er" her way through the discussion. Then you'd want her to be prepared to propose solutions that meet both your needs, not just hers. In essence, you would want her to get familiar with Chapter 15 so she could be ready for a positive, productive meeting with you and listen to your side of the story.

✔ **Set a goal for the discussion that allows the employee to get back on track and motivated to reach team goals.** Keep her focused on what's going well and what needs to be improved. Then be open to hearing what she has to say. If her ideas don't lead to the outcomes you want, you can always be more direct later in the conversation, but initially see if she has any ideas about resolving whatever problems the two of you are having. Let her be a part of the solution so she has more buy-in and follows through with whatever pledges you make to each other.

✔ **Think about your part in the trouble.** Being at odds with a subordinate is frustrating. Oftentimes, putting the entire onus for the problem on the employee is easier than taking personal responsibility — especially if you're genuinely unaware of the negative impact that particular words or actions may have on him. Do a little self-assessment — check out the information in Chapter 4 about how managers can unknowingly contribute to a conflict.

Being open to addressing your own behavior helps you create a management style that brings out the best in your employee, instead of resorting to playing the power card and insisting that she do everything your way "because you said so." Don't, however, own up to anything if you don't know what you're supposed to own up to.

Creating a positive environment

Because you're the boss, you have to be a little more mindful of the environment you ask a subordinate into — especially given that the topic of conversation is about the conflict between the two of you. Work to put her at ease. Follow the general process for a one-on-one conflict meeting (refer to Chapters 15 through 17), and weave these suggestions in as you go:

✔ **Open the meeting by acknowledging the tension or difficulties between the two of you.** She may be expecting you to say something akin to "You need to straighten up, buddy." If, instead, she hears you say, "Donna, the last few weeks haven't been easy for either of us and I'm sure it comes as no surprise that we're having some difficulties," she'll appreciate that you're setting the tone for a positive discussion.

✔ **Explain, if relevant, where your work responsibilities may be getting in the way of the relationship.** For example, have you been too busy on a large project to really work with her on addressing smaller conflicts that have now escalated? Have outside factors distracted you from your usual management role?

✔ **Own up to your share of the frustrating dynamics in your work relationship.** Perhaps you've played favorites or not given her the same respect you give her co-workers. Or perhaps you've been aware of the problems and let them grow while you considered your next move.

✔ **Commit to a new approach.** Tell her you're willing to create a different working relationship that you'd like her to help build. Express what you'll be doing to change it from its current status.

✔ **Be open to her suggestions for a different relationship.** This may be a tough spot in the conversation, but see it through. It's likely your employee sees you differently than you see yourself, so it may be difficult to listen as she ticks off your shortcomings. Resist being defensive and using your position to justify your actions. You may find a nugget of truth in what she's telling you that'll allow you to expand on some of your managerial strategies and help you build your career. Just because the information is coming from an underling doesn't mean it's of no value to you.

✔ **Apologize when and if necessary.** I'm not suggesting you say you're sorry for something you didn't do, offer a blanket apology with no meaning, or think you have to apologize because it's part of the process I recommend. But if during your conversation your employee tells you that she feels personally slighted by your behaviors, a sincere apology starts to repair past misgivings and affirms your commitment to building trust. Just keep it simple without adding in complicated excuses. Include a description of what you're sorry for, an assurance that it won't happen again, and a request for an opportunity to make it up to the injured party.

✔ **Ask for the changes you'd like to see between the two of you.** Clearly, honestly, and respectfully describe what you'd like to see from her that will change the relationship for the better. Phrase your requests with what you want her to do instead of what you want her to *stop* doing. For example, say, "I'd like you to return from lunch by 1:15 every day" instead of "Stop being late all the time."

Focus on the task, not personal shortcomings

Having a discussion in which you have to mesh attitude with tasks, mesh behaviors with team goals, or tie an employee's communication style to end results can get complicated. I mediated a case in which a manager was disappointed in his employee's performance and attitude on the job. He had repeatedly told her she wasn't doing her job, to no avail. Each time the employee was asked to perform a task, she would look to her job description and snap back that it wasn't her job, causing the two of them to clash on a daily basis.

During the mediation, the manager listened to the employee's point of view and came to understand how important continuity and security were to her. He realized that she wasn't using the official job description as a way to get out of work — she was using it as something she could count on in an otherwise ever-changing work environment.

When the manager commended her for her performance on the tasks she did well and spoke in terms of the position and its requirements and not her personally, the air in the room changed, the body language between the two became more relaxed, and they jumped into solving problems. Both saw how they could use the document in a positive way, and the manager approached future requests by saying, "This position requires these tasks" rather than saying, "You're not performing up to par."

If you think a conflict conversation with a subordinate may be especially difficult because of the nature of the tension or the fact that it's been going on for quite some time, prepare for the meeting by talking it through with a trusted source, such as a supportive supervisor or a Human Resources representative. Use brainstorming meetings not as a way to strengthen your position but as a way to prepare for the best possible outcome and plan how to track your success. Plus, if you discuss the situation confidentially with HR, you can ask about any boundary issues and get coaching on how to comply with company policies and employment laws. Chapter 13 covers common internal resources that can help you prepare for tough conversations.

You're the one applying a mediation process to the conversation. Your subordinate may not have as much tact or skill when it's time for her to communicate her concerns. Help her by

- ✔ **Using the reflecting and reframing skills from Chapter 7 and modeling as best you can the way you'd like her to speak to you.** In this conversation, lead by example and create a framework for future dialogue.

- ✔ **Reminding her of the meeting's goal.** Do this by refocusing the conversation and her comments toward future actions that you both can control and build on versus staying stuck in the past.

- ✔ **Being mindful of your responses.** How you respond to poor communication on her part can mean the difference between a successful outcome and a firestorm rolling down the hallway. Your ability to defuse aggressive approaches without aggravating the situation allows more information to be shared and will lead to better working agreements. Decide not to react defensively. Think about how she may represent the discussion to others, and create the opportunity for her to speak highly of you and the process.

Keeping your power in check

A smart manager once told me that those with real power don't need to remind others. Because you're in a position of power over your employee, you have the muscle to intimidate, push, and demand that she do what you say. You also have the ability to frame your conversation as a productive learning experience for both of you.

Power starts with location. If you're sitting behind your big desk, which sits a good foot above the little chair you've placed her in, you're already setting the tone for a disciplinary meeting even before you utter a word. Your subordinate will appreciate your efforts to level the playing field a bit, so move to a table where the two of you can see eye to eye (literally and figuratively!) or sit on the couches at the café down the street. Create a comfortable environment for both yourself and your employee by applying the tips in Chapter 16. Taking responsibility for your actions or admitting that you were affected by her actions is easier in a comfortable, private setting in which phones aren't ringing and other staff aren't knocking on the door with "just a quick question."

Create the emotional space for your employee to be forthcoming about what she's willing to do to repair your relationship. A subordinate commonly acquiesces to her manager's position out of fear. Be sure she's not agreeing just to agree and get it over with. That sort of caving feels good in the moment but has the real probability of enraging you down the line when she doesn't follow through with something she agreed to do. Help her feel comfortable about sharing her point of view by letting her know that you're in this together (at least for now) and you're open to finding a long-term solution. Tell her that the best way to achieve that goal is for the two of you to put an equal amount of input, perspective, and ideas on the table. If appropriate, suggest that there will be no negative consequences when you both come clean about the situation.

Switch up how you think about power when it comes to subordinates. Start by erasing the idea that power is self-serving. Your power isn't only for your own betterment or just to prove that you're in charge. True, sometimes you have to exert strength in decision making or perform triage when emergencies arise. But applying your power to a conflict discussion with an employee by exhibiting a "just do it and shut up" stance may cause you to lose her respect and diminish your ability to influence her as time goes by (or when it really counts). Your power is expanded, not eroded, when you make room for her perspective. Using "my way or the highway" as your only approach focuses on the fight for power rather than the problem. Instead, open the floor to your employee and hear her out; it takes a certain level of command to step back and let an employee come up with answers.

Considering nerves

It should come as no surprise to you that, when you call a meeting, your employee will experience some level of worry or stress because she's not sure what to expect, what topics will be covered, or what approach you'll take. And with all the preplanning and prepping you're doing, you're likely to feel a little nervous yourself!

Your employee may be a little jumpy, her ability to process information may be slowed, and you can probably expect her to be overly defensive. Her emotions may even take over, which means her ability to reason will be low.

Try the following tips to keep you both cool, calm, and collected:

✔ **Slow down the conversation.** Neither of you needs to get every detail of every event that has taken place between the two of you out in the first five minutes of the meeting. Let her know you have as much time as it takes.

✔ **Ask her to take a deep breath with you.** Taking a moment to breathe and focus at any point in the conflict discussion — as many times as is needed — is a way for you to acknowledge the nerves in the room, and it allows you the chance to calm any anxiousness you may be experiencing yourself.

✔ **Ask questions to understand her point of view.** If she doesn't seem to be making sense or is putting multiple thoughts together that appear unrelated, ask some open-ended questions so she has an opportunity to clarify her position. Help her focus on one thought at a time without making comments on her scattered approach.

✔ **Be aware of your own defensiveness.** If your employee's voice is cracking and her hands are shaking to the point where she'd never pass the final exam with the bomb squad, and yet she's able to blurt out her dissatisfaction with the way you organize the schedule, now's not the best time to tell her you think she's dumber than a stump (actually, there's probably never a good time to tell her that!). Instead, go back to the tactic of asking open-ended questions to pinpoint what *about* the scheduling process doesn't work for her.

✔ **Use language to focus on the goal of the meeting.** Reduce butterflies for your subordinate by being clear about what you want to accomplish and using *we* and *us* language to indicate you're in this together and she doesn't have to come up with all the answers.

Used correctly, word choices that denote collaboration are far more inviting and allow you to reach the same goal: to improve performance and outcomes. You'll still discuss what she needs to do to accomplish the goals, but the conversation can now be focused on future requirements that she can control. Here are a few examples to get you started:

• Instead of stating, "I wanted to call this meeting so we can discuss how to improve your performance," say, "I'd like us to discuss what's happening with the project and share ideas for reaching the projected goals."

• Instead of saying, "We need to talk about your attitude," say, "I've noticed some tension between us and I'd like to talk about how we can improve our working relationship."

There's a difference, though, between setting the stage that you're working on the conflict together and using *we* in the royal sense of the word, which is condescending. For example, you wouldn't want to say, "We seem nervous" when you really mean "You seem nervous."

Addressing Conflict with a Peer

On the surface, it may seem easy enough to treat an equal like an equal, but when you're angry or frustrated, not building armies or creating competitive situations around personal conflicts with another manager can be tough. For the good of your own career aspirations, resist the urge to one-up a peer or compete for the limelight; instead, work to keep a level playing field as much as possible.

How you approach a colleague about an ongoing conflict depends on a number of factors. Take into consideration how well you know her, how often you interact, and how important the working relationship is to you. Use the steps for a one-on-one conflict discussion I suggest in Chapters 15 through 17, and then adapt your conversation with the following information.

Respecting a peer's position

When you think about all the managers in your organization and what each of you brings to the table, a diverse set of talents and capabilities probably comes to mind. Companies benefit from having dissimilar managers who bring with them a multitude of work and life experiences, varying lengths of service, different educational backgrounds, and a variety of communication styles. Even establishments that are strictly regimented in the way they do business don't have cloned, robotic employees running each of their departments in the exact same way. So when you approach another colleague about a conflict the two of you share, first take into account how the top brass may value her unique skill set — even if her talent isn't quite evident in your eyes!

Consider that you may not truly understand what it takes for her to work with her unique staff and manage the intricacies of her programs, just as she most likely doesn't know what it takes to walk in your shoes. Focusing on your own team's goals and, in the process, inadvertently affecting another team is common. Give her a little latitude by going into a one-on-one conflict discussion with an open mind about her actions and the motivations behind them. She may be protecting her flock just as you're safeguarding yours. Respect her priorities, the pressures of her job, and any deadlines she may have looming, and carve out an adequate amount of time to address fully whatever problems you're having.

Even though you're a manager, you're not *her* manager. Be mindful of the tone you take, and err on the side of using the same decorum you would use with a superior. If she's in management now, there's always the chance she'll one day manage you, so think beyond your current problems and consider who or where she'll be tomorrow.

Being sensitive to location

Both you and your peer want to retain the respect of your respective staffs and the company at large, so meet in a private place, especially if your disagreements have been public up to this point. Even if you think she's 100 percent wrong, allowing for some dignity and the opportunity to save face demonstrates to the higher-ups that you're capable of having a focused, productive conversation without creating fallout that disrupts others. For general information about choosing a good location for a conflict conversation, see Chapter 16.

Preserving the working relationship

If you share the same grade level or sit on the same dotted line on the organizational chart but don't know the other manager well enough to talk with her on an ongoing basis, or if you merely think of her as someone you have to tolerate once or twice a year, you may choose not to bother approaching her with a formal mediation process over a minor disconnect. However, if the two of you getting along matters to those above you (and it probably does), take the time to resolve the conflict in order to eliminate the possibility of any negative talk about you to superiors. Keep your reputation intact.

If you know your peer well, the issues may be easy to address and the two of you can get back on track, keeping your professional relationship undamaged before anyone is the wiser. Having a discussion with someone you consider a friend may actually be tougher — but rest assured that addressing conflict and keeping friendships aren't mutually exclusive. The level of respect you're willing to give her, the amount of interest you show in her proposed solutions, and your combined abilities to tackle the problem without personally destroying each other will serve as an excellent example for your respective teams.

A good motivation for addressing difficulties with a peer is to consider who else is talking about your problems. Think about the effect this conflict can have on your career and your reputation, and work to resolve the issue as soon as you can. Don't let the rumor mill take on a life of its own. Gossiping and speculating about dueling managers can be great sport! If the conflict between you and your colleague is affecting even one person in the workplace, you run the risk of the impact being discussed not just horizontally but vertically as well.

You may need to consider if the topics at hand are ones your peer can even affect. If the two of you decide it's really out of your hands, at the very least express your interest in keeping — and growing — a working relationship with her. That way, when a problem arises that you *do* have some control over, you've set the groundwork to address it with each other without letting it escalate. Similarly, if she can control something and chooses not to (even after your openness to partner with her on solutions), *you* may need to change the way you interact with her instead of asking *her* to change her behavior. Your reputation will be better for it.

Having One-on-One Conversations with Your Boss

You may have heard the story about the employee who tells his buddies that he's going to discuss concerns *about* his boss *with* his boss. The colleagues respond by asking if his résumé is current and hope he has at least eight months of savings in the bank. In essence, they're saying, "Are you kidding? You can't talk to your manager about his performance issues — it's easier to quit than it is to have *that* kind of conversation!"

How you attempt to resolve a conflict with your manager may depend on both short-term and long-term goals, though I encourage you to think more long term than short. Even if you know in your heart of hearts you're just here for the short term, burning a bridge with your boss is never a good idea. Leaving with dignity and knowing that you gave it your best shot will keep you from being an outsider if you ever cross paths again.

Weighing the pros and cons of asking for a meeting

I'm all for talking things out — I'm a mediator after all! I'm the first to suggest a meeting and ask clarifying questions, and I have no problem having a difficult conversation because my experience tells me it's worth it. However, I recognize that you may not yet have the same mindset, especially when it comes to having a tough conversation with your boss. You may want to know the hard and fast rules about when (or when not) to open yourself up to possible repercussions with someone who has the power to end your career with the organization.

The fact is, you know your situation better than I do, so you have to decide for yourself what you're willing to do. To help you weigh your options, though, I can give you some points to consider that I've gathered through various mediation cases.

When it may be a good idea to meet

A productive meeting with your boss can be a relief and can motivate you to be the best you can be. But if you're not sure you're ready to tackle a discussion about the conflict between the two of you, here are some motivations for a meeting you may want to consider:

- ✔ **You're determined to stay with the organization.** If you want to establish yourself as an integral part of the management team, your boss can help you do that, so work with her, not against her. If you're so frustrated that you can't imagine respecting her anytime soon, try respecting the position instead.

- ✔ **One or both of you are relatively new to the position, and you got off to a bad start.** Building trust and taking time to share and relate to a new boss while you work through minor conflicts is important. Set the stage for an ongoing relationship by asking her opinion, valuing her input, and offering your insights as well. Show her that you're capable of having honest and respectful conversations when needed. Going to a superior with a concern or complaint is much easier when you've already laid the groundwork.

- ✔ **You're concerned about your reputation.** You may not continue your employment under this manager, but slinking away without making an effort to repair a damaged reputation may not be in your best interest. At the very least, try to clarify your actions and work to clear the air.

- ✔ **Values such as respect and dignity have been violated.** If you're at a point in your life in which you'd like to get more out of your job than just the paycheck and want to focus on what you value — respect, trust, cooperation, and the like — having a conversation may be worth your time. Be genuine in your approach and provide specific examples of how her actions have affected you. Merely saying, "I value respect and I don't feel respected" may leave her a little bewildered and thinking you're just there to complain.

- ✔ **The situation is impossible to overlook and can no longer be ignored.** If this conflict is negatively affecting your quality-of-life and has started to seriously impact personal relationships or is robbing you from sleep, and if you're willing to address it at any cost, then by all means go for it. However, don't ignore the process from Chapters 15 through 17 and make sure to be mindful of your approach, tone, and willingness to listen.

When you should consider holding off

I almost always think it's a great idea to address conflict with anyone. Almost. I'm not saying to never have the conversation, but here are some examples of times when you may consider waiting to ask for a meeting to talk about your difficulties:

- **Tempers are ratcheted up.** When emotions are high, reasoning is low. If you want the best possible outcome, consider your timing. Trying to paint your boss into a corner isn't a good idea — and doing it when steam is pouring out of her ears is a really bad idea.

- **All the relevant issues and players have yet to be revealed.** If there's a chance the story is still unfolding, hold off a bit until you feel more comfortable with the facts and figures involved.

- **You're showboating.** Be careful not to fight battles on behalf of others just for the sheer experience. Yes, you want to represent your team or your subordinates as best you can, but having co-workers put you up as the sacrificial lamb isn't in your best interest. Decide for yourself whether the conflict is really yours and if you would feel as compelled to take it on if no one else was urging you to do so.

- **The situation is in flux.** If there's a chance your manager (or you) may be reorganized into a different department or is leaving the company, or if the very issue you're in conflict over may be solved without the two of you, hang tight for a while. Meanwhile, conduct yourself professionally and keep your reputation intact.

- **You want to deliver a diatribe and aren't ready to hear her out.** Showing up to a meeting to discuss your problems with nothing more than a laminated list of complaints will only frustrate her, especially if you're complaining about things outside of her control. Even if she does have the power to change things and you rush in with directives about what she ought to do, you run the risk of her not being able to see any perspective but her own and, subsequently, asking you to move on. Consider a venting session with a trusted confidante instead.

Redefining your concept of power

You are not powerless — ever. You may not like some (or any) of your options, but you always have a choice, even with a superior. Here are just a few ways in which you have power in what may seem like an otherwise powerless situation:

- **You have the power to expand your boss's perspective.** When you approach a conversation with your manager believing that you have some knowledge that's beneficial to resolving a conflict, you'll have a more productive discussion than you would if you went in asking what the heck your boss was thinking. Knowledge is power, and there's no way your manager can have a 360-degree view without you. She can benefit from your perspective, so at the very least you have the power to share what you know. And, at a minimum, what you know is how her actions, attitudes, or behaviors have affected you.

✔ **You have the power not to act like a victim.** If you go into a discussion already defeated and acting the victim of your manager's power, you're essentially creating your own reality. Not acting the victim, though, doesn't mean being arrogant and disrespectful — it means giving some thought to the areas of the conflict you can control and working to improve them.

✔ **You have the power to tread lightly.** Keep the raging to yourself and, instead, channel your energy and power into doing what's right for you. If after sincere attempts to resolve a conflict with your manager you conclude that the two of you just don't mesh, you may have to rethink the traditional concept of power (refer to the earlier section "Keeping your power in check" for some insight). If letting her think she has won or choosing to defer to her experience and decisions will calm things down, do so in a respectful way. Going over her head or behind her back, or attempting to sabotage her in any way, erodes your integrity. Use your power to control your attitude, your work product, and your destiny.

Changing the status quo

A new manager was told by his colleagues that a particular vice president was impossible to work with and to avoid her at all cost. All her co-workers had a story about a bad experience they'd had with her, and they did everything they could to steer the new manager away from working with the top brass.

Instead of accepting that his future would be the same as his co-workers' experience, the new manager tried creating respectful working relationships with everyone he met. He went out of his way to greet and smile at those in upper management. Over time, the VP started asking him questions about his projects, and he gave a brief description about a new product or development that his team was focusing on. During a meeting a few months into the job, the VP turned to the manager and asked his opinion of an idea that others were discussing. She had begun to trust him, his ideas, and his insight. The two developed a mutually beneficial working relationship.

Years later, the VP unknowingly made an offhand remark about the manager's team. Because of the existing relationship, the manager didn't feel forced to accept the slight without an explanation. He was able to call a meeting with the executive in which he shared with her how her comment had affected him. She was genuinely surprised and apologized for speaking without thinking. Their relationship was stronger for it, and when the VP left the company a few years later, the manager remained with the knowledge that creating his own lasting relationships was not only a possibility but also a smart move.

Making the most of your time

Like you, your boss is busy, so use the time you have with her wisely by following these tips:

- ✔ **Let her calendar trump yours, and ask for a block of time that will allow for an in-depth conversation with few distractions.**

- ✔ **Have a specific goal in mind for the meeting.** Do you want to address a particular incident, or are you more interested in speaking in general terms about your working relationship? Either way, come prepared with specific examples.

- ✔ **Write down and prioritize what you want your boss to know before you start the meeting.** If you're especially anxious about the conversation, you could forget and miss a great opportunity to talk about what's most important to you.

- ✔ **For every complaint or issue you bring up, suggest at least three (yes, three) solutions.** Coming in with nothing makes you sound like a whiner, coming in with only one solution may be misinterpreted as an all-or-nothing ultimatum, and having only two solutions doesn't show the range of your capabilities. Presenting three solutions opens the door for her to add more, and then the two of you can work together to refine the proposals.

- ✔ **Be the first to apologize if you've erred.** Get your mistakes out in the open, on the table, and out of the way.

- ✔ **Strategically admit your limitations so she can no longer use them against you.** If you're constantly defending yourself, you miss the opportunity to look at a behavior and choose whether to change it. You also miss the chance to build your résumé with educational opportunities.

- ✔ **Graciously accept any apology she makes, and don't hold her to an impossible standard.** She may be above you in rank, but she's still human, and admitting mistakes is tough. Give her some credit if she's able to say she's sorry.

Part V
The Part of Tens

The 5th Wave   By Rich Tennant

"She's not a bad manager. Just keep your head down, do your work, and try not to get between her and her cubs."

In this part . . .

I list some things that anyone can control, even in the most difficult of times. Not to keep picking on managers (although I did write this book for you), but I also address why some people have a difficult time when it comes to dealing with conflict. Finally, I provide some unprecedented wisdom from experienced mediators.

Chapter 19

Ten Things You Can Control When You're in an Unresolved Conflict

In This Chapter

▶ Looking at your responses to conflict

▶ Emphasizing the positive

▶ Focusing your energy on what's important

Finding resolution is ideal, but what do you do to maintain your sanity when a conflict drags on? If you can't count on others to work with you to resolve the problem, look for things you *can* control. Finding the power to change what you can provides relief and comfort during a difficult time. Plus, it gives you something positive to focus on!

Your Plan for the Future

Consider what's important to you and follow a strategy for a period of time that feels comfortable. Your plan may include leaving your current work environment, either through a transfer within the company or by leaving the company for good and moving on. Or you may decide that staying where you are is the best thing to help you reach your goal for a secure retirement, or continued health benefits, or a shorter-term benefit like a good letter of recommendation. Whatever the choice, decide when, why, and how you'll approach your plan. Knowing what you want your future to look like helps you look past the current situation and focus beyond temporary problems.

Your Perspective

It's easy to get so wrapped up in a conflict that you lose all perspective about the situation. This is especially true when the conflict is at work and you're experiencing it every single day. Dealing with a persistent difficulty can become the routine — until you make the choice to change how you look at the problem. Stop and reassess your point of view.

Ask yourself whether you can find a learning opportunity somewhere in this situation. Perhaps the conflict is a chance for you to step outside yourself and extend a little compassion to the other person. Or maybe if you purposefully and mindfully examine what's going on, you can honestly say, in the scope of things, that the disagreements aren't really that important to you.

Your Responses

I'm sure you know from experience that you can't control the other person's actions, thoughts, or feelings. Try as you might — and I suspect you've tried a lot of different things — his behavior remains unchanged. It's frustrating, challenging, and disappointing to feel like you're the only one making an effort, but the good news is that no matter what he's doing, you always have the option to control your own responses.

Try changing how you react to what's happening, and look for ways to respond to hot button topics that won't escalate your anxiety or cause your blood pressure to spike through the roof. Consider who you want to be and choose your responses accordingly.

Your Investment

Think about how long you've lived with this conflict and how much effort you've put into trying to control every aspect of the problem. Then consider the reality that sometimes, in trying to control everything, you lose your ability to control anything! Do you want to be more emotionally invested than everyone else? Maybe the answer is yes, and that's fine if it's working for you. But if your answer is no (or even a shaky maybe), then try to reduce your investment in the drama. Spend less time thinking about it, talking about it, and engaging in it.

Your Role in the Conflict

As difficult as it is to admit to others that you have some responsibility in the conflict, it can be equally difficult to admit that fact to yourself. Self-assessment — and by that I mean more than 30 seconds of superficial introspection — requires you to step outside of your thoughts and feelings and consider how your actions and reactions look to others. Consider the impact of your actions, and honestly identify your role in the conflict. Ask yourself, "What have I said or done, or *not* said or done, that has kept this conflict going?"

When you have your answer, see if it's something you're willing to change. Change may not happen overnight, and you may need the assistance of friends, family, or professionals to help you through the transition, but you'll never be able to change your role if you don't take the time to identify what it is. No need to continue being the bully, the one who stirs the pot, or even the victim. If it takes two to tango and you're no longer willing to dance, the conflict has no choice but to diminish.

Your Expectations

When your expectations don't fit the situation, even though you've tried everything you can imagine to make them fit, give serious thought to changing your expectations.

Notice that I said *change,* not *lower.* For example, someone who has spent ten years at a company expecting to be promoted will be disappointed if she's turned down year after year. If she changes her expectation from being promoted to being acknowledged as an integral employee, the yearly bonus she receives may meet her new needs.

Similarly, you may carry around a set of expectations for yourself and put those expectations on others. Is it possible that your expectations are causing your frustration and the conflict to continue? I'm not talking job performance issues here, but rather personal preferences for how another person behaves. Your frustrations will decrease when you stop holding others to standards they don't know they're being measured against. I often coach employees to get a new yardstick!

Your Energy

Changing where you focus your energy can provide a huge relief from the stress of conflict. I believe that unresolved conflict (and unresolved emotions!) can be a black hole for energy: You can give and give without any guarantee you'll see that energy investment returned to you. Instead of putting 110 percent of yourself into the conflict, consider your alternatives at work or in your personal life. What do you enjoy? What gives you peace or a sense of well-being? What projects would satisfy you? Look for a different outlet for your attention and put your energy there. Cleaning out your closet and donating the clothing, putting together a proposal for a creative project at work, or jumping back into the classes at the gym are all great ways to channel energy and emotions.

Your Own Story

When I read a good book, I create what I call "the movie in my head." I'm the casting director, set designer, and director all in one. When it comes to the problems at work, you essentially do the same by choosing how you depict the scene to yourself and others.

If I were asked to recount a conflict I'm mediating, my summary would come from a broader and more objective viewpoint than the viewpoint of those involved. I might say that both people are having a difficult time, that both are emotional, but that both really want to do what's right for the company. If one of the parties were asked the same question, he'd probably describe it very differently. When you're not emotionally involved in a problem, you can see both sides, so take that ability to be objective and apply it to your own situation.

After you work through the initial emotions of a conflict (not all the emotions, just the initial ones), you can decide how this particular story will play out and how you'll speak about it. Give an account without elevating or victimizing anyone. When a co-worker or supervisor asks about specifics, consider an honest but hopeful response such as, "It's a difficult time right now, but I'm learning a valuable lesson about expectations," rather than, "Yet again I'm the victim and no one cares."

Your Method for Processing

You can keep the impact of a conflict to yourself and stuff your emotions away, or you can choose to find a constructive way to process what's happening. Talking with a mentor, family member, friend, clergy, and professionals can be very helpful, and you can do a lot on your own as well. Keeping a journal, writing letters you'll never send (my personal favorite), working out vigorously, or even slinging rocks at the tree in the backyard are all productive ways to process your emotions and perspective of an otherwise unproductive situation.

I particularly like the example of a co-worker who was devastated by the news that a project she had put her heart and soul into was being taken over by another department. The news came on a Friday afternoon, and she challenged herself, by Monday morning, to find ways the change would benefit her. She spent a few minutes (that's all it took!) making a list. She decided that she would have more time to spend with her family, she'd be able to participate on a committee she had her eye on, she could finish the marketing plan for the event idea she'd been tossing around, and so on. Find what works for you and have at it!

Your Character

Sure, you follow directions and have job functions you're responsible for, but no one can *make* you *do* anything. When you say, "He just makes me so (fill in the blank) that I *had* to (fill in what terrible past response or action you took)," you're giving the other person control over your moral fiber. Take personal responsibility and give no one else the power to *make* you behave in a way that is unbecoming, unethical, or dishonorable. Show your best side and not an unchecked series of poor reactions.

Chapter 20

Ten Reasons Managers Give for Not Addressing Conflict

. . . .

In This Chapter

▶ Avoiding issues deliberately

▶ Being reluctant or unable to address conflict

▶ Fearing consequences

. . . .

*O*ver the course of providing mediation services, I've heard a lot of rationale for managerial inaction. Whenever I hear someone say he's done nothing, I remind him that doing nothing *is* doing something — it's making a decision to ignore a conflict that's evident to at least one person, and possibly many more.

In this chapter, I list the ten statements (in no particular order) for not addressing conflict that I hear most often from managers. If you find yourself repeating one of these statements, use the tips I give you in this book to determine and find the resources you need, hone your coaching skills, have a productive conversation with a colleague, or try a new approach to an old problem.

I Don't Really Know How

Managers — especially new managers — tend to be at a loss the first time a conflict arises and it doesn't just sort itself out. Finding the right language and the right techniques to use at the right time takes finesse. For some people, that dexterity comes naturally, but for others, perhaps even you, it's a learned skill that comes with experience, training, and opportunity. This book is a great place to start! Check out Chapter 5 to gain insight into how to evaluate the details of a conflict, and see Chapters 13 and 14 to consider internal and external resources.

I Don't Want to Open a Can of Worms

No one ever wants to be the first person to notice that the toilet is overflowing in the restroom. Maybe that's a bad analogy, but you may feel that if you address a conflict, your suspicions about bad behavior and work performance will be proven true, and you'll have to deal with it — all of it. Consider the impact on others (and the company) if you sit back and do nothing.

I Haven't Been Successful Before

Losing hope and a willingness to commit to problem solving are common responses when a manager feels that his efforts are all for naught. If previous attempts at resolution haven't gone well, others may have lost trust in your abilities. Trying something new may be exactly what's needed.

Perhaps you just haven't had the right help or training. Confer with colleagues, your HR contact, or outside conflict resolution specialists. Chapters 13 and 14 deal with asking for help and reviewing possible options.

Problem? What Problem?

While some managers see problems and "wish" them away, others like to stay completely in the dark. You can't be expected to address something you don't know exists, right? Maybe you're busy, or the work is getting done so you think everything is fine, or you're an off-site manager who isn't able to see the day-to-day drama at the work site. Keep an eye on how your team interacts, the language choices they make, how they speak to you about one another, and whether specific individuals work a little too hard at not working together.

Addressing smaller issues at the onset is a lot easier than facing larger problems later on.

I Don't Know Where to Start

Taking the time to assess a situation and make a plan burns up energy and attention. It's smart to sit back and consider your next steps instead of jumping into a conflict willy-nilly, but inaction doesn't get you any closer to resolution. Develop a plan with clear goals in mind, and get whatever help you need to put it into action. Start with Chapters 2 and 3 to determine possible underlying issues or emotions, and then flip to Chapter 4 to consider how you may be contributing to the difficulty. Find a mentor, HR employee, or an outside expert who can help you break what may seem like an overwhelming situation into manageable pieces.

It's Not My Business

Hey, whatever is happening between Seth and Lauren is something they're just going to have to work out on their own! You may not be sure why they can't get along, and you may think that what you don't know won't hurt you. Not true. If it affects the business, it *is* your business.

I'm Not a Babysitter

People have different managerial styles, and some like to take a more hands-off approach. These managers go into the workplace with the philosophy that their employees are adults and they should be able to resolve differences like adults. You may believe that you're there only to make sure the work gets done — not to hold hands or babysit employees. Changing your perspective from "babysitting" to "mentoring" gives you an opportunity to hone your leadership abilities.

I Have Real Work to Do

You know as well as I do that managers are busy. They have meetings to attend, budgets to review, inspections to conduct, paperwork to file, and on top of that, staff to oversee. They don't always have enough time in the day to get everything done, and when a manager has to put his work down and step in to resolve a dispute, it can be distracting and frustrating. Addressing personnel issues, though, is an important part of being an effective manager. In fact, it may be one of the first questions asked of you in your next job interview. Have something positive to say about your abilities in this area.

1 Don't Want to Have to Fire Anyone

Conflicts shouldn't be knock-down, drag-out fights in which the winner takes all. It's possible for two people in an argument to turn their disagreement around and walk away the better for the conversation. Just because two employees aren't getting along doesn't mean the only answer is to fire one of them. You have plenty of other options, and the more you work with each of them to brainstorm solutions, the more you expand your choices.

If, after your best efforts, it's clear that it would be best for an employee to move, be sure to keep other employees focused with the tips I lay out in Chapter 10. Grace and dignity in an otherwise difficult situation are a matter of choice, but you can help ease an outgoing employee's distress by modeling positive behaviors and attitude. Chapter 19 covers ten things anyone can control in the midst of conflict.

1 Don't Want to Look Bad

Before you were a manager you were an individual contributor — a subordinate. You had to watch your step and keep your reputation intact if you were going to be promoted. So it makes sense that you now want to be careful about anything that could adversely affect the way others view you. But being overly concerned about being seen as an ineffective or weak manager who can't handle his people doesn't help you create a reputation as a problem solver. Co-workers see it, even if you think you're doing a good job of masking the problems. Simply put, ignoring conflicts on your team affects your reputation in a negative way.

Chapter 21

Ten Pearls of Wisdom from Professional Mediators

In This Chapter
▶ Listening carefully to all parties
▶ Focusing on similarities
▶ Steering the conversation toward a solution

Seeing a conflict through to a positive resolution can be life-changing — it certainly has been for me. It's empowering to help others, and yourself, through a difficult time whether you're at work, at home, or at play. My goal with this chapter is to share what I know about mediation and conflict and to take advantage of the fact that I know some really accomplished and insightful mediators. My hope is that some of this expertise will help you turn problems around in your everyday life without having to become an expert in conflict resolution. So I made a list of things I thought you should know, talked to my friends about their best advice, and put it all together to give you these bits of information that I hope you find helpful.

Value the Process as Much as the Outcome

Achieving resolution and securing a signature on an agreement form may be an obvious sign that a conflict conversation has gone well — unless, of course, you steamrolled over the parties and forced them to acquiesce because you wanted to quickly put the surface issues behind you. Striving to improve a working relationship gives you more than a momentary solution. A mediation process that allows the parties to come away with an understanding of the real issues can also deliver broader benefits, such as more collaboration between the two parties, an increase in creativity, and a boost in productivity.

Accept That Her Truth Is Her Reality

Acting as the judge, jury, and executioner isn't the point of mediating conflict. The purpose of the discussions isn't for you to find out who's telling the truth and who's lying — for the people involved, the stories they share *are* the truth. Work within a person's point of view to help her find resolution.

Rapport Matters

Presenting yourself professionally and being open to input from all sides creates a comfortable environment for both parties to be honest with you about what's happening and what they're willing to do to resolve the difficulty.

Get off to a good start by being genuinely interested in the perspectives from all the people involved in the conflict.

Be Present and Available

Give your full attention to the individuals sitting in front of you during a conversation about conflict — not the computer, not your phone, not the knock on the door. Put the golden rule into play and give others the same care and attention you'd want in the same situation.

Find Common Ground for More Success

People in conflict have a tendency to focus only on differences, and these differences are what keep them fighting. Rather than concentrate on what's dividing them, find the things that bring them together. Common interests and values can be the stepping stones to finding solutions that work for both people. Mediators who are able to keep their clients focused on common interests have successful outcomes more times than not, and you can too. Even if a problem is between you and another person, if you can approach the discussion from the viewpoint of the things you have in common, you stand a better chance of the other person relaxing and hearing what you have to say than you do if you only want to discuss your differences.

Be Aware That This Isn't the Participants' Best Moment

People in conflict aren't at their best! Feelings such as hurt, fear, frustration, and anger can drive a person to ridiculous behavior sometimes. That doesn't mean that underneath these feelings a colleague isn't a decent person just trying to get by. Give her the benefit of the doubt, even if you can't see her best qualities at the moment.

Silence Is Golden

Silence is one of my favorite tools! Don't rescue employees when they sit in stony silence. The more uncomfortable they get, the more you demonstrate to them that this is their conflict. If you speak to end the silence, you may take away an opportunity for them to share something important.

The same is true when you're one of the people involved in a conflict, but be careful not to come across as stubborn or defiant. Use your communication skills to ask about the other person's perspective, and then wait for her answers.

Be Curious

Curiosity may have killed the cat, but it's one of a mediator's best tools! My favorite questions start with, "Help me understand . . ." and "I'm sorry, I'm not quite sure what you meant when you said. . . ." This gets a person talking so I can listen for what's really important to her — that is, her *values*. (See Chapter 2 for a more in-depth discussion of values.) Priceless!

Fear Rules the World

Giant egos, rude behavior, and bully tactics all come down to the fear of losing something. The bigger the reaction, the bigger the fear. Work to uncover what a co-worker may fear from the conflict and strive to allay her concerns.

Look to the Future

Staying in the past is much like circling the drain; around and around we go. Asking parties to share their perspective (what brought them here) is a good way to start a mediated conversation. Everyone needs a chance to tell her side of the story, but repeating (and repeating and repeating) what happened 19 Tuesdays ago doesn't resolve anything. When you feel the perspective has been heard, move to address it properly by focusing the conversation on what she'd like to see on the next Tuesday, what that looks like for her, and how she thinks she could make that happen.

Index

• H •

• I •

Business/Accounting & Bookkeeping

Bookkeeping For Dummies
978-0-7645-9848-7

eBay Business
All-in-One For Dummies,
2nd Edition
978-0-470-38536-4

Job Interviews
For Dummies,
3rd Edition
978-0-470-17748-8

Resumes For Dummies,
5th Edition
978-0-470-08037-5

Stock Investing
For Dummies,
3rd Edition
978-0-470-40114-9

Successful Time
Management
For Dummies
978-0-470-29034-7

Computer Hardware

BlackBerry For Dummies,
3rd Edition
978-0-470-45762-7

Computers For Seniors
For Dummies
978-0-470-24055-7

iPhone For Dummies,
2nd Edition
978-0-470-42342-4

Laptops For Dummies,
3rd Edition
978-0-470-27759-1

Macs For Dummies,
10th Edition
978-0-470-27817-8

Cooking & Entertaining

Cooking Basics
For Dummies,
3rd Edition
978-0-7645-7206-7

Wine For Dummies,
4th Edition
978-0-470-04579-4

Diet & Nutrition

Dieting For Dummies,
2nd Edition
978-0-7645-4149-0

Nutrition For Dummies,
4th Edition
978-0-471-79868-2

Weight Training
For Dummies,
3rd Edition
978-0-471-76845-6

Digital Photography

Digital Photography
For Dummies,
6th Edition
978-0-470-25074-7

Photoshop Elements 7
For Dummies
978-0-470-39700-8

Gardening

Gardening Basics
For Dummies
978-0-470-03749-2

Organic Gardening
For Dummies,
2nd Edition
978-0-470-43067-5

Green/Sustainable

Green Building
& Remodeling
For Dummies
978-0-470-17559-0

Green Cleaning
For Dummies
978-0-470-39106-8

Green IT For Dummies
978-0-470-38688-0

Health

Diabetes For Dummies,
3rd Edition
978-0-470-27086-8

Food Allergies
For Dummies
978-0-470-09584-3

Living Gluten-Free
For Dummies
978-0-471-77383-2

Hobbies/General

Chess For Dummies,
2nd Edition
978-0-7645-8404-6

Drawing For Dummies
978-0-7645-5476-6

Knitting For Dummies,
2nd Edition
978-0-470-28747-7

Organizing For Dummies
978-0-7645-5300-4

SuDoku For Dummies
978-0-470-01892-7

Home Improvement

Energy Efficient Homes
For Dummies
978-0-470-37602-7

Home Theater
For Dummies,
3rd Edition
978-0-470-41189-6

Living the Country Lifestyle
All-in-One For Dummies
978-0-470-43061-3

Solar Power Your Home
For Dummies
978-0-470-17569-9

Internet

Blogging For Dummies,
2nd Edition
978-0-470-23017-6

eBay For Dummies,
6th Edition
978-0-470-49741-8

Facebook For Dummies
978-0-470-26273-3

Google Blogger
For Dummies
978-0-470-40742-4

Web Marketing
For Dummies,
2nd Edition
978-0-470-37181-7

WordPress For Dummies,
2nd Edition
978-0-470-40296-2

Language & Foreign Language

French For Dummies
978-0-7645-5193-2

Italian Phrases
For Dummies
978-0-7645-7203-6

Spanish For Dummies
978-0-7645-5194-9

Spanish For Dummies,
Audio Set
978-0-470-09585-0

Macintosh

Mac OS X Snow Leopard
For Dummies
978-0-470-43543-4

Math & Science

Algebra I For Dummies
978-0-7645-5325-7

Biology For Dummies
978-0-7645-5326-4

Calculus For Dummies
978-0-7645-2498-1

Chemistry For Dummies
978-0-7645-5430-8

Microsoft Office

Excel 2007 For Dummies
978-0-470-03737-9

Office 2007 All-in-One
Desk Reference
For Dummies
978-0-471-78279-7

Music

Guitar For Dummies,
2nd Edition
978-0-7645-9904-0

iPod & iTunes
For Dummies,
6th Edition
978-0-470-39062-7

Piano Exercises
For Dummies
978-0-470-38765-8

Parenting & Education

Parenting For Dummies,
2nd Edition
978-0-7645-5418-6

Type 1 Diabetes
For Dummies
978-0-470-17811-9

Pets

Cats For Dummies,
2nd Edition
978-0-7645-5275-5

Dog Training For Dummies,
2nd Edition
978-0-7645-8418-3

Puppies For Dummies,
2nd Edition
978-0-470-03717-1

Religion & Inspiration

The Bible For Dummies
978-0-7645-5296-0

Catholicism For Dummies
978-0-7645-5391-2

Women in the Bible
For Dummies
978-0-7645-8475-6

Self-Help & Relationship

Anger Management
For Dummies
978-0-470-03715-7

Overcoming Anxiety
For Dummies
978-0-7645-5447-6

Sports

Baseball For Dummies,
3rd Edition
978-0-7645-7537-2

Basketball For Dummies,
2nd Edition
978-0-7645-5248-9

Golf For Dummies,
3rd Edition
978-0-471-76871-5

Web Development

Web Design All-in-One
For Dummies
978-0-470-41796-6

Windows Vista

Windows Vista
For Dummies
978-0-471-75421-3

How-to?
How Easy.

Dummies products make life easier!

DVDs • Music • Games •
DIY • Consumer Electronics •
Software • Crafts • Hobbies •
Cookware • and more!

For more information, go to
Dummies.com® and search
the store by category.

FOR
DUMMIES
Making everything easier!™